REBUILDING AMERICA'S CITIES

REBUILDING AMERICA'S CITIES

A policy analysis of

THE U.S. CONFERENCE OF MAYORS

prepared under the leadership of

ERNEST N. MORIAL, MAYOR OF NEW ORLEANS AND
PRESIDENT, U.S. CONFERENCE OF MAYORS

and

MARION BARRY, JR., MAYOR OF WASHINGTON, D.C.
AND
CHAIR, SPECIAL
COMMITTEE ON A NATIONAL URBAN POLICY

by

EDWARD M. MEYERS, PROJECT DIRECTOR

BALLINGER PUBLISHING COMPANY
Cambridge, Massachusetts
A Subsidiary of Harper & Row, Publishers, Inc.

International Standard Book Number: 0-88730-051-0

Library of Congress Catalog Card Number: 85-30780

Printed in the United States of America

Library of Congress Cataloging-in-Publication Data

Morial, Ernest N.
Rebuilding America's cities.

Includes bibliographies and index.
1. Urban renewal—United States. 2. Urban policy—United States. 3. Community development, Urban—United States. I. Barry, Marion, 1936- . II. United States Conference of Mayors. III. Title.
HT175.U59 1986 307.3'4'0973 85-30780
ISBN 0-88730-051-0

CONTENTS

LIST OF FIGURES

LIST OF TABLES

LIST OF ABBREVIATIONS AND ACRONYMS

AAA	Area Agency on Aging
AFDC	Aid to Families with Dependent Children
AFDC/UP	Aid to Families with Dependent Children/ Unemployed Parent
CAAs	Community Action Agencies
CBO	Congressional Budget Office
CCC	Community Credit Corporation
CDBG	Community Development Block Grant
CED	Committee for Economic Development
CETA	Comprehensive Employment and Training Act
CSBG	Community Services Block Grant
DISC	Domestic International Sales Corporation
DLA	Defense Logistics Agency
DOD	Department of Defense
DOL	Department of Labor
DRG	Diagnostic Related Group
ECIA	Education Consolidation and Improvement Act
EDA	Economic Development Administration
EHAP	Experimental Housing Allowance Program
EITC	Earned Income Tax Credit
ERISA	Employee Retirement Income Security Act
ESAA	Emergency School Aid Act
ESEA	Elementary and Secondary Education Act
FAUS	Federal Aid Urban System
FHA	Federal Housing Administration
FNMA	Federal National Mortgage Association

GA	General Assistance
GAO	General Accounting Office
GRS	General Revenue Sharing
GSA	General Services Administration
HoDAG	Housing Development Action Grant
HUD	(Department of) Housing and Urban Development
IDB	Industrial Development Bond
IRS	Internal Revenue Service
ITA	Individual Training Account
JTPA	Jobs Training Partnership Act
LEAs	local education agencies
NCIC	National Center for Innovation in Corrections
NEA	National Education Association
NGA	National Governors Association
NIE	National Institute of Education
NIJ	National Institute of Justice
OCR	Office of Civil Rights
OFCCP	Office of Federal Contract Compliance Programs
PHAs	Public Housing Authorities
PSA	Planning and Service Area
RAM	Reverse Annuity Mortgage
RFC	Reconstruction Finance Corporation
SBA	Small Business Administration
SCEP	Senior Community Service Employment Program
SEAs	state education agencies
SMSA	Standard Metropolitan Statistical Area
SSBG	Social Services Block Grant
SSI	Supplementary Security Income
STAA	Surface Transportation Assistance Act
TJTC	Targeted Jobs Tax Credit
UDAG	Urban Development Action Grant
UI	Unemployment Insurance
UMTA	Urban Mass Transit Administration
VA	Veterans Administration
WEEA	Women's Educational Equity Act
WFC	War Finance Corporation
WIC	Special Supplemental Program for Women, Infants and Children
WIN	Work Incentive Program

PREFACE

In June of 1985, the U.S. Conference of Mayors held its 53rd annual meeting in Anchorage, Alaska. In these meetings mayors continue to guide national urban policy in economic development, housing, education, tax reform, health, transportation, intergovernmental fiscal relations, and international trade, through the development of specific policies in a formal legislative process.

The Conference of Mayors is composed of Democratic and Republican mayors of large, medium, and small cities in the North, East, South, and West, ranging from New York City to Farmers Branch, Texas. The mayors have placed aside their political differences and agreed to a policy position that would halt the drastic federal budget shifts from urban-directed programs, while maintaining those programs at the prior year's levels. With such a budget freeze, national policymakers and other citizens could then examine the effectiveness of urban policies and programs at the frozen level, for a year or longer.

This policy position of U.S. mayors was important in the development of a fiscal year 1986 federal budget, which in many ways followed much of the mayors' guidance.

At the Anchorage conference mayors also voted unanimously to accept a national urban policy report, which has been developed over the past thirty months by a special committee, as a useful resource tool in the exploration of future urban policies. Policies in this report are based on resolutions adopted over the years by mayors through the formal policy processes of the Conference in annual meetings.

This is not to say that U.S. mayors have deliberated upon every statement in this report; they have not. Nonetheless, the mayors offer the report to the public in hopes that the policy background and history, the charts and data, and the policy options discussed herein will be useful to readers as they examine the full variety of urban policy topics during the budget freeze period.

THE PRESIDENT'S NATIONAL URBAN POLICY REPORT

Every two years, through the U.S. Department of Housing and Urban Development, the president issues the President's National Urban Policy Report. We encourage citizens to read those reports, to gain an understanding of federal executive branch concepts and policies for cities during both Republican and Democratic administrations.

Naturally, mayors, who are on the front lines in the battle for improved urban conditions, will from time to time have different views from those of the federal executive branch. In this, the first urban policy report from mayors' perspective, the main concern is how our federal policies affect urban citizens.

SELF-SUFFICIENCY VERSUS FEDERAL PROGRAMS

One theme repeated by both major political parties, by conservatives and progressives alike, and by people of all incomes and races, is the need for urban populations to achieve self-sufficiency. No one benefits from a dependency on government—neither the low-income family nor the taxpayer who foots the bill.

Mayors throughout America encourage our teenagers daily to avoid dropping out of school, pregnancy, drugs, alcohol, and crime, and turn instead to jobs, education, community involvement, and family responsibility. We encourage those who receive public assistance to try a variety of innovative job and training programs, and we often provide child care to them at little or no cost until family debts are brought under control. We do what we can about the deplorable housing conditions that stifle family morale, to shape communities that are as free as possible from the influences that breed poverty and despair. We encourage businesses that long ago abandoned central cities to return and rebuild our communities along with us.

As we visit the neighborhoods of our cities, we find community leaders, parents, civic groups, clergy, and educators working side by side with us voicing the same theme: Urban citizens must lift themselves from poverty.

The goal of self-sufficiency is much more universally accepted than is the set of policies designed to achieve it. We have yet to develop a societal consensus about the role of the more affluent communities in building the health of economically distressed central cities. At one extreme, one can simply draw a circle around populations with high concentrations of poverty and ask those within the circle—the urban residents—to somehow pay the price. This means higher police costs to combat the higher crime rates. It means greater per capita educational expenditures than found in affluent areas to overcome learning disadvantages due to the unstable family and community environments produced by poverty. It means greater per capita health care expenditures because the higher urban unemployment rates leave more people, proportionally, without private health insurance. It means greater public service levels for the urban elderly, many of whom did not have the opportunities to build their assets that the more affluent elderly enjoyed.

All of these conditions result in higher taxes inside cities than outside. The middle and upper income citizens and businesses that remain inside the urban circle must pay the price because those outside the circle are choosing not to share those costs.

Millions of urban residents continue to pay these growing local tax bills, and mayors are eternally grateful to them. But what of the millions who cry "Enough!" and move away, leaving those behind to pay deeper and deeper shares of their discretionary income? When the burdens became too great, when corporations and the middle class find it impossible to stay, and when the concentrations of poverty are so intense, the daily encouragement we offer citizens to achieve self-sufficiency often seems futile. We win the battle with hundreds of families through new employer attraction strategies, innovative educational concepts, drug counseling efforts, and the like. But, at the same time, hundreds of other families slip forever from us.

The central question of this report is: What is the share of responsibility that affluent communities have to those with heavy poverty concentrations? The evolution of economically and racially segregated communities could not have been possible without explicit federal, state, and local government decisions over the years that shaped housing, employment, zoning, and civil-rights policies. Urban citizens must achieve self-sufficiency primarily on their own. But it seems to us that government must tear down the artificial barriers that impede citizens' progress. The free market forces will not, by themselves, undo past and present injustices unless some of the underlying assumptions are revised.

Some of the policies discussed in this report are virtually free of cost. For example, full enforcement of equal opportunity laws now on the books would have a minimal pricetag. In fact, national economic revitalization of unprecedented proportions would likely ensue as new consumers and business owners create massive additions to the national income stream and the job base. Other policies do have pricetags, for example, infusion of capital assistance to economically distressed central cities must be of sufficient magnitude to sway business locational decisions. One must weigh the cost of such an economic stimulus against the costs to society of maintaining jobless residents in lives of dependence.

Several other issues are raised and analyzed in this book. We should decide as a society what job training policies are needed to assure that urban residents will compete successfully for the new jobs in today's increasingly skilled job market. The nation seems to have made a commitment to retain housing subsidies for middle and upper income citizens through the tax system, but we should determine what level of housing assistance should be extended to the lower income group as well. Past years of educational assistance to the economically disadvantaged have produced significant achievement gains—should we continue this investment in our youth? In what form, and at what level?

Public assistance reform has not been on the national agenda for some time, yet the same interstate disparities and insufficient links to job training are still with us. There is still as much a need as ever to devise a cost-effective system to reduce these problems. It is also time to reorient our health systems, employment patterns, and housing policies to meet the needs of the rapidly growing elderly segment of our society.

The American public is starting to realize that serious structural readjustments are needed in the criminal justice system. We need to consider whether some nonviolent offenders should serve their sentences outside of prison complexes to relieve overcrowing. For those inside prison walls, we should decide whether they will be given the opportunity (or the requirement) to hold jobs or at least to receive intensive education and job training while in prison. Or can we afford only to store them?

We have subsidized and accommodated the private automobile in a variety of ways for years. But can we approach a semblance of such support for mass transit? Placing rhetoric aside, let us determine with some precision our obligation to those without cars, to clean air, to energy conservation, and to relief from traffic congestion.

And finally, we should examine the role that the federal government as an entity can play in improving urban conditions. Its own contracting policies can assure equal employment opportunities among all races and both sexes, at all wage and salary levels, in the thirty-million jobs controlled by federal contractors and subcontractors. Federal contracts could also be used to funnel resources to high-unemployment areas and to build minority-owned businesses at a surprisingly low cost.

These issues are, or should be, at the top of our nation's domestic policy agenda. Nearly 30 percent of America's population lives in central cities, while 75 percent lives in metropolitan areas, which directly depend on their central cities' vitality for their well-being and their very identities. Building the strength of central cities takes careful and conscious planning—just as a strong national defense, agricultural progress, or environmental quality requires thoughtful planning to ensure success.

Ernest N. Morial
Mayor of New Orleans
and
President, U.S. Conference of Mayors

Marion Barry, Jr.
Mayor of Washington, D.C.
and
Chair, Special Committee on a National Urban Policy

ACKNOWLEDGMENTS

Ed Meyers directed this urban policy project; authored Chapters 1, 2, 3, 4, 6, 12, and 16; collaborated in the drafting of the other chapters; and served as the manuscript's editor.

Many contributed to the research and drafting of this book. Kay Ostberg wrote the "Historical Basis for Affirmative Action" (pp. 125-127), while Diane Flannigan Montgomery provided policy guidance for Chapter 6. Larry F. Weston collaborated with the project director to draft Chapter 7.

Chapter 8 was drafted by LaMar Haynes, while Thomas C. Joe was the principal contributor to Chapter 11. Mary Lee Allen, Helen Blank, and Sara Rosenbaum assisted in the research for Chapters 9 and 12.

Cheryl Fish assisted in the drafting of Chapter 13, while Walter S. Smith collaborated with the project director in drafting Chapter 14. Dr. Judith Schloegel wrote the sections on "Alternatives to Incarceration" and "Prison Industries," pp. 251-252. Robert G. Stanley collaborated with the project director to draft Chapter 15.

Melvenna Avent and Christopher Sjorup provided considerable administrative assistance, Kathleen M. Burke provided editorial assistance, and Richard F. Groner provided graphics support. Warren H. Suss Associates of Jenkintown, Pennsylvania, advised us on procurement outreach centers as a means of obtaining Defense contracts. Jerry Fastrup of the U.S. General Accounting Office provided technical guidance on targeted fiscal assistance proposals. David Shea, University of Maryland intern, assisted in researching Chapter 16.

1 OVERVIEW OF MAYORS' NATIONAL URBAN POLICY REPORT

This survey of urban policies has been compiled in an era in which the overriding concern of the general public is not urban deterioration but a federal budget that is drastically out of balance with current revenue authority. Few policymakers today are taking a stand for major new spending programs, no matter what the degree of necessity may be. America's mayors join with the president, Congress, and the majority of Americans in recognizing that continuing large federal deficits pose a serious threat to the economic health of our country. These deficits can be reduced by curtailed spending and increased revenues.

In view of this urgent need to bring the federal budget as closely into balance as possible, the U.S. Conference of Mayors' Executive Committee adopted a resolution in 1985 that endorsed a spending reduction through a freeze for at least one year on all non-means-tested programs in the federal budget and for increased revenues from measures other than the personal income tax. In this way, our nation would have a balanced approach to controlling federal deficits. Urban-directed programs such as general revenue sharing, urban development action grants, subsidized housing, mass transit assistance, student loans, and jobs programs could be retained at current levels rather than being sharply reduced or eliminated altogether.

Gramm-Rudman-Hollings legislation enacted in December 1985 went beyond the freeze, providing for domestic and defense reductions that would produce a balanced budget by 1991. This legislation places greater pressure against urban programs or, alternatively, requires Congress to face the reality of restoring some tax revenues.

Every two years, the U.S. Department of Housing and Urban Development (HUD) produces the President's National Urban Policy Report. As an example of recent federal urban philosophy, the 1982 report stated that the federal executive branch "intends to devolve the maximum feasible responsibility for urban matters to States and through them to their local governments, and to limit federal government responsibilities to those matters where a clear national interest is at stake."[1]

This mayors' national urban policy report is issued to support the view that it is clearly in the national interest to strengthen urban vitality. In this, the first urban policy report produced by mayors, the major urban policies and programs are examined. A discussion of their history, costs, and usefulness to the public is presented, as policymakers consider the direction of the nation during Gramm-Rudman-Hollings and the proposed period of the budget freeze.

Mayors believe there will be much common ground upon which to develop a strong urban policy. The viewpoints of both political parties, urban and suburban residents alike, can be accommodated in future budgetary decisions. For example, the President's 1984 Urban Policy Report recognizes the problems of particularly distressed cities: "Those cities which have been dependent on mature basic industries, and which contain much aging and unmodernized plant, will probably lag in their recovery and require special measures at all levels of government to overcome their specific liabilities."[2]

One such special measure offered by the federal executive branch is the urban enterprise zone, which would provide tax and other incentives to stimulate business location and retention and stimulate the hiring of economically disadvantaged citizens. The U.S. Conference of Mayors has enthusiastically endorsed the concept of the urban enterprise zone. The zones should complement the effectiveness of the other measures that are rebuilding urban economies.

TRENDS IN URBAN CONDITIONS

To be sure, urban America continues to serve as the center of commerce and culture. Many downtown areas are by now in the midst of extensive, exciting, tasteful, and diverse renovation. Cities are unrivaled as financial, educational, tourist, and entertainment centers. Even urban governments' fiscal conditions are not as deficit ridden as they once were, since many local governments, over time, have learned to scale back their efforts to correct structural economic and social imbalances. Government at all levels—federal, state, and local—is adjusting to the urban deemphasis. Most Americans seem to assume that the urban trends are improving over time—very slowly, with recessionary setbacks from time to time, but improving nonetheless over the long haul.

Mayors, therefore, face perceptual obstacles in presenting their case for remedies to the urban conditions. Most Americans routinely assume that poverty is being slowly eradicated. Americans assume that the income gap between the races is closing and that economic equality among the races, while still distant, is nonetheless certain. These perceptions enable the general public to remain complacent and to postpone until another day the arduous task of building thriving central cities. Despite the general perceptions, however, many of the trends continue to deteriorate over time, as they have for three decades.

We have heard much about the "urban crises." Following the conflagrations in Newark, Watts, Detroit, Washington, and other cities, the nation had an explicit crisis to address. In contrast, today the "crises" are more individualized: disintegration of the family, crime rates double those of twenty years ago, rampant drug addiction and alchoholism, increased homelessness, growing poverty, and additional generations who are economically dependent on government. Unfortunately for mayors and urban residents, the nation can save budgetary expenditures in the short run by cutting back on urban programs—and "get away with it" only because the deterioration is incremental, not sudden or symbolic. We still have sufficient economic segregation in the United States so that, in the absence of the rebellions of decades past, the majority of Americans are not excessively inconvenienced by declining urban conditions. Over time, the failure to act results in structural problems of such magnitude that it is little wonder that many refuse even to acknowledge their existence.

Chapter 2 explores urban conditions in some depth. The following is an overview of the key trends.

Population Drain. Between 1975 and 1980, 80 of the 153 largest cities surveyed lost population. Many cities lost considerable numbers of their citizens in the last decade (for example, St. Louis, 27 percent; Cleveland, 24 percent; Buffalo, 23 percent; Detroit, 21 percent; and Pittsburgh, 19 percent). Meanwhile, suburbs gained 18 percent in population in the last decade. Residents lost to the suburbs, moreover, usually have much higher incomes than those remaining.

Increasing Poverty in Cities. One of every five city residents lives in poverty—more than double the suburban rate. In many hard-pressed urban centers, the poverty rate within cities can be ten times the proportion found in their suburbs.

Two-thirds of black and Hispanic children in female-headed households live in poverty. Alarmingly, the number of female-headed households has increased more than 50 percent in the last decade. The odds of those children breaking out of the poverty cycle during their lifetimes are low, given the level of commitment being made to them. In cities, where there are now 12.9 million poor, the poverty rate has increased from 15.7 percent in 1979 to 19.8 percent in 1983.

Wide and Growing Income Gaps between City and Suburb. Suburbs have a 32 percent advantage over cities in median family income; the gap is 44 percent in the largest cities. The city-suburban income gap was 20 percent in 1969 and 13 percent in 1959. In 1949 city residents had greater income (and greater taxpaying ability) than suburban residents.

Table 1-1. Percentage Change in Real Disposable Income, 1980-1984.

	Income Quintile				
	Bottom	*Second*	*Third*	*Fourth*	*Top*
Black families	−7.0	−8.2	−3.7	−0.6	−0.1
All families	−7.6	−1.7	+0.9	+3.4	+8.7

Growing Racial Income Disparities. The proportion of black families earning under $10,000 is greater today at 34 percent than it was (in constant dollars) in 1970, when the proportion was 28 percent. The ratio of black-white median income is even lower today (at $56 per $100 of white income) that it was in 1970 (at $61).[3] Moreover, 26 percent of black families headed by high school *graduates* live in poverty, while just 22 percent of white families headed by someone with an eighth-grade education or less live in poverty. In fact, black male *college* graduates have a lower median income than white male *high school* graduates. The United States is hardly "bending over backward" to change, as the myths would have us believe.

According to a 1984 Urban Institute study, black family disposable (after tax) income declined among all income classes over the last five years (in constant dollars), in contrast to the general trend for all families.[4] Low-income families, regardless of race, fared poorly in 1980 through 1984 (refer to the large percentage income declines of families in the bottom and second-from-the-bottom income quintiles in Table 1-1). However, black income has also declined among middle and upper income families as well—in contrast to the general trend where the incomes of the middle and upper classes have increased over the four-year period. Cities, which have a high proportion of minority and lower income people, lost considerable ground over those four years.

Structural Unemployment in Times of Economic Expansion. The general economic recovery has reduced the nation's unemployment rate to 7.1 percent (as of September 1985), with 8.1 million people unemployed. The administration forecasts unemployment rates between 6 and 7 percent the rest of the 1980s.

Historically, these unemployment rates are high for periods of economic expansion, reflecting growing structural (as opposed to cyclical) unemployment. More importantly, an overall unemployment rate of 7 percent can mask some serious problems among segments of the population and nation. Double-digit unemployment in Gary, Cleveland, Dayton, Detroit, New Orleans, Miami, Toledo, Oakland, Buffalo, Newark, and other citites may be even more significant today than it was during the recession, since continuing high rates in times of recovery and expansion are indicative of long-term economic decline. Will the nation's employment and economic policies play in Peoria, where the unemployment rate today is 12.4 percent?

Moreover, an unemployment rate among blacks of 15.3 percent—2.5 times the white rate—indicates a serious structural imbalance among population groups. Such a rate is depression level and would undoubtedly call for immediate and substantial federal action if such a rate would pertain to the majority population. Moreover, the general unemployment rate of 7.1 percent, the black rate of 15.3 percent, and the Hispanic rate of 10.4 percent do not include discouraged workers—those who have dropped out of the labor force altogether, discouraged over not finding work.

Homelessness and Hunger. Chapter 7 of this book notes increases in homelessness of 20 percent, 30 percent, 50 percent, and more in major U.S. cities, with many local governments unable to cope with sharp increases in demand. Chapter 10 notes increases of more than 70 percent in the demand for emergency food assistance, fully half of the cities surveyed reporting an inability to meet the demand.

Remaining Gaps in Educational Achievements. Urban schoolchildren have made remarkable progress in recent years, cutting suburban advantages by half or more in math and reading proficiency tests. Nonetheless, reading and math proficiency scores are still much higher in the suburbs than in cities among older youth. Currently, only 45 percent of economically disadvantaged children receive targeted federal education assistance. Urban school systems and their children have suffered a disproportionate share of funding cuts in recent years, absorbing 25 percent of federal funding declines while having only 11 percent of the nation's enrollment.

Crime Rates at Excessive Level. Reductions in the nation's crime rate of 17 percent over the past four years have lulled some into a false sense of security. The crime rate today is still double the level of twenty years ago. The crime rate in cities is more than double the rate of the suburbs and more than four times the rural rate.

Unfairly High Urban Tax Burdens. Under our system of government, jurisdictions that have opened their doors to people of all income levels must pay a disproportionate share of the financial burdens to treat the wide variety of social and economic problems associated with poverty. On average, city residents pay 23 percent more in local taxes per capita than do suburban residents. Some distressed cities exceed this average tax disparity figure by wide margins.

Shift of Political Influence to Suburban Districts. It is only in relatively recent times that urban interests have been soundly out-voted. Today there are 79 urban congressional districts, 228 suburban districts, and 128 rural. As recently as 1970, cities held a 148- to 144-seat advantage over suburban interests in Congress. Political might is turning federal priorities away from those who need help the most. Urban contingents in Congress are no longer able to enact urban remedies; instead they must depend on the wisdom and compassion of others to awaken to the trends and take necessary action for the greater good of the nation.

OVERVIEW OF FEDERAL ACTIONS AFFECTING CITIES

Millions of urban citizens face a situation where no level of government claims to have the capacity to redirect the urban trends which, increasingly, are closing off the opportunities of mainstream America to them. Grants to state and local governments have declined from an 11.7 percent share of the federal budget in 1978 to a 6.2 percent share in 1985 (see Figure 1-1). This translates to a 1985 loss of $52.7 billion a year.

These grants to state and local governments—including education, transportation, housing, social services, training and employment, and economic development assistance—are today funded at a level that is less than one-half the amount spent for interest on the federal debt. As recently as 1980, these forms

Figure 1-1. Changing Federal Budget Priorities.

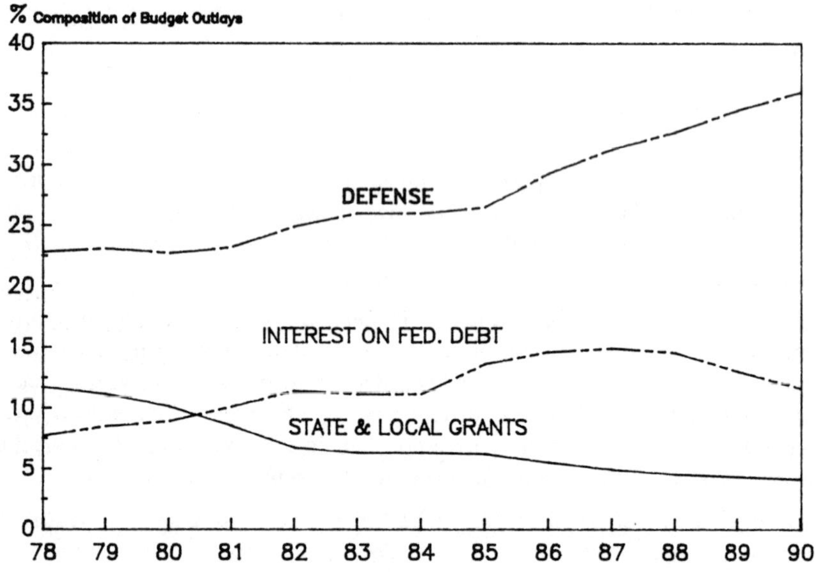

Source: U.S. Office of Management and Budget, *Historical Tables for the President's Fiscal Year 1986 Budget* (Washington, D.C.: U.S. Government Printing Office, 1985), Table 6-2. Note: Projections for 1986 to 1990 are as proposed by the President.

Figure 1-2. Budget Authority for Defense, 1976-1990 (*proposed*).

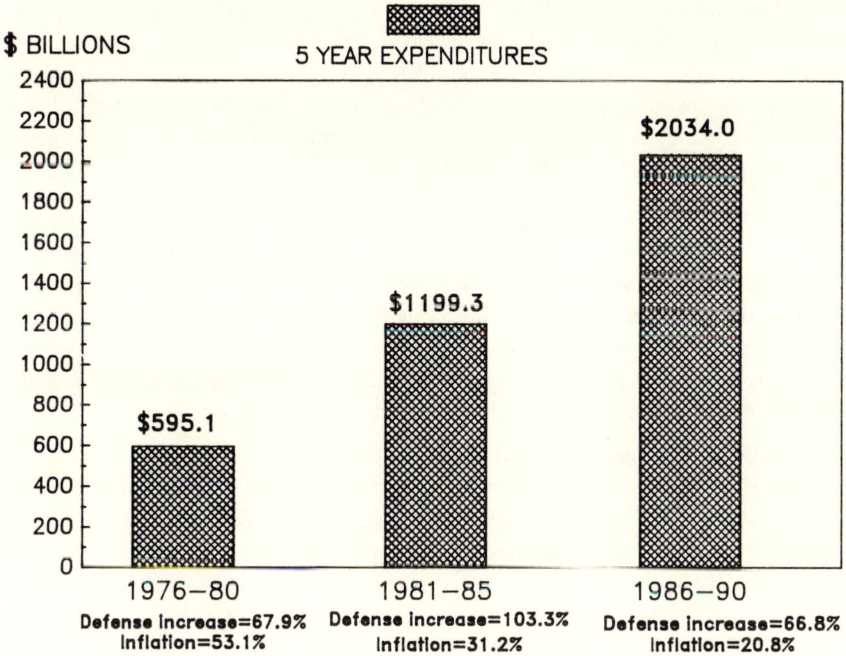

Source: U.S. Office of Management and Budget, *Historical Tables for the President's Fiscal Year 1986 Budget* (Washington, D.C.: U.S. Government Printing Office, 1985), various tables. Note: 1986-90 projections are as proposed by the President.

of assistance to state and local governments exceeded interest by a rather wide margin.

The funds that have been directed away from domestic programs have shifted primarily to defense expenditures—which have risen from 22.8 percent of federal outlays in 1978 to 26.5 percent in 1985 and are projected by the administration to rise to 36 percent by 1990—as well as to interest on the federal debt.

In Figure 1-2 it is shown that defense spending totaled $595 billion between 1976 to 1980, at levels that increased somewhat faster than inflation. Between 1981 and 1985, however, defense spending totaled nearly $1.2 trillion, increasing more than *triple* the rate of inflation. Defense spending is projected in the FY 1986 federal budget also to increase by more than triple the rate of inflation between 1986 and 1990, with over $2 trillion in expenditures during that time period. Fiscal 1986 congressional budget actions indicate that these increases will be moderated in coming years. A budget freeze period would provide an opportunity to conduct a thorough examination of the defense spending levels required to meet national security objectives an examination that many assert has not as yet been attempted.[5]

Federal spending as a whole is greater in 1986 as a percentage of gross national product (23.3 percent) than it was in 1980 (at 22.9 percent). There has been no overall austerity program in recent years; rather, the difference has been a change in spending priorities. According to an Urban Institute study, "Not since 1932 has there been such a redirection of public purposes."[6] This redirection has affected cities and their residents in all areas:

- Rebuilding decaying communities is of crucial importance to cities. Combating crime, educational deficiencies, drug abuse, and the full array of social maladies found in central cities starts with a decent living environment. Yet, federal housing assistance has been cut by over 60 percent since 1982. Moreover, a two-year moratorium on virtually all forms of housing assistance was proposed by the President in the 1986 budget, although Congress enacted an additional 7 percent reduction in housing assistance for 1986.
- Another key to achieving fulfillment and economic independence is a job. However, employment and training funds have been cut by more than half since 1980. The President's 1986 budget proposed additional cuts of 22 percent in jobs programs, including the elimination of the WIN training program for welfare recipients and Jobs Corps, the intensive youth job-training program in a residential setting. Congress restored most of those cuts, reducing jobs programs by an additional 8 percent.
- The other key to self-sufficiency is education. However, education's share of the federal budget has declined from 2.4 percent in 1979 to 1.8 percent in 1986, costing urban school systems billions of dollars. The President proposed to decrease federal education programs by an additional 17 percent in 1986 although Congress enacted a 2 percent cut.
- The highly successful, job-generating Urban Development Action Grant (UDAG) program, which encourages capital infusion in cities, was proposed for elimination in the fiscal year 1986 budget. This program and Community Development Block Grants (CDBGs) have lost considerable ground to inflation in recent years. Congressional 1986 actions retained UDAGs at 75 percent and CDBGs at 90 percent of 1985 levels.
- Child care ranks with the above keys to achieving self-sufficiency. The decline in child care assistance is a major cause of poverty in female-headed households. More than a third of single-parent families, where that parent is employed, lives below the poverty level. The Title XX Social Services Block Grant, the primary source of child care funding, has been reduced 24 percent in five years from the funding levels that would have prevailed under previous policies.

- Other measures that have been reduced from previously planned funding levels include child nutrition, reduced 28 percent; Aid to Families with Dependent Children, 14 percent; and food stamps, 14 percent.[7]
- Federal crime-fighting assistance to state and local governments is only one-fifth the level it was in 1975. Jurisdictions with high levels of poverty—and therefore high levels of crime—have had to divert scarce resources needed for education and other means of building self-sufficiency to put those funds into police, judicial, and correctional systems.
- Federal public transit funding makes bus and rail systems affordable to citizens, so that cities can serve as efficient centers of commerce and culture. High transit fares literally drive people to suburban shopping centers and business sites. Transit operating assistance has already declined by 21 percent since 1980, total elimination now being urged by the executive branch. In 1986 Congress retained operating assistance at 1985 levels.
- Federal revenue sharing allocations are just 25 percent of their 1972 levels, in inflation-adjusted dollars.[8] This program was also proposed for elimination in the president's 1986 budget, although Congress adopted a one-year-only retention of revenue sharing for 1986.
- The combination of tax and domestic policies has especially affected cities, with their disproportionate levels of low-income citizens. The lowest income Americans lost 7.6 percent of their disposable income between 1980 and 1984; the highest income citizens gained 8.7 percent in disposable income during the same period.[9]

One need not be an economist or sociologist to understand the damage. The net effect of all of these changes is clearly destructive to cities, with their large numbers of lower income people who are struggling to overcome disadvantages that were overwhelming in scale even prior to these domestic policy revisions.

Over a longer term, several national policies have favored suburban over urban development. The massive federal highway system has aided dispersal of population. Retail shopping centers are made possible by our nation's subsidized accommodation to the automobile. Tax policies over time favored investment in housing over other development, especially the higher priced, lower density construction of single-family homes (which would not be feasible for many without property and interest tax deductions). Defense and other federal procurement is placed disproportionately outside urban, high-unemployment areas, and this trend is accelerating. Above all, a financing structure has evolved over the years that requires the residents of high-poverty areas to pay a disproportionate share of the costs for treating poverty—while those who have the financial means for mobility can and do escape this heavier tax burden simply by moving across a jurisdiction's borders. Weak equal opportunity policies which are rarely enforced also place at a disadvantage cities that have high proportions of those subject to discrimination while favoring jurisdictions having populations that benefit from the status quo.

GUIDING PRINCIPLES IN FORMING URBAN POLICY

Three guiding principles provide the foundation for this mayors' national urban policy report.

1. *Budget Freeze.* Mayors have sought a freeze on all non-means-tested programs for at least a year, during which the future direction of urban and other programs should be thoroughly evaluated. Policies offered for future years should also have reasonable pricetags, in view of the need to control federal deficits over an extended upcoming period.
2. *Self-Sufficiency for All People and Regions.* Policies that move people from dependency on government to economic independence are proposed by mayors. Moreover, policies are offered that remove the excessive financial burdens on urban centers having a disproportionate share of poverty, unemployment, and related problems. Improvement is possible only when the financial burdens are shared equitably among all levels of government.
3. *Private Sector Emphasis.* A primary lesson learned over the last several years by mayors and urban analysts, progressives and conservatives alike, is that governments cannot solve socioeconomic problems without a strong private sector partnership. This report recognizes the need to support and strengthen the service delivery systems run by local governments in urban areas. Nonetheless, entry-level government jobs cannot keep pace with the employment needs of the millions of urban residents who are victims of structural unemployment. Similarly, keeping people at a subsistence level through public assistance leads us nowhere.

Private sector employment has far greater potential. Business management and ownership opportunities for those now excluded help even more. A 15 or 20 percent government leverage to stimulate private sector development adds much more to the income stream than a 100 percent government investment in some government program. Mayors' policies therefore emphasize the private sector, not only to help urban citizens but also to boost the competitive abilities of U.S. enterprise.

SUMMARY OF MAYORS' POLICIES

Following is a summary of mayors' urban policies. These policies have been adopted over the years by the U.S. Conference of Mayors through the established, formal policy processes of the organization.

National Urban Development Bank

The cornerstone of mayors' policies is capital infusion into economically disadvantaged areas. Public capital assistance would be leveraged to stimulate five to twenty times those levels in private sector investments. In this way, businesses are attracted and retained, and jobs are created. Moreover, the bank's infrastructure division would reduce the critical backlog in the repair of bridges, waterways, port facilities, roadways, and prisons.

Mayors are often asked why public funds should be used to subsidize "economically inefficient" areas and firms. First, subsidies from all levels of government are already high for nonproductive public assistance types of programs. Economic development and jobs are needed to reduce these public subsidies.

Second, cities are "inefficient" not for any inherent reason but simply because the nation's intergovernmental fiscal structure forces cities to shoulder a disproportionate share of poverty-related burdens. The general public has a responsibility to remove artificial barriers to competition and produce a more efficient balance so that all sectors have an opportunity to grow and prosper.

Third, subsidy levels are already enormous for private sector assistance to affluent businesses in affluent areas. Chapter 3 provides dozens of examples of tax breaks, research and development grants, credit corporations, and federal banks that today give $100 billion a year in assistance to healthy corporations in areas that have little poverty and unemployment. The National Urban Development Bank is intended to help move individuals, cities, and entire regions from dependence to self-sufficiency. The bank would be capitalized at $5 billion per year for four years, after which time it will offer loans to firms, on a competitive basis, from loan repayments, without the need for further public contributions.

The bank is modeled after the highly successful but relatively small-scaled Urban Development Action Grant program, a program that is worthy of continued support based on its track record.

Targeted Fiscal Assistance to Economically Distressed Areas

In Chapter 4 mayors recommend retaining general revenue sharing through the budget freeze period recommended by mayors and consideration of a targeted fiscal assistance program at some future point.

Those cities with the greatest levels of unemployment and poverty are the very ones that are forced to lay off employees, reduce services to their citizens, and increase taxes. As economic conditions deteriorate over time, the tax base dwindles and social needs mount, necessitating further drastic budget reduction measures. Such measures have accelerated urban problems by forcing from the cities taxpaying citizens and businesses, in a never-ending downward spiral that has continued for two to three decades in many cities.

A targeted fiscal assistance program would help restore fiscal balance to the nation's intergovernmental structure. The costs of poverty—a national problem—can be shared more equitably. Taxes can be restored to levels comparable to those found in the more affluent jurisdictions. Services that help build self-sufficiency can be retained. Jobs can be created in the private and public sectors.

National Employment and Training Policies

It is incredible to mayors that the nation has never put a strategy together to achieve full employment. With the $24 billion a year spent by the U.S. Department of Labor or the $2 billion spent by Commerce, some sort of action plan would seem in order. We have national legislation, the Humphrey-Hawkins Act of 1978, which requires the development of a comprehensive and consistent policy to achieve a 4 percent full employment level, but that act has not as yet been implemented.

Numerous urban centers have double-digit unemployment in times of economic recovery and expansion, while their suburbs have just 3 percent or 4 percent unemployment. All major urban centers have double-digit unemployment if one were to count, as part of the unemployed, the large numbers of discouraged workers (no longer in the labor force) found disproportionately among lower income citizens. The nation tolerates too well these enormous imbalances as well as clearly excessive unemployment rates among minorities and youth. Federal employment and training programs only reach, by official estimate, 3.7 percent of the eligible population (the unemployed, economically disadvantaged).[10] Moreover, state and local governments receive no national guidance whatever on what skills they should train citizens to achieve, what training program designs are most effective, or how to treat dislocated workers. The federal government has made no attempt to track and prepare for technological trends.

In Chapter 5 mayors propose a national employment and training policy, which would identify economic and technological trends; determine long- and short-term education and training needs; develop workable affirmative action measures to ensure equal opportunities for minorities, women, the economically disadvantaged, youth, aliens, refugees, and ex-offenders; and determine the appropriate roles of the various levels of government and the nongovernmental sectors in achieving full employment.

After a budget freeze period, consideration could be given to a private sector job creation program to reduce unemployment by a minimum of one percentage point, to be targeted to the economically disadvantaged. Overall job training funding could be restored at least to prior Comprehensive Employment and Training Act (CETA) levels.

Equal Opportunity

Over time, waves of political philosophy come and go. There are progressive, conservative, liberal, reactionary, and a variety of other beliefs. Whatever school of thought is in the ascendancy, mayors call for an explicit national commitment to equality of opportunity in the United States for all races and both sexes. Explicit plans to achieve equal economic opportunity and full integration of the U.S. labor force and society have not been drawn by any major political party. Instead, policymakers rely on natural evolution, as if time itself will someday bring needed reform.

Over the past several administrations, there has been inadequate leadership in achieving equal opportunity and often not even mention of the urgency for progress in human rights. In very recent years, what gains have been won have been explicitly attacked. Goals and timetables, designed to overcome systematic discrimination, are no longer sought by the federal government. Over the last three years, there has been only one debarment (i.e., loss of federal contract or a ban on a firm's ability to bid on future government contracts) due to failure to achieve or maintain fair hiring patterns. The dollar amount of back pay awards in discrimination cases has declined dramatically. Meanwhile, as demonstrated in Chapter 2, the income, poverty, and unemployment gaps between whites and minorities are growing wider over time, in proportional as well as absolute terms.

U.S. urban centers have been used as repositories for the effects of centuries of abuse. Cities are expected to solve injustice caused by the larger society and somehow marshall the resources to pay for the solutions. In this way, more affluent jurisdictions can turn their attention and resources to quality education, recreation centers, industrial parks, and so on to perpetuate their advantages. This peculiar moral and fiscal arrangement accounts for the alleged economic inefficiency of cities as much as anything else. Conversely, a sincere national commitment to equality of opportunity can do more to help cities than any other action the nation can take.

In Chapter 6 mayors call for presidential and congressional leadership in building a consensus for equality of economic opportunity among all races and both sexes. This leadership includes the development of a specific, achievable national affirmative action strategy with legislation, executive orders, and other means to achieve fully representative levels of minorities and women at all salary levels in the private and public sectors.

The federal government has enormous power at its disposal to achieve these goals. With 75,000 private sector establishments doing business with the federal government and thousands more subcontractors, together employing over 30 million people, the federal government can successfully insist on fair employment patterns. Goals and timetables to achieve such fairness should be vigorously enforced. Mayors support equal pay for work of comparable value, in opposition to abnormally low wages in sex-segregated "women's work" types of jobs. Debarment should be used for firms with poor affirmative action policies and records.

Our nation can never be truly open to all as long as minority-owned firms have less than 1 percent of the gross receipts for U.S. businesses as a whole. Goals and timetables for a fair share of contracting with minority-owned businesses should be initiated for all federal agencies, including subcontracting goals for all federal contractors.

The federal government could give consideration to business incentives, through the tax system, to achieve fair representation of minorities, women, and the handicapped at all salary levels—a human investment tax credit.

Housing

In Chapter 7 mayors call for a reexamination of our nation's housing policies. Because of growing federal deficits, a reorientation toward defense spending and spiraling housing costs, our nation's subsidized housing programs have been slashed by more than half. New construction and substantial rehabilitation of low-income housing have been virtually halted.

Subsidized housing for the low income is considered by some a luxury that the nation can no longer afford. However, the annual housing subsidy in 1985 to middle and upper income households, through homeownership tax deductions, was nearly four times the subsidy levels provided to the low income through federal housing programs.

Rental housing costs are a family's primary expenditure and therefore a major contributor to poverty among those with little disposable income. A good living environment is essential to lifting oneself out of poverty. Today, only a quarter of eligible families receive housing assistance, and long two-year-plus waiting lists for housing assistance are the norm.

Various experiments in housing subsidy are proposed at the federal level, usually involving a reduction in resource commitment. Mayors are receptive to improved or different forms of housing subsidy, as long as a supply of decent, safe, sanitary, and affordable housing is available to all income classes. Ensuring such a supply, however, will inevitably mean retaining and ultimately increasing (after the budget freeze period) resource commitments. In Chapter 7 mayors urge funding the comprehensive public housing modernization program at adequate levels, additional units of rental subsidies, new construction, and rehabilitation of low- and moderate-income subsidized housing so that the future supply does not run dry.

Education

In Chapter 8 mayors call for retaining federal investment in urban children during the budget freeze period, with consideration for added commitments in the future. Unequal economic opportunity starts with educational inequality. In recent years the correlation between the quality of education and the size of parental bank accounts has grown increasingly strong, as federal funds to economically disadvantaged school systems have been losing ground to inflation. States are not replenishing the lost federal revenues, leaving urban school systems no choice but to cut local efforts sharply.

We can measure tangible educational achievement gains since federal education support for urban school systems has increased over the levels of an earlier era. Math and reading skills attainment by urban children increased dramatically from a decade ago, and the proportion of minority college students has doubled.

Federal education funding cannot by itself overcome the effects of broken families, joblessness, and poverty, but it is an essential basis for self-sufficiency. The foundation for future educational gains is today threatened because of funding deficiencies that inevitably will widen all of the urban-suburban disparities and jeopardize all of our institutions.

Mayors propose retaining "Chapter I and II" educational budget levels and student loan programs through the budget freeze period, with annual increases thereafter which, at a minimum, keep pace with inflation. The Chapter II formula should provide funding on the basis of need. After the freeze period, additional funding of math, science, and vocational education could be considered to ensure that students and U.S. businesses can meet the high technology needs of today and tomorrow. Handicapped children should receive the necessary federal funding to carry out the mandates of the law.

Mayors call for passage of federal desegregation assistance legislation to provide equal educational opportunities for minority children and to support enforcement of existing desegregation laws. Desegregation efforts have been diluted since the consolidation of the Emergency School Aid Act into the Chapter II Block Grant.

Mayors also urge adequate funding of the Bilingual Education Act so that limited or non-English-speaking students are not shut off from the mainstream of American society. The "sink or swim" method of education, without bilingual assistance, results in too many educational drownings.

Finally, mayors vigorously oppose tuition tax credits, educational vouchers, and other proposals that promote segregation by race and income, create constitutional conflicts between church and state, reduce services to economically disadvantaged students, and devastate the already struggling urban school system. The relatively small amount per family that a tax credit would provide cannot help the low income attend private schools. It merely offers public resources to encourage enrollment of middle and upper class students in private schools. These resources are needed to improve public school systems.

Social Services

Because of shifting federal priorities—and a resistance to "handouts" to impoverished citizens—federal social services funding has been reduced considerably in recent years. In fact, social services funding today is 40 percent less than the 1979 level in real (inflation-adjusted) dollars, and 11 percent less in absolute dollars. In Chapter 9 mayors call for restoration of funding of the Social Services Block Grant after the budget freeze period.

What is not recognized enough is that much of the social services funding is essential to reduce long-term domestic spending. Social services often reduce dependency on public assistance programs; prevent the continuation of family problems; defer or prevent costly institutionalization; and generally help individuals, families, and communities cope with the varied effects of poverty. Thus, homecare, transportation, homemaker, meals-on-wheels, and other services can keep people in their homes and communities rather than in publicly subsidized institutions at a far greater cost. Adolescent pregnancy prevention can lead to reduction in welfare and health service expenditures. Similarly, day care for children can free a parent to obtain work or job training. Foster care enables placement of a child in a home setting, reducing adjustment problems. Adoption services provide the maximum feasible stability for a child, preventing a host of social problems later. Counseling and protection in child abuse cases can help prevent in the child the development of a variety of maladies. Other social services include assistance to drug and alcohol abusers, boarding home services, emergency services, independent living for the handicapped, multiservice programs for the aged, and social services in corrections institutions.

Human services programs are supported by a wide variety of federal, state, and local government and private funding sources. They are provided by a similarly wide range of agencies. Often there is little coordination between the planning for and funding of services that benefit the residents of a given community. Providing social services funds directly to local governments having the capacity to deliver social services could go a long way toward reducing these difficulties.

Child care is emerging as a human services issue of the very highest priority because of the changing composition of the U.S. labor market. Only 19 percent of women with children under age eighteen were in the labor force in 1947; in contrast, 60 percent of women with children were employed in 1982—a threefold increase in thirty-five years. The costs of child care keep many working mothers in poverty and prevent others from seeking and holding a job. After the budget freeze period, consideration could be given to an annual earmark for child care, to be added to the Social Services Block Grant.

Food and Nutrition

The debate over whether there is hunger in the United States is bizarre to mayors. The nation's mayors see clear, unmistakable evidence of hunger in their cities every day. Tens of thousands of people do not line up for cheese in the cold of winter or the heat of summer unless they have no alternative, unless they need food and do not have the money to buy it. Growing numbers of people, including many families with children, do not come to soup kitchens unless they must, unless they have nothing to eat and nowhere to go.

In October 1982, the Conference of Mayors conducted a survey which found that only 43 percent of the emergency service needs—for food, shelter, and emergency medical help—were being met in cities. In June 1983, the Conference developed case studies on hunger in eight cities across the nation. Despite differing local economic conditions and rates of unemployment, all of the cities examined had experienced dramatic increases in the demand for emergency food assistance; only three of the eight cities were able to serve all of those in need of food assistance. A 1984 survey of cities nationwide revealed a 70 percent increase in the demand for food assistance in just one year.[11] Even though local actions provide food banks, food hotlines, surplus food distribution systems, and the like, the problem of hunger is continuing to grow in cities. The economic recovery is not "trickling down" to those in greatest need.

The hardships caused by deep cuts in federal food programs were exacerbated by simultaneous cuts in other federal assistance programs designed to help low-income persons: Aid to Families with Dependent Children (AFDC), low-income energy assistance, and subsidized housing programs, to name a few. Many families facing unemployment, often for the first time, have found that they cannot provide for their families' needs once their unemployment benefits are depleted, and they are not eligible for government assistance. An enormous number of new soup kitchens and food pantries have opened their doors in the past three years. The lines at these emergency centers have multiplied and, in most cases, the doors must close before all those seeking assistance can be served.

Of deepest concern are the numerous children from female-headed households and other children who are growing up in poverty, without the nourishment needed to prevent stunted physical and educational growth. Despite growing poverty, 3 million fewer children receive school lunches each day than was the case a few years ago.

The provision of food for the hungry is the most minimal and elemental commitment a government can make to citizens. In Chapter 10 mayors call for the retention of food and nutrition programs at least at congressionally adopted fiscal 1985 levels during the freeze period. Ultimately, the fundamental food assistance programs—namely, food stamps, child nutrition, and WIC (Special Supplemental Program for Women, Infants and Children)—should be supported as entitlement programs. In this way, all those who are eligible for and in need of the assistance can receive it. Medicaid cost increases could be eased somewhat over time as nourishment increases child health; moreover, infant mortality would be reduced. In building such a nutritional network, care should be taken to ensure that emergency food assistance is available for those having immediate needs.

Public Assistance Reform

In Chapter 11 mayors urge federalization of public assistance, consistent with mayors' policies adopted over many years. Nowhere is the controversy over intergovernmental responsibility drawn so clearly as in the case of public assistance or "welfare." States and cities that have disproportionate numbers of the poor are themselves invariably at a fiscal disadvantage compared to states and cities having few poor. The fiscally impoverished states and cities cannot compete with the more affluent jurisdictions, and create improved conditions for economic development, when they must pay out disproportionately large shares of their revenues for public assistance and the vast array of related rehabilitation and correctional costs associated with poverty. Federalization of public assistance is one way to reduce fiscal handicaps and better share the costs of treating poverty among affluent and impoverished jurisdictions alike. In this way, we improve opportunities for balanced economic growth among all states and cities. Poverty should be recognized as a national responsibility, and the federal government is the only instrument that can provide equitable sharing of this responsibility among all Americans.

Federalization would replace the current patchwork of local-state-federal public assistance programs which have a variety of payment levels and regulations. For example, the maximum AFDC payment for a three-person family in Tennessee is $138; in Minnesota it is $524. Eleven states require their cities and towns to share in AFDC costs, adding to the fiscal responsibilities of such overburdened central cities as New York City, Newark, Denver, Oakland, Baltimore, Cleveland, and many others, as well as Washington, D.C., which has state funding responsibilities.

As a consequence of the financial inability (or unwillingness) of overburdened state and local governments to pay for public assistance costs, AFDC benefits have lagged far behind inflation, declining 33 percent in real dollar value from 1970 to 1985.

Mayors recommend establishment of a single federally funded income maintenance program with a national minimum benefit level designed to provide a decent standard of living for families and individuals who cannot reasonably be expected to work. This includes such persons as many of the handicapped, single parents with young children, and those with major health or emotional problems. Benefit levels should be standardized nationally with regional cost-of-living adjustments.

By spreading the public assistance burdens among all Americans, states and cities will have more resources to combat the variety of social and economic problems resulting from the alarmingly high poverty rates. To ease additional financial burden on the federal government, perhaps arrangements could be devised to provide for state contributions into a national fund.

To help reduce public assistance costs in the long run, the national employment and training policy (Chapter 5) should include specific strategies to enable people to proceed from a life of dependence on government programs to self-dependence, by means of training, work experience, and job placement programs for those AFDC recipients able to work. This proposal goes well beyond "workfare," in that meaningful training and career opportunities are offered in areas of endeavor chosen by citizens rather than compulsory employment in low-skill, dead-end jobs.

Health

Mayors agree with the need to curtail health costs. If left unchecked, Medicare (which insures 26 million elderly and 3 million disabled) and Medicaid (which serves 20 million low-income citizens) can easily increase 15 percent or more each year. Comprehensive revisions to the health care system are essential, and further changes in benefit levels as well as hospital and physician payments are inevitable. While these reforms are being developed, mayors urge that the health needs of those presently excluded or insufficiently covered be considered.

Over the decades preceding the 1980s, the nation had been progressing steadily toward some form of universal health coverage, as the federal government accepted ever-growing responsibility in health care for the indigent. The dream that everyone could have access to affordable health care once seemed achievable. However, the current outlook is not as optimistic.

Today, more than 12 percent of Americans—21 million adults and 7 million children—are considered medically disadvantaged. They lack health insurance, and they needed health care in the previous twelve months but were unable to obtain it.[19]

Medicaid is usually thought of as the health safety net for the low income. To the contrary, over half of the nation's population living in poverty are ineligible for Medicaid. A variety of low-income individuals, children in two-parent families below the poverty level, first-time pregnant low-income women, the working poor, plus millions of people with incomes just above the poverty level are often shut out from any form of public or private health insurance.

As an example of the uninsured, 80 percent of those without a job for a year are without health insurance. Equally significant, about half of all those uninsured are employed. Most tragic of all in its discriminatory implications for America's health system, 59 percent of the poor and near-poor blacks and 62 percent of the poor and near-poor Hispanics were uninsured all or part of the year.[13]

Nor does Medicare mean that the health problems of the elderly are provided for. In fact, the elderly pay 29.9 percent of their total health costs directly out of pocket, not even counting the Medicare premiums they pay. Again, it is the poor who are disadvantaged by the health systems. The elderly with annual incomes of $5,000 or less pay an average of 21.5 percent of their incomes on medical care, compared to 3.1 percent paid by the elderly with incomes over $20,000.[14]

We still live in a time when the capability of remaining in good health is strongly correlated to one's financial means. While cost containment methods continue to be devised, mayors seek an improved balance in our health care systems.

Eventually, the nation should move toward federal assumption of the full health care costs of all medically indigent. In this way, we ensure that all Americans accept an equal share of these costs rather than expecting jurisdictions with large numbers of impoverished people to pay a disproportionate share. While the nation moves toward this long-term goal, several intermediate steps can be taken.

Some 12 million Americans are among the working poor, the vast majority of whom lack public or private health coverage. Legislation could require the expansion of private health insurance to the workplace for all, with some federal subsidy when necessary. Employers and employees (on a sliding scale, depending on income) would primarily bear the cost.

The nation could also consider extending health insurance to the more than 5 million unemployed citizens who lack health insurance. Employers and current workers, as well as public funds, could help create an insurance pool for the unemployed. Moreover, at a cost of $3 billion annually, consideration should be given, after the freeze period, to extending Medicaid to the nearly 4 million low-income citizens not now covered.

At a much lower cost than universal health coverage for the low income, the nation could improve federal support for hospitals that treat the uninsured. At a cost of $6 to $7 billion a year, public hospitals can be reimbursed for services rendered free to the uninsured, and private hospitals can be given the needed economic incentive to accept patients of all income levels. Concomitantly, private hospitals must be required to accept a fair share of the poor; presently, "dumping" of patients having low incomes on public hospitals is a common practice.

Mayors also seek adequate federal funding for public disease prevention and clinical programs that impact on urban areas, including drug abuse, alcoholism, rodent control, lead-based-paint-poisoning prevention, AIDS screening, VD control, and tuberculosis programs. Because of insufficient local resources to treat the wide array of urban concerns, many of these public health problems are allowed to run rampant.

In an all-too-real sense, our nation's inequitable health policies are epitomized by the excessive and disproportionate rate of infant mortality among minorities and the low income in general. Nationally, mortality among black babies is double the rate of white babies. In some cities this black-to-white ratio can be as high as six to one. In some sections of cities, the infant mortality rates are as high as in the poorest, most underdeveloped nations of the world.

In fact, forty-four states reported reductions in prenatal and delivery systems following implementation of the maternal and child health block grant, and concurrent funding reductions, in 1982. Moreover, twenty-six states do not provide Medicaid coverage to pregnant women and children in poor two-parent families; ten states do not cover first-time pregnant women. Half of the women of child-bearing age have no health insurance of any kind. This is one of those issues that should be shocking to Americans but which receives almost no attention from those who are able to obtain adequate maternal care for their own families. Through Medicaid, Maternal and Child Health block grant reforms, and nutrition assistance supplementing greater local efforts, these infant death rates must be substantially lowered.

The Urban Elderly

In Chapter 13 mayors consider policies for the urban elderly. Many of the reforms needed are comprehensive, requiring thoughtful, intergovernmental planning, at which our nation has never been very successful. Most of the recent budget reductions affecting the elderly have long-term consequences, hindering the ability of the elderly to live independently and remain active in their communities. This is precisely the area where further attention is needed.

For example, the nation has not given sufficient attention to finding suitable employment opportunities for older workers. The national employment and training policy (Chapter 5) should include such strategies. Moreover, the Social Security Act should be amended to reduce penalties for working beyond the "retirement age."

A new Community Health and Support Services Act could be established to provide comprehensive, community-based health and support services, enabling the older person to receive a level of health and social care required for remaining independent in the community for the longest possible time. The existing health care system encourages spiraling costs by emphasizing institutionalized, acute, and long-term care over preventive or in-house care. Most low-income elderly spend 20 percent and more of their income on health care. To make ends meet, they average 35 percent fewer physician visits and 27 percent fewer prescription drugs than do the more affluent. Without adequate community-based care, health is allowed to deteriorate, and long-term care is required. When this occurs, seniors are likely to spend themselves quickly into Medicaid eligibility, costing governments at all levels considerably more than the cost of programs that foster independent living. To reduce these problems and costs, federally financed in-home health and support services should be expanded, with increased local flexibility and involvement.

One of the best ways to obtain "community-based" care is through families and friends. Federal tax incentives can encourage such help.

Mayors insist that attempts to cut Medicaid costs by increasing the age of eligibility above sixty-five must be strongly resisted. Such proposals are blatantly discriminatory against blacks and other minorities. Because of poorer health care, difficult living conditions, hypertension, nutrition problems, and the like, the life expectancy of minorities is much lower than that of whites; for example, black males have a life expectancy of just 65.2 years compared to 71.6 years for white males. Raising the age of Medicare eligibility would reduce life expectancy even further.

Mayors of older, high-density urban centers are all familiar with the long waiting lists that the elderly confront when they try to receive some help with their housing costs. Often the lists are years long—an injustice to this group, for whom time is the most precious of all goods. Consideration should be given to reforming the nation's housing policies, after the freeze period, to subsidize an additional 20,000 units a year for the elderly and handicapped. Moreover, tax and other incentives should be developed to encourage a 200,000-unit increase in the nation's supply of housing for older Americans from all sources, private and public. As part of these reforms, a national demonstration program on alternative living arrangements for older persons should be implemented, promoting closer coordination of community support services and preventive forms of health services.

Crime-Fighting Assistance

We have seen a significant 17 percent reduction in the nation's crime rate over the past four years. Nonetheless, crime levels are still double what they were just two decades ago. Crime remains one of the largest threats to urban well-being, for urban residents as well as suburban commuters and out-of-town visitors, requiring concerted pressure by all levels of government.

The causes of crime extend beyond urban boundaries; they are national in scope. One cannot hold a city culpable for having excessive poverty, joblessness, and other factors correlated with high crime rates any more than one can justifiably praise a suburban jurisdiction for freeing itself from those conditions. Yet, cities are required to divert a much larger share of their resources for their police and other criminal justice systems, compared to more affluent jurisdictions.

Ten years ago $480 million was allocated in federal crime control assistance to state and local governments. Today that level of commitment has declined to about $60 million. In Chapter 14 mayors recommend consideration of a federal policy, which, after the proposed budget freeze, would restore the federal share of crime-fighting responsibility. The vast majority of funds should reach local crime-fighting forces, with a minimal level supporting federal and state administrative and research functions. The discretionary grant program should be prioritized on the basis of a jurisdiction's crime rate, a measure that standardizes the number of offenses on the basis of population.

The discretionary grant programs could be used to support such programs and initiatives as: (1) halting or dramatically reducing the illegal sale and distribution of controlled substances; one recent study indicated that 354 Baltimore heroin addicts committed 775,000 crimes in a nine-year period; (2) developing workable means to alleviate prison crowding, including alternatives to incarceration for nonviolent offenders; (3) ensuring the transfer of successful technologies developed around the country to local jurisdictions; (4) treating the complex problem of family violence; and (5) providing funding to state and local jurisdictions responding to emergency situations. The Atlanta child murders were a tragic case of the need for greater emergency assistance.

Moreover, mayors once again express their support for gun control, including national legislation that would ban the manufacture, sale, importation, and private possession of handguns, except for use by law enforcement personnel, the military, and sport clubs. At a minimum, Congress should adopt a national handgun registration law and enact mandatory minimum sentences for firearms-related crimes. Although many jurisdictions have enacted their own gun control laws, they have had limited success because, without federal legislation, they can offer no real control of the transportation of weapons across jurisdictional lines. Mayors originally proposed such national action in their resolution of 1972.

Transportation

In Chapter 15 mayors recommend long-term, consistent federal government support for transportation, with adequate resources, in recognition of the pivotal, catalytic role the federal government plays in the federal-state-local-private transportation network. The uneven, roller coaster, faltering commitment of the federal government in recent years necessarily weakens the ability of other levels of government and the private sector to maintain their share of the responsibilities to transportation needs.

The entire nation—not just city residents—uses the transportation systems of cities to reach the urban marketplace, jobs, education, and cultural centers. Therefore, the responsibility for urban transportation rests in the hands of the total public. Without adequate support, the essence of cities as efficient aggregations of people, commerce, structures, and ideas is threatened.

Mayors recommended that the federal government continue to provide transit capital assistance and do so in a multimode fashion: assistance for bus purchases, modernization of rail systems, and new rail systems. New rail projects in such cities as Detroit, Los Angeles, Houston, Pittsburgh, Miami, Atlanta, and the District of Columbia must go forward. The full level authorized in the Surface Transportation Assistance Act of 1982 is a minimum funding level for capital assistance. This act for the first time earmarked federal gasoline tax money for public transit, at one cent per gallon or $1.1 billion per year. Mayors enthusiastically endorse this financing tool.

Federal mass transit operating assistance, which pays for only 10 percent of total local transit operating costs, must be continued as a useful federal tool to help communities meet their overall transportation needs. Without such support, jurisdictions would have no choice but to increase bus and rail fares beyond the level of affordability for many and reduce service, creating an overdependency on the private auto with its side effects of air pollution, traffic congestion, and inefficient land use. Operating assistance at $870 million in FY 1986 is just 79 percent of the FY 1980 level of $1.1 billion and only 58 percent of that level in inflation-adjusted dollars. During the budget freeze period recommended by mayors, capital and operating assistance should be retained at 1985 levels rather than trimmed by 67 percent, as proposed by the president in the FY 1986 budget. Congress accepted the mayors' recommendations for a freeze in operating assistance for 1986, with a 14 percent reduction in capital assistance. These actions set the stage for a close examination of transportation assistance in 1987. In future years consideration should be given to increasing mass transit assistance at a minimum by annual price index adjustments.

Mayors recommend that transit service for the elderly and handicapped should be enhanced by all levels of government. Local governments should have the option of tailoring those transportation systems to meet their own community needs. For example, some cities may find that a separate transit system for the elderly and handicapped better meets their needs than federally mandated mechanical lift devices for all buses.

Federal Procurement Policies

The federal government is one of the nation's greatest economic forces, its budget amounting to nearly 25 percent of the gross national product. Obviously, the federal government is more than a passive monitor of economic growth and equity; its own actions determine who fares well and who does not. Targeted federal procurement of goods and services is one route to achieve balanced growth, so that areas of sluggish economic activity and heavy unemployment can better participate in economic recovery and growth.

In Chapter 16 mayors recommend a reasonable goal of 10 percent of federal government purchases to be targeted to high-unemployment areas. Moreover, a fair share (e.g., 10%) of goods and services should be procured from minority-owned and operated firms.

Strategic weapon systems are often difficult, and in many cases impossible, to target. These high-precision goods can be largely exempt from the procurement goals. However, procurement goals for the Defense Logistics Agency (involving nonstrategic services and supplies) should be strengthened.

To accomplish these goals, procurement outreach offices could be targeted to high-unemployment areas, with no additional federal funding, to seek actively contracts for businesses located in those areas. Currently, federal funding establishes procurement outreach centers in relatively affluent as well as distressed areas.

Targeting federal procurement adds enormous benefits at little cost: the Defense Logistics Agency awarded 61,203 contracts to firms in labor surplus areas between 1981 and 1984 and had to pay a price differential (averaging just 1.7%) on only 1,194 of these contracts. The cost per job created in these high-unemployment areas was just $1,326 which is only a third of the cost per job in traditional job programs.[15]

Finally, mayors recommend that all levels of government use caution in contracting out so as not to jeopardize the jobs of vulnerable, nonsupervisory members of the public workforce, thus exacerbating urban unemployment.

COSTS OF PROPOSALS

The proposals contained in this report—for a National Urban Development Bank, targeted fiscal assistance, job and training programs, equal opportunity enforcement, housing programs, education funding, federalization of public assistance, support for social services, increased food and nutritional programs, senior citizens services, anticrime efforts, health reform, transportation, and targeted federal procurement—have cost estimates attached to them whenever possible.

With adoption of the budget freeze resolution, mayors have sought no increases in urban-directed, non-means-tested programs in fiscal year 1986 and the duration of the freeze period. During the freeze period, future urban investment options should be considered, including those proposed by mayors, as summarized in this book.

Mayors caution against adding the cost of all programs together to form one large future pricetag. It is unlikely, to say the least, that all proposals could be adopted in any one fiscal year after the budget freeze period. Moreover, mayors are more than willing to work with the executive and legislative branches to analyze and discuss which of the policy proposals should be funded, revised, reduced, or eliminated. For example, mayors have for years proposed federalization of welfare costs (Chapter 11) as a way to redistribute the poverty burden more equitably among all jurisdictions. If this policy reform is ultimately enacted, it could well reduce the extent of a targeted fiscal assistance program (Chapter 4), at least insofar as state participation is concerned. Similarly, support for equal opportunity proposals (Chapter 6) would inevitably reduce funding of human services, housing assistance, food and nutrition, and many other programs over time. Proposals to stimulate private sector investment (Chapter 3), if fully funded, could reduce the level of job creation program funding.

MEASURES TO REDUCE THE FEDERAL DEFICIT

The mayors' budget freeze resolution, adopted in March 1985 by the Conference of Mayors' Executive Committee, also provides for "increased federal revenues from measures other than the personal income tax." The increased revenues would be placed in a trust fund and devoted exclusively to deficit reduction.

By a combination of a budget freeze, which would restrain defense expenditures as well as urban programs, and some revenue increases, the federal budget would be placed on a sounder basis.

Defense Expenditures

It is not essential that we continue to pour 12 percent and 13 percent a year federal expenditure increases into the defense industry. An Urban Institute study considers the political swings in budget policies over time:

> . . . one can easily imagine some future administration tackling an "overgrown" defense budget rife with "fraud, waste, and abuse" in much the same way the current one has tackled the non-defense budget. Indeed there are already signs of waning public support for this dramatic shift in priorities and growing concern among experts about the scale and composition of the build-up—both of which appear to have been chosen with little thoughtful analysis.[16]

This study estimates that if defense spending were to continue to increase annually, but only at the rate of inflation instead of seven or more percentage points a year above inflation, then a savings of $68 billion a year could be realized by the time of the fiscal year 1989 budget. Moreover, an international arms reduction agreement could produce considerably greater savings.

If one is persuaded that the military buildup is of such urgency that it must proceed at a pace greater than inflation, growth at a rate of 3 percent a year *above* inflation would still yield a $28 billion a year savings by 1989 when compared to administration plans. Such a growth rate would still enable military expenditures to increase another full percentage point as a share of the gross national product by the end of this decade.[17]

Congressional actions on the 1986 budget could signal a major turning point in spending priorities. The president's proposal for a 10 percent defense expenditure increase was trimmed by Congress to 1 percent in 1986, with future increases substantially in excess of inflation now uncertain at best.

Federal Tax Increases

The federal tax reductions of 1981 are accounting for nearly all of the federal deficits. The 1986 revenue loss resulting from the 1981 tax reductions is estimated in the federal budget at $210.8 billion, a sum that by itself exceeds the projected 1986 federal deficit of $175 billion.[18] These reductions are enacted to produce economic recovery, according to supply-side (as well as traditional Keynesian) reasoning. Now that the recession has ended, some restoration of tax revenues may be in order to produce federal budgets that are as close to being balanced as possible.

Mayors have taken no position on the types of tax increases that might be necessary; however, there are several likely candidates for consideration. As a result of federal tax changes, chiefly involving depreciation and investment deductions and credits, the effective corporate tax rate has been reduced from 33 percent in 1980 to under 16 percent today. Some restorations are being considered in 1986 tax reform legislation, so that a greater share of the tax burden would be shifted from individuals to corporations. Other revenue-raising possibilities include elimination of income averaging ($7 billion), increased alcohol and cigarette taxes ($6 billion), and a variety of other "loophole closings," tax simplification, and reform measures which could total $20 billion.[19] Restoration of a portion of the individual income tax cuts would of course yield considerably greater revenue.

Once the federal deficit and budgets are brought under control, decisions for the future can be reached by reviewing and refining options presented in this and other reports. A rational analysis of our trillion-dollar federal budget should indicate that development of our nation's full human potential through education, job training, economic development, and other urban policies is affordable, given an inclination to build them into national priorities.

NOTES TO CHAPTER 1

1. U.S. Department of Housing and Urban Development (HUD), *The President's National Urban Policy Report, 1982* (Washington, D.C.: HUD, 1982), p. 57.
2. U.S. Department of Housing and Urban Development (HUD), *The President's National Urban Policy Report, 1984* (Washington, D.C.: HUD, 1984), p. 63.
3. U.S. Bureau of the Census, Current Population Reports, Series P-60, No. 149, *Money Income and Poverty Status of Families and Persons in the United States: 1984* (Advance data from the March 1985 Current Population Survey) (Washington, D.C.: U.S. Government Printing Office, 1985), p. 10.
4. John L. Palmer and Isabel V. Sawhill, eds., *The Reagan Record: An Assessment of America's Changing Domestic Priorities* (Cambridge, Mass.: Ballinger Publishing Company, 1984), pp. 329, 332.
5. U.S. House of Representatives, House Committee on Budget, *President's FY 1986 Budget* (Washington, D.C.: U.S. Government Printing Office, 1985), p. 65.
6. Palmer and Sawhill, p. 1.
7. Ibid., pp. 185-86.
8. Richard P. Nathan, Testimony before Senate Subcommittee on Intergovernmental Relations, April 5, 1983, p. 4; updated by Figure 4-1.
9. Palmer and Sawhill, pp. 20, 228, 329.
10. Gary Walker et al., "An Independent Sector Assessment of the Job Training Partnerhsip Act" (Washington, D.C.: National Commission for Employment Policy, March 1984), p. 102.
11. U.S. Conference of Mayors (USCM), Task Force on Joblessness and Hunger, "Status Report: Emergency Food, Shelter, and Energy Programs in Twenty Cities" (Washington, D.C.: USCM, January 1984), pp. 1-2.
12. The Robert Wood Johnson Foundation, "Updated Report on Access to Health Care for the American People" (Princeton, N.J.: The Robert Wood Johnson Foundation, 1983), pp. 8-9.
13. National Health Law Program, "In Poor Health: The Administration's 1985 Health Budget" (Los Angeles: National Health Law Program, 1984), p. 17.
14. Refer to Chapter 10 for a full discussion.
15. Conversations with staff of Defense Logistics Agency, Department of Defense, October 1985.
16. Palmer and Sawhill, p. 26.
17. Ibid., p. 130.

18. Office of Management and Budget, *Budget of the U.S. Government, FY 1986* (Washington, D.C.: U.S. Government Printing Office, 1985), pp. 4-7; deficit estimate from the Congressional Budget Office (CBO), *The Economic and Budget Outlook, An Update* (Washington, D.C.: CBO, August 1985), p. 74.
19. Office of Management and Budget, pp. 118-298.

2 TRENDS IN THE SOCIAL AND ECONOMIC CONDITIONS OF AMERICAN CITIES

The era of concern for cities—the 1960s and parts of the 1970s—has been eclipsed in recent years by other issues: foreign policy, inflation, the nuclear freeze, and so forth. However, one should not gain the impression that the "urban crisis" has vanished or even diminished. The trends have accelerated since the era of concern. Although some downtowns are showing renewed signs of vitality and the back-to-the-city movement is restoring close-in housing in many cities, the problems of poverty, population and business loss, crime, race disparities, housing deterioration, and unemployment all remain at unacceptable levels.

POPULATION

In 1950, 59 percent of all residents of metropolitan areas lived inside the central cities of those metropolitan areas and 41 percent lived in the suburbs. By 1980 this situation had been reversed: 40 percent of metropolitan area residents lived in cities and 60 percent lived in the suburbs.

During the 1970s city population increased just two-tenths of 1 percent, and suburban population increased 18.2 percent. Although the decade of the seventies was a break-even period for city populations as a whole, many central cities lost significant numbers of people (see Table 2-1). These trends continued into the 1980s, although population declines were less drastic in most cases.

In viewing the urban population declines in Table 2-1, it should be kept in mind that the U.S. population as a whole increased 10.5 percent between 1970

Table 2-1. Population Loss, Selected Cities, 1970-1980 and 1980-1984 (*percentage change*).

City	*1970-1980*	*1980-1984*
St. Louis	-27.2	-5.5
Cleveland	-23.6	-5.0
Buffalo	-22.7	-5.6
Detroit	-20.5	-10.5
Pittsburgh	-18.5	-5.3
Louisville	-17.5	-3.1
Washington, D.C.	-15.7	-2.5
Cincinnati	-15.0	-4.0
Minneapolis	-14.6	-3.5
Atlanta	-14.1	+0.2
Newark	-13.8	-5.7
Philadelphia	-13.4	-2.5
Baltimore	-13.1	-3.0
Boston	-12.2	+1.4
Kansas City	-11.7	-1.1
Milwaukee	-11.3	-2.5
Chicago	-10.8	-0.4
New York	-10.4	+1.3

and 1980 and 4.2 percent between 1980 and 1984. It is encouraging that in Table 2-1 cities, New York and Atlanta have registered modest increases in the 1980s, after double-digit percentage losses in the 1970s. Nonetheless, it is chilling to realize that Detroit's population declined from 1,514,000 to 1,089,000 between 1970 and 1984, while St. Louis experienced a decline from 622,000 to 429,000 in the same period.

Of the 181 cities having 100,000 or more in population, 84, or 46 percent, lost population or showed no gain between 1970 and 1980. Between 1980 and 1984, 31 percent of the 176 cities having more than 100,000 in population showed a decline. Therefore, the extent of urban population decline may be lessening somewhat. However, most of the large, old, high-density cities continue to experience considerable population drain.

Brookings Institution's urban analysts indicate that:

> Declines in population can be desirable if the area is overcrowded to start with—as were most cities as late as 1950. But initial falls in population . . . often start self-reinforcing effects that tend to perpetuate them well beyond relief of overcrowding. For this and other reasons, the amount of decline in most cities since 1980 has imposed negative impacts upon their residents and upon the nation as a whole. Many of these impacts result from the disproportionate concentration of low-income residents that typically accompanies falling big-city population.[1]

POVERTY

Population drains from cities usually occur among those who have acquired the financial means for mobility. Those left behind are often those who are most dependent upon government for help. However, as the tax base is diminished by the loss of the middle income population, the local government is financially unable to provide the services needed for citizens of any income level.

We are all familiar by now with the self-perpetuating effects of further tax increases and service cutbacks as cities attempt to cope with these population changes. More and more of the middle and upper-middle income citizens are driven out, while lowest income citizens have less and less of an opportunity to escape from the effects of concentrated poverty.

One of every five central city residents lives in poverty. Since this is an average figure, many of the most distressed cities have even larger concentrations of poverty. On average, the poverty rate is more than double in cities than it is in their surrounding suburbs; however, it is not unusual to find five or ten times or more the poverty rate in cities than in their suburbs.

Poverty is a growing problem in cities and nationwide. Between 1978 and 1984 the national poverty rate increased from 11.4 percent to 14.4 percent, with 1983 having the peak poverty rate of 15.3 percent. Even with the nearly one percentage point decline in 1984, the poverty rate equals the rates of the late 1960s. Moreover, more than 66 percent of black children and 71 percent of Hispanic children in female-headed households live in poverty, and the numbers of these households have grown by more than 50 percent in the past decade alone. In cities, where there are now 12.9 million poor, the rate has increased from 15.7 percent in 1979 to 19.8 percent in 1983. The urban poverty rates of recent years are higher than in any year given in census reports dating back to 1959.[2]

Strong and continued economic expansion is likely to correct some of the upsurge in national poverty data; however, cyclical economic upswings by themselves cannot reduce substantially poverty rates in cities, since heavier levels of poverty are becoming too deeply imbedded in the urban culture.

In sharp contrast to the current federal thesis that urban problems should be solved at the state and city levels, the Brookings authors state:

> One of the continuing social functions of large cities—helping society cope with and upgrade its poorer citizens—will require sustained infusions of outside resources, especially from the federal government. Dealing with poverty requires income-redistribution policies, and such policies simply cannot be effectively carried out by local and even state governments.[3]

INCOME DISPARITIES

The median family income of central city residents in 1983 was $22,286, compared to $29,397 for the suburbs, a differential of 31.9 percent. For metropolitan areas having over 1 million in population, the disparity is even greater at 44.3 percent.[4] These income differentials make it exceptionally difficult for cities to capture the resources necessary to treat urban problems and compete effectively with suburbs in creating a climate that attracts residents and businesses. Suburbs have achieved this competitive advantage because of zoning and housing policies that have excluded lower income citizens. Targeted assistance to cities is necessary to overcome the adverse effects of such policies so that all may fairly share in the cost of treating poverty and other urban problems.

The trends are toward ever greater levels of urban-suburban income disparity. The disparity of 31.9 percent in 1983 compares to a 26.7 percent income gap in 1979. The gap was 21.9 percent in 1969 and just 17.9 percent in 1959.[5]

Only 25 percent of the U.S. white population lives in cities; 58 percent of the black population and 50 percent of the Hispanic population lives in cities. Therefore, cities and their residents are especially affected by discriminatory employment practices. Black median family income in 1984 was just 56 percent of white income—a ratio that has fallen considerably from the 1970 level of 61 percent.[6] Myths of racial progress notwithstanding, the income gaps between the races have been widening considerably in recent times.

Exacerbating the adverse income trends in central cities in recent years has been (1) a change in federal domestic and economic policies which has further increased the income gaps in the nation, and (2) a change in tax policy, which has had a similar effect. An Urban Institute study indicates that, largely as a result of domestic spending cuts, corporate and individual income tax changes that favor the more affluent, and monetary policies that have focused on producing sharp reductions in inflation at the expense of high levels of unemployment, the income gaps have all widened in recent years. The Urban Institute states that, "some widening of the income distribution would have taken place from 1980 to 1984" irrespective of federal policy actions. "But the peculiar policy mix of tax and benefit reductions" chosen by the executive and legislative branches exacerbated the trend. The policies "helped the affluent but not the poor or the middle class."[7]

The policies of recent years have worked to the disadvantage of cities, removing billions of dollars from the urban income stream. Conversely, the additions to the income stream in affluent jurisdictions lead to greater expenditures for goods and services in those areas, which create jobs, which in turn create still more income through this multiplier effect.

Between 1980 and 1984 families in the lowest quintile of income lost 7.6 percent in real (inflation-adjusted) disposable income. Families in the second-

Table 2-2. Percentage Changes in Real Disposable Income for Families, 1980-1984.

	Income Quintile					*All Income Levels*
	Bottom	*Second*	*Third*	*Fourth*	*Top*	
Elderly	+6.2	+6.8	+8.4	+9.2	+11.2	+9.5
Two-earner (husband-wife) families	-6.7	-0.1	+2.5	+4.9	+10.1	+4.3
Female-headed (non-elderly) families	-12.0	-9.3	-4.8	-1.9	-0.2	-3.3
Black families	-7.0	-8.2	-3.7	-0.6	-0.1	-2.1
All families	-7.6	-1.7	+0.9	+3.4	+8.7	+3.5

Source: John L. Palmer and Isabel V. Sawhill, eds., *The Reagan Record, An Assessment of America's Changing Domestic Priorities* (Cambridge, Mass.: Ballinger Publishing Company, 1984), pp. 332-33.

from-the-lowest income quintile had their disposable income decline by 1.7 percent during that time. Middle income people had a slight (0.9%) disposable income gain from 1980 to 1984. In contrast, the fourth income quintile (the "upper-middle" and "lower-upper" income families) gained 3.4 percent, and the top quintile (the highest income) gained 8.7 percent in real disposable income from 1980 to 1984. Some of these trends would have occurred anyway; however, the Urban Institute attributes much of this phenomenon to federal domestic and tax policies. For example, 4.1 percent of the 7.6 percent income decline for the lowest income was attributed to federal policies.[8]

Table 2-2 gives a breakdown of disposable income changes, 1980 to 1984, for various types of demographic groups. The elderly were the biggest gainers because Social Security benefits increased by over 7 percent, in real terms, during that period (reflecting a lag in benefit adjustment of earlier cost-of-living increases). Note that black families and female-headed households of all races experienced real disposable income declines among all income levels; moreover, those demographic groups lost ground relative to the patterns experienced by all families. The Urban Institute attributes *all* of the real declines in black family income to federal policies implemented between 1980 and 1984. Much of the decline experienced by female-headed households is attributed to federal policies as well.[9]

The tax reductions of 1981 particularly aided the affluent and widened the competitive disadvantages faced by lower income families. The average-income family received an annual tax reduction of $829, amounting to 3.9 percent of their disposable income. However, the upper income (top income quintile) received an average reduction of $2,429, amounting to 5.9 percent of their income. In contrast, the lowest income received no help at all from the tax reduction. Lower-middle income families only received a reduction of 1.4 percent of their income.[10] The Urban Institute indicates that if they had included the substantial business tax reductions, the liberalized treatment of Individual Retirement Accounts, and the reductions in gift and inheritance taxes, then all of the above income disparities would be widened further. It should be noted that the tax burdens could have been equalized to a greater extent if, for example, the personal exemption and the earned-income tax credit were adjusted to help the lower income along with higher income Americans.

EMPLOYMENT

Between September 1982 and June 1983 unemployment rates were in double digits nationally, reaching a high of 10.7 percent in November and December 1982. As the nation recovered from the 1981-1982 recession, unemployment fell considerably, to just over 7 percent as of this writing.

Nonetheless, as cyclical unemployment has declined, structural unemployment remains high in many central cities. Table 2-3 is a sampling of double-digit unemployment in large and smaller cities in the North, South, East, and West.

Table 2-3. Unemployment Rates, Selected Cities, July 1985.

Gary, Indiana	18.3%	Joliet, Ill.	11.7%
Compton, Calif.	16.4	Jersey City, N.J.	11.5
Fairbanks, Alaska	16.4	New Orleans, Louisiana	11.5
Waterloo, Iowa	15.5	Decatur, Ill.	11.5
Laredo, Texas	15.3	Hammond, Ind.	11.4
Youngstown, Ohio	15.2	Dayton, Ohio	11.4
Canton, Ohio	15.1	Galveston, Tex.	11.3
Brownsville, Tex.	14.5	Akron, Ohio	11.0
Detroit, Mich.	13.4[a]	Toledo, Ohio	10.4
Modesto, Calif.	13.4	Reading, Pa.	10.4
Camden, N.J.	13.3	Cincinnati, Ohio	10.3
Cleveland, Ohio	13.3	Buffalo, N.Y.	10.2
Rockford, Ill.	13.0	Niagra Falls, N.Y.	10.1
Beaumont, Tex.	12.9	Pueblo, Colo.	10.1
Stockton, Calif.	12.6	Miami, Fla.	10.0
Peoria, Ill.	12.4	Oakland, Ca.	10.0
Racine, Wisc.	12.0	Birmingham, Ala.	9.7
Newark, N.J.	11.8	Chicago, Ill.	9.6
El Paso, Texas	11.7		

a. Detroit rate as of June 1985 (latest data available).

Source: Bureau of Labor Statistics, Local Area Unemployment Statistics, September 1985 (printout by request).

In a summer 1984 survey (well into the economic recovery) of 388 cities by the National League of Cities, 22 percent of cities reported double-digit unemployment.[11]

The end of each recession leaves unemployment rates in many cities higher than they were at the end of the previous recession. The structural problems of employers shutting down or relocating, continuing discriminatory employment patterns, and lack of sufficient job skills, along with deficiency of training programs to meet the needs of today's rapidly changing job market, are combining to create a condition of clearly excessive unemployment in many cities. This condition will remain in times of national recession, recovery, and economic expansion alike, unless more comprehensive actions are taken.

These excessive urban unemployment rates would be considerably higher if the nation counted discouraged workers. This group includes those who have dropped out of the labor force, discouraged over not finding work. They are not counted officially as unemployed. A Washington, D.C. Urban League survey in the summer of 1983 found that 48.7 percent of all low-income citizens aged sixteen to sixty-four were not in the labor force; they were discouraged workers, public assistance recipients, disabled, or retired. For middle and upper income citizens (those having annual family incomes of $20,000 or more), this out-of-the-labor-force rate was only 15.5 percent.[12] A good portion of the difference between these two out-of-the-labor-force rates can be attributed to unemployment problems, even though this group is not included in the official unemployment rate data. The labor force drop-out rates are considerably more acute in cities, with their high proportions of low-income citizens, than in the more affluent suburbs. It is unfortunate for cities and urban citizens that the full extent of the unemployment conditions are not recognized in the federal data, since the higher rates would more likely spur greater action.

In the first six months of 1984 the U.S. labor force grew by 1.8 percent when compared to the first six months of 1983. However, in a sample of twenty-four major U.S. cities, the labor force actually declined by 1 percent during this same recovery period.[13] Some of these differences are due to continuing urban population losses; however, another portion must be attributed to the discouraged worker phenomenon.

Historically, and indeed currently, minorities have disproportionately shouldered the nation's unemployment burdens. This pattern especially affects cities as shown in Table 2-4. Black unemployment as of September 1985 was 15.3 percent compared to a white rate of "only" 6.1 percent. This rate is depression level by any standard and should be alarming to national policymakers. Unfortunately, there are few national reinvestment strategies targeted to areas of high unemployment, and job and training programs have been slashed drastically. Cities suffer economically from heavy unemployment, while the personal toll in terms of family break-up, acute depression, drug abuse, alcoholism, and crime can be enormous. It has been estimated, for example, that a sustained 1 percent

Table 2-4. Unemployment Rates by Race, Selected Years, 1948–1984.

Year	*Total*	*White*	*Minority*
1948	3.8	3.5	5.9
1950	5.3	4.9	9.0
1955	4.4	3.9	8.7
1960	5.5	4.9	10.2
1965	4.5	4.1	8.1
1970	4.9	4.5	8.2
1979	5.8	5.1	11.3
1983	9.6	8.4	17.8
1984	7.5	6.5	14.4

increase in unemployment produces a 4.1 percent rise in suicides and 4 percent rise in prison admissions.[14]

Many of today's unemployment problems can be traced directly to employers' leaving central cities. In 1958 the central cities' share of retail trade was 62 percent; by 1977 this share had declined to 42 percent. Again, this is an average figure; many cities experienced much more precipitous declines. For example, in 1958 Detroit had 51 percent of its metropolitan area's share of retail trade. By 1977 that share had declined to 19 percent. The drop was nearly as steep in Philadelphia, from 51 to 29 percent.[15]

Cities, as manufacturing centers, are particularly affected by the relative lack of growth nationally in manufacturing jobs. Moreover, cities have a significantly lower proportion of what manufacturing jobs remain, compared to years past. In 1960 central city manufacturing employment constituted 33 percent of all U.S. manufacturing employment. By 1978 this figure was only 26 percent.[16]

For particularly severe cases of job flight, examine the case of the nine largest metropolitan areas in the Northeast and Midwest as shown in Table 2-5. Cities of these metropolitan areas lost 17 percent of their population and 29 percent of their employment base during 1950 to 1980; at the same time, their suburbs gained 102 percent in population and 146 percent in jobs.

A Brookings Institution study indicates that "it is unrealistic to assume that most unemployed persons could soon move to more economically dynamic areas, even if public assistance for such moves was available," adding that "many growing metropolitan areas deliberately create barriers to the entry of low-income households."[17] It is impractical for government to encourage and subsidize millions of the unemployed to abandon cities and the multibillion-dollar infrastructure that is already established for them and to send them to places where there is no welcome mat and where job prospects for the untrained may be slim. It may also not be a sound policy on ethical grounds. As another author states:

> If the American society values "free choice" above all else, then government policy must be more responsive to the choice of individuals not to move as to

Table 2-5. Decentralization of Jobs and People in the Nine Largest SMSAs in the North and East, 1950-1980.[a]

	1950				1980				Percentage Change 1950 to 1980	
	Central City		*Suburban Ring*		*Central City*		*Suburban Ring*			
	Amount	*Percentage*	*Amount*	*Percentage*	*Amount*	*Percentage*	*Amount*	*Percentage*	*Central City*	*Suburban Ring*
Population[b]	19,169	64.0	10,630	36.0	15,839	42.0	21,463	58.0	-17.0	+102.0
Employment[b]										
Manufacturing	2,812	69.0	1,241	31.0	1,605	43.0	2,092	57.0	-43.0	+ 69.0
Retail trade	1,267	74.0	452	26.0	860	38.0	1,408	62.0	-32.0	+212.0
Wholesale trade	734	90.0	78	10.0	473	51.0	459	49.0	-36.0	+488.0
Selected services	531	83.0	106	17.0	847	56.0	665	44.0	+60.0	+527.0
Total	5,344	74.0	1,877	26.0	3,785	45.0	4,624	55.0	-29.0	+146.0

a. The nine Standard Metropolitan Statistical Areas (SMSAs) are: New York; Chicago; Philadelphia; Detroit; Washington, D.C.; Boston; Pittsburgh; Baltimore; and Cleveland.

b. Figures are in thousands.

Source: Computed from data in the U.S. Census of Population 1950 and 1980 (prelim.); U.S. Census of Business, 1948; U.S. Census of Manufacturers, 1947 and 1977; U.S. Census of Services, 1977; U.S. Census of Wholesale Trade, 1977; and the U.S. Census of Retail Trade, 1977. Arthur F. Schreiber and Richard B. Clemmer, *Economics of Urban Problems* (Boston: Houghton Mifflin, 1982).

> the choice of moving. Since capital growth can contribute to the growth of the locality then there are options for greater involvement of the federal government in creating better local environments.[18]

A sustained economic stimulus of cities can turn the trends around, for balanced economic growth where all sectors and all people contribute.

EDUCATION

In years past the educational gap between cities and their suburbs was large in those cities with heavy minority populations. However, educational attainment progress over the past decade has been significant. In 1970 the median school years completed for adults of 25 and older in the nation as a whole was 12.1 years and only 9.8 years for blacks—a 23 percent differential. By 1983 the national average was 12.6 years of schools, compared to 12.2 years for blacks—a difference of just 3 percent.[19]

Much of these extraordinary gains is unquestionably due to substantial increases in federal educational outlays during that period—from $9.2 billion in 1970 to $26.8 billion in 1981.[20] Many of these funds were targeted for loans and grant programs to economically disadvantaged students and school districts.

Other educational performance measures also indicate substantial gains among urban residents. Among nine year olds, suburban youths scored 12.5 percent higher in reading proficiency tests than large-city students in 1974-75, but by 1979-80 that differential had shrunk to 5.4 percent; for thirteen year olds the differential diminished from 15.8 percent to 9.2 percent.

In math proficiency assessment scores we see the same trends. Among nine year olds, suburban youths scored 15.2 percent higher in math scores than large-city youths in 1977-78; by 1981-82 that differential had declined to 9.6 percent. For thirteen year olds the difference had diminished from 14.9 percent in 1977-78 to 12.2 percent by 1981-82.[21]

These remarkable gains in just a few years are being threatened by national policymakers who ignore the facts and claim that federal educational expenditures have little or no tangible benefit. Education's share of the federal budget of 1.8 percent in 1986 was a steep decline from a 2.4 percent share as recently as 1979. Had that same relative share been maintained, education funding would be $24 billion in 1986, rather than $18 billion—a difference of $6 billion or 25 percent.[22]

Despite the recent achievement score gains, much progress remains to be achieved in urban school systems. There are still significant math and reading score deficiencies between city and suburb among the older (e.g., seventeen-year-old) students, who did not gain the benefit of federal educational programs in their early years. Whites are 1.7 times as likely as blacks and 2.4 times as likely as Hispanics to become college graduates (1985 data). On the other hand, blacks are 1.8 times as likely as whites to become high school dropouts, while Hispanics are three times as likely.[23] Educational gaps are closing, but progress cannot be accelerated without federal assurances of equal educational opportunities.

CRIME

The nation has seen an encouraging 17 percent decrease in crime over the past four years (1980-1984). Much of this decrease is due to increased awareness among citizens in avoiding crime situations, engraving their property with identification marks, and banding together in "neighborhood watch" organizations. The reductions may also be due in large part to decreases in the proportion of the population in crime-prone (14-24) years, as well as substantial increases in the prison population, keeping crime-prone persons out of society, and increased police department effectiveness.

Despite the recent improvements, the crime rate is still more than double today what the levels were twenty years ago. Moreover, the crime rate in cities of 250,000 and more in population is 106 percent greater than in the suburbs of U.S. cities and more than quadruple the crime rates of rural areas.

For 1985, $69 million was allocated to state and local governments for crime-fighting assistance—about 2 percent of the Department of Justice budget. In contrast, ten years previously, $480 million was granted to state and local governments—about 23 percent of the department's budget.

With continually increasing fiscal problems, cities have few or no discretionary funds to compensate for this drastic cutback in federal support for crime-fighting efforts. A much stronger federal-state-local partnership is essential.

TAXES AND FISCAL HEALTH

Because cities must treat a full array of poverty-related and other urban problems, the taxes of city residents are inevitably higher than those of suburban residents. In the suburbs most of these types of funding needs are effectively obviated by zoning and housing policies. Table 2-6 demonstrates this fundamental inequity.

City residents on average pay 23 percent more in local taxes than do suburban residents. This ratio has remained relatively constant over the years. Some distressed cities, of course, exceed this average tax disparity figure by wide margins.

Without federal actions that redistribute significant resources to assist those jurisdictions and people that need help the most, we find a situation where one can escape the burdens of paying for social and economic problems simply by

Table 2-6. Per Capita Taxes of Central Cities and Suburban Residents of Sixty-eight Largest Metropolitan Areas.

	1970	*1977*	*1981*
Central city	$233	$411	$501
Suburbs	$179	$336	$407

Source: U.S. Advisory Commission on Intergovernmental Relations (ACIR), *Central City-Suburban Fiscal Disparity and City Distress, 1981* (Washington, D.C.: ACIR, forthcoming), Table 5.

moving across an arbitrary boundary of the city limits. As domestic spending programs are substantially reduced, these inequities are widened.

In 1984, twenty-four states enacted permanent tax increases, twenty-one states projecting permanent increases for 1985.[24] Moreover, in twenty-two of twenty-seven mostly larger cities surveyed by the Urban Institute in 1981 through 1984, the nonfederal tax burdens increased, often sharply. Tax increases were steepest in the industrial areas that suffered the most adverse effects of the recession.[25]

A 1985 survey of 150 cities' fiscal conditions found a weak tax base in many of our urban centers. For example, 1985 general fund revenue growth was expected to be slower than inflation in 65 percent of midwestern cities and in 56 percent of northeastern cities. Business taxes were expected to grow more slowly than inflation in 61 percent of all cities, including 79 percent of midwestern cities and 78 percent of northeastern cities. Property taxes were projected to grow more slowly than inflation in 51 percent of all cities, including 71 percent of midwestern cities.[26]

Of all cities surveyed, 72 percent expected expenditures to grow faster than inflation at current service levels; 53 percent expected general fund revenues to outpace inflation. Therefore, cities on average are experiencing a more rapid growth in expenditures than in revenues.

Despite these weaknesses in the tax base, many states and cities are likely to record budget surpluses, and some will reduce their tax levels. Nonetheless, cities (and certain states) with heavy unemployment and other forms of economic distress are likely to continue to have high tax rates and greater possibilities for budget deficits, relative to more affluent jurisdictions.

It should be recognized that a city's (or state's) surplus or deficit level does not provide a clear signal of its ability to cope with the vast array of urban problems. A city's budgetary status simply indicates how well that jurisdiction is able to live within the fiscal parameters it sets for itself. Most cities will freely acknowledge that they cannot substantially improve urban conditions within existing resources parameters; they can attack some of the symptoms of poverty but few of the causes.

Most major cities have gone through a decade or more of employee layoffs and constant tax increases to produce balanced budgets. In view of those fiscal conditions, it is unrealistic to expect cities to compensate for federal reductions in education, employment, economic development, health, housing, social services, and other programs. It simply cannot and will not happen. With federal action, urban conditions can be considerably improved; without such actions, further substantial deterioration is inevitable.

POLITICAL INFLUENCE

A recent Brookings study of cities summarized succinctly the basic problem of funding:

> Most large cities need continuous infusions of federal aid because they provide services to a disproportionate share of the poor. Targeting federal aid to the neediest cities has been one way of providing such aid. But it is likely to be undermined by the weakening political power of big cities as their populations subside, and it has been greatly curtailed in recent years. Nevertheless, the basic need remains and will increase in the future.[27]

Political might is turning federal priorities away from those who need help the most. This shortsighted philosophy cannot build a strong and united nation. It can only provide temporary financial gain to those who already have an advantage in competing for their share and more of U.S. affluence.

The *Congressional Quarterly* has designated 79 congressional districts as urban—where 60 percent or more of the population of the district resides in the central city of a metropolitan area—228 as suburban, and 128 as rural. Therefore, urban interests are potentially outvoted by more than five to one on issues affecting cities. As recently as 1970, cities held a 148- to 144-seat advantage over suburban interests in Congress.

Of historical curiosity, a 1971 report of a wealthy suburban county predicted with full accuracy the future tide of events:

> The accurate representation [as a result of the Supreme Court "one man-one vote" reapportionment] should challenge the existing complexion of many pieces of federal legislation aimed at improving the economic and social ills of American society. Domestic programs in the areas of housing, transportation, welfare, health maintenance, farm subsidies, education, law enforcement, revenue sharing and the environment should increasingly reflect both the governmental and the personal needs of suburban voters rather than central city or rural interests.[28]

They could at least have gloated a little less. After examining the adverse effects of federal policies upon millions of city residents—and upon millions more of suburban residents who depend upon healthy central cities—mayors urge the adoption of policies that build strength in all sectors of U.S. society.

NOTES TO CHAPTER 2

1. Katherine L. Bradbury et al., *Urban Decline and the Future of American Cities* (Washington, D.C.: The Brookings Institution, 1982), p. 4.
2. U.S. Bureau of the Census, Current Population Reports, Series P-60, No. 138, *Characteristics of the Population Below the Poverty Level: 1981* (Washington, D.C.: U.S. Government Printing Office, 1983), various tables; U.S. Bureau of the Census, Current Population Reports, Series P-60, No. 145, *Money Income and Poverty Status of Families and Persons in the United States: 1983* (Washington, D.C.: U.S. Government Printing Office, 1984), p. 3; and U.S. Bureau of the Census, Current Population Reports, Series P-60, No. 149, *Money Income and Poverty Status of Families and Persons in the United States: 1984* (Washington, D.C.: U.S. Government Printing Office, 1985), p. 21.
3. Bradbury et al., p. 12.
4. U.S. Bureau of the Census, *Money Income and Poverty Status: 1983*, p. 5. The median income for central cities in all metropolitan areas was computed from data supplied in Table 1.
5. Ibid., and U.S. Bureau of the Census, *1980 Census of the Population,* "Characteristics of the Population: General Social and Economic Characteristics," U.S. Summary (Washington, D.C.: U.S. Government Printing Office, 1983), Table 118; U.S. Bureau of the Census, *1970 Census of the Population*, Vol. 1, "Characteristics of the Population," Part 1, Section 1, U.S. Summary (Washington, D.C.: U.S. Government Printing Office, 1973), Table 116; U.S. Bureau of the Census, *1960 Census of the Population*, Vol. 1, "Characteristics of the Population," Part 1, U.S. Summary (Washington, D.C.: U.S. Government Printing Office, 1963), Table 101.
6. U.S. Bureau of the Census, *Money Income and Poverty Status: 1984*, p. 10.
7. John L. Palmer and Isabel V. Sawhill, eds., *The Reagan Record: An Assessment of America's Changing Domestic Priorities* (Cambridge, Mass.: Ballinger Publishing Company, 1984), p. 345.
8. Ibid., p. 329.
9. Ibid.
10. Ibid., p. 326.
11. National League of Cities (NLC), "Employment Problems and America's Cities" (Washington, D.C.: NLC, August 1984), p. 1.
12. Unpublished survey conducted by Washington Urban League. Low income applies to those with incomes under $4,000. The labor force dropout rate is nearly as severe (42.1%) for those with incomes of $4,000 to $10,000.
13. Analysis by James Cooper, D.C. Department of Employment Services, for Mayors' National Urban Policy Report, September 1984.

14. M. Harvey Brenner, "The Social Costs of Economic Distress," *Consultation on the Social Impact of Economic Distress* (New York: American Jewish Committee, 1978), pp. 3-6.
15. W. Walzer and Glenn Fisler, *Cities, Suburbs and Property Taxes* (Cambridge, Mass.: Oelgeschlager, Gunn & Hahn, 1981), p. 200.
16. Unpublished HUD data.
17. Bradbury, p. 283.
18. Gordon L. Clarke, *Interregional Migration, National Policy and Social Justice* (Totowa, N.J.: Rownan and Allanhead, 1983), p. 17.
19. U.S. Bureau of the Census, *Statistical Abstract 1985*, p. 134.
20. Ibid., p. 136.
21. National Center for Education Statistics, *Digest of Education Statistics 1982* (Washington, D.C.: U.S. Department of Education, May 1982).
22. Office of Management and Budget, *Fiscal Year 1986 Budget, Historical Tables* (Washington, D.C.: U.S. Government Printing Office, 1985), Tables 5.2 and 5.3.
23. U.S. Department of Labor, Bureau of Labor Statistics (BLS), *News Release 85-355* (Washington, D.C.: BLS, September 2, 1984), Table 2.
24. Data from unpublished report of the National Association of State Budget Officers, May 1984, conversation with Dr. J. Miller.
25. Palmer and Sawhill, p. 247.
26. National League of Cities (NLC), *City Fiscal Conditions and Outlook for FY '85* (Washington, D.C.: NLC, March 1985), pp. 27-33.
27. Bradbury, p. 15.
28. Nassau County, N.Y. Executive office, *Counties: New Suburban Power and Influence* (Mineola, N.Y.: Nassau County, 1971), pp. 13-15.

3 INCREASING PRIVATE SECTOR INVESTMENT IN URBAN CENTERS

Regardless of political party membership, income level, race, or philosophical leanings, a consensus has developed in our nation that the key to family and urban well-being is full participation in the economic mainstream. This means an end to our present system of economic exclusion of urban citizens, millions of whom are maintained at a minimal subsistence level in a condition of dependency on government.

As Jesse Jackson said in his address to the 1984 summer meeting of the U.S. Conference of Mayors in Philadelphia, "The people are crying out not for social service, but for fundamental social change." Social services may be essential under today's conditions to enable a citizen to reach a point where he or she can take advantage of opportunities available, but it is the ultimate in government waste if social services are provided in the absence of opportunity.

Without substantial private sector urban investment, true "welfare" of urban areas and citizens is impossible. Rev. Jackson noted that, "we cannot violate the laws of investment and rebuild urban America. We will reap what we sow. If we invest in the suburbs and in foreign cheap labor markets, and not in our cities, our cities will die."

In other chapters of this book, proposals are advocated to build a healthier U.S. workforce.

- In Chapter 4 mayors advocate targeted fiscal assistance to cities based on unemployment rates. That proposal is primarily intended to assist governments in economically distressed urban centers to maintain essential services and avoid layoffs and tax increases which drive businesses and middle income citizens out of cities. The funds would have the additional purpose of increasing employment by 500,000 persons.

- Chapter 5 proposes a national employment and training policy to ensure that the labor force acquires the skills to perform the jobs of today and tomorrow. Subsidized jobs programs are advocated to meet immediate needs, reducing unemployment by a minimum of 1 percent. Reforms in the current dislocated worker program are offered.
- Chapter 6 calls for the development and implementation of national affirmative action strategies, to develop specific initiatives to achieve fully representative levels of minorities and women, at all wage and salary levels in the private and public sectors. Reforms in affirmative action enforcement policies in federal contracting and minority business assistance are advocated.
- Chapter 11 proposes an expansion of job-training opportunities for public assistance recipients who seek employment.

However, those recommendations cannot be successful without the creation of new jobs through economic development in urban centers. In this chapter mayors propose the establishment of a National Urban Development Bank or similar credit mechanism to finance a significant increase in industrial and commercial development in central cities. In this way, we can encourage full partnership of the private and public sector. This partnership cannot evolve without some economic stimulus to ensure sufficient levels of private-public ventures.

Federal investment strategies currently provide economic stimuli to energy suppliers, railroads, airlines, shipbuilding, space exploration, telecommunications, agriculture, exporters, and many other sectors. In fact, the surge in recent years in government investment in defense industries could be construed as an industrial policy in favor of defense corporations. Many favored federal investment strategies are now under close scrutiny to see if they should be reduced or discontinued. Over time, this examination will inevitably reduce or eliminate targeted investments in several, but not all, favored industries. A good case can be made that economically distressed urban centers should be included in the federal portfolio of targeted investment strategies. Investments in urban centers, through an urban bank or other financing mechanism, can do more to improve the employment, productivity, and balance of trade prospects of the nation's economy than nearly any other targeted economic development strategy.

Additionally, mayors support existing economic development tools: urban development action grants, community development block grants, Economic Development Administration grants, Small Business Administration assistance, and industrial development bonds. Federal assistance targeted at present to urban economic development is but a small fraction—1.5 percent—of federal assistance to all U.S. business. Large-scale corporate tax credits and deductions, loans, loan guarantees, and direct expenditures are well established in many economic sectors but are still at a modest level with respect to targeting urban development assistance. The potential for revitalization of the urban job base is not being sufficiently cultivated. The current economic development tools are essential to cities and should be retained, fully funded, and eventually expanded.

Mayors call for the development of national industrial strategies to plan for sustained economic growth, moderate wild swings in business cycles, enhance international trade, achieve full employment, and involve fully minorities and women in the management and production of our nation's goods and services. The Departments of Commerce, Labor, Housing and Urban Development (HUD), and Treasury, with Congress, governors, mayors, other policy organizations, business, and labor should participate, using existing resources, in developing the strategies. The National Urban Development Bank, or other financing mechanism, should provide leadership and would serve as the implementation mechanism for the strategies adopted.

SUMMARY: NATIONAL URBAN DEVELOPMENT BANK

Following are examples of possible elements of an urban development bank:

1. *Sufficient Capitalization.* The bank could be capitalized initially with a minimum of $5 billion per year over a four-year period. In addition, the bank could be authorized to issue debt instruments of $50 billion per year, thereby providing a $55 billion annual infusion into urban economies for loan guarantees and low-interest financing assurance to state and local governments and businesses in economically distressed areas. These revolving funds would be repaid to the bank for reuse beyond the initial capitalization period.
2. *Separate Divisions for Business Development and Infrastructure.* Because different types of analysis and different methods of allocating funds are required in business and industrial development and in repairing infrastructure, two separate divisions (or two separate banks) should be formed.
3. *Targeting of Investment.* To help ensure that all sectors of the nation and economy have a meaningful opportunity for recovery, job retention, and prosperity, bank assistance should be targeted. Criteria for bank financing could include some level of per capita income, employment growth (or loss) rates, unemployment rates, and population growth (or loss).
4. *State and Local Decisionmaking.* State and local economic development corporations, banks or agencies, on behalf of their chief elected officials, would work with local businesses in financial packaging for National Urban Development Bank assistance. State and local decisionmaking for development projects should be retained.
5. *Leveraging.* The bank should supply 10 percent to a third of the funds required by business, and in some cases, less than that. This provision ensures a

market test for the ability of the firm to repay the loan, and it helps public financing funds go much further than they would under full financing.

6. *Targeted Jobs Program and Affirmative Action.* Businesses that seek financing as well as publicly conducted infrastructure programs must be required to submit plans that include providing a certain proportion of jobs and training to the unemployed and underemployed. In addition, these plans must include strong affirmative action goals to ensure that minorities and women are fully represented. The goals should provide for fair hiring of minorities and women at all salary levels.

7. *Board of Directors.* Most models of the development bank provide for an interagency corporation, with secretaries of HUD, Commerce, Labor, and Treasury directing the corporation. Such interagency direction provides for coordination of the federal programs related to bank actions, with links to funding within those programs.

Following is a brief summary of the major benefits of adopting National Urban Development Bank legislation:

- *Stimulates Economy.* The bank would stimulate the economy in all parts of the nation (and not just in areas of heavy defense industry concentration as is the case with much of present federal spending), providing jobs and increased disposable income, especially in areas experiencing serious structural economic problems. Those areas would have a better chance to join the productive economic mainstream rather than hinder economic recovery as they presently do.

  As the nation expands economically, a development bank is needed to stimulate investment. As stated by Amitai Etzioni, director of The George Washington University Center for Policy Research: "[E]ven if interest rates are brought down and deficits slashed, there will still be a need for development banks. The American economy has developed several structural deformities which need treatment and will not self-correct just because the economy will be back on its feet."[1]

- *Creates Jobs.* Since bank financing would be targeted to high-unemployment areas, it would reduce unemployment and, moreover, build job skills that are lacking among many of the currently unemployed. To cite an example of the bank's employment impact on an urbanized state, Governor Thomas Kean of New Jersey estimated that the infrastructure portion alone of development bank implementation would create 120,000 jobs in his state, enough to reduce New Jersey's unemployment rate by more than three percentage points.[2] This rate can be reduced still further as industries are encouraged and retained by the bank.

- *Increases Productivity and Reduces Business Failure.* The 31,334 business failures of 1983 were at the highest level since the depression era and are a

24 percent increase over the 1982 recession year's level of 25,346.[3] Long-run productivity growth has declined sharply in recent decades (see further discussion below), and U.S. capital formation (business investment) is at low relative levels compared to other nations. The bank proposal would help revitalize U.S. businesses. As Senator Hollings stated in introducing similar legislation, "the Bank is not a cure-all, but neither is it a band-aid."[4]

- *Repairs Nation's Infrastructure.* The proposal would provide a good start in reducing America's multibillion-dollar infrastructure backlog, providing the nation's cities and businesses with renewed basis for sustained growth.

- *Complements Other Legislation.* The proposal for a National Development Bank in the President's National Urban Policy Report of 1978 also included expanded Urban Development Action Grant (UDAG), Community Development Block Grant (CDBG), and Economic Development Administration (EDA) grant authority, which would complement bank loan guarantee and financing capabilities. The grants "would cover expenditures for land assembly, site preparation, rehabilitation and equipment." The combined efforts of the grants would reduce a firm's financing cost considerably in high-risk urban areas and coordinate all forms of economic development assistance.[5] The bank would also overcome what is probably the primary concern of the urban enterprise zone concept: provision of the capital that firms urgently need to remain, locate, or expand in enterprise zone areas.

A National Development Bank would build on and help meet the objectives of existing federal program. As stated by Representative Frank Guarini, "We have probably 300 programs that are responsible for 56 percent of all money loaned in our society, and it is all fragmented. . . . [I]f you had a [a development bank] in place, it would coordinate in a more specific direction . . . building up our industrial sector or making industrial policy."[6]

THE CAPACITY OF PRIVATE-PUBLIC PARTNERSHIPS TO REBUILD CITIES

To our knowledge, no one has tallied the total effects of corporate involvement to improve deteriorating urban conditions. Indeed, it seems impossible to do so. Whatever the level, the results are impressive.

There are perhaps 3,500 to 4,000 examples of public-private partnerships to rebuild central cities and accomplish other vital purposes, as estimated by Partnerships Data Net, Inc. These include such bank industry initiatives as Security Pacific National Bank's low-interest loans which total more than $85 million to help low-income families rehabilitate their homes and neighborhoods; commercial development loans in Boston by several leading banks, where Community Development Block Grant funds join with bank loans on a one-to-three basis, and bank participation in community development corporations, Small Business Administration guaranteed loans, and Minority Small Business Investment Companies.

A group of several insurance companies formed a $2 billion Urban Investment Program to help build riot torn cities, leading to 116,000 new housing units, over 40,000 jobs, health care facilities, nursing homes, parks, and day care centers. Aetna of Hartford has committed more than $11 million in below-market housing financing in several cities, and other insurance companies have had similar mortgage programs for low-income citizens.[7]

Private venture capital pools, made up of investments from pension funds, corporations, wealthy individuals, insurance companies, bank trust departments, and other sources, have stimulated investments in urban areas and sometimes in economically distressed areas (although these types of investments are predominately suburban oriented). And of course several large corporations have combined with urban governments to obtain Urban Development Action Grants (e.g., Sears Terminal in Chicago) or simply have developed urban tracts on their own, with city cooperation but without excessive dependence on grants to accomplish their major objectives (e.g., Detroit Renaissance's massive economic development effort).[8] Nonetheless, one would have to conclude from all the data that, under the present network of financial incentives, the vast majority of investment in business location and expansion, commercial development, and housing is made in the suburbs—away from the high-unemployment areas having the greatest need for investment. The price of land is cheaper, there is good proximity to buying power, there is room for parking and future expansion, downtown is nearby, the tax burdens are less, the crime rate is lower, pressures to integrate the workforce and contribute to societal well-being are less, and projected returns on investments are often greater in the suburbs.

Despite the impressive track record built by concerned corporations, the existing free market forces are not likely to change the investment patterns. As stated by the Committee for Economic Development (CED), a national "nonprofit, nonpartisan and nonpolitical" independent research and educational organization of 200 business executives and educators:

> In fiscally hard-pressed cities, local governments are limited in their ability to provide the mix of public investment and private incentives necessary for effective participation in partnerships with their private sectors. Federal assistance to economically and fiscally distressed cities through programs with sufficient flexibility to respond to unique local needs may be necessary for effective local government participation in development partnerships.[9]

Nor can corporate charitable contributions be the answer. The President's Task Force on Private Sector Initiatives in 1982 set as its first and only tangible goal a doubling of cash contributions to charitable organizations engaged in public service.[10] This is not likely to happen. As pointed out by CED:

> The substantial reduction in corporate tax [in 1981] will increase the cost of giving to corporations for each dollar of contribution. New depreciation deductions, research and tax credits, and the opportunity to shift tax burdens to firms with losses will eliminate the tax liability of some firms, thereby diminishing the tax-related incentive for charitable giving. However, the [1981] act raises the maximum allowable deduction for charitable giving from 5% to 10% of pretax profits, and the lower tax liability presumably will increase the resources available to firms from which contributions would be made.[11]

On the bright side, if the task force goal of doubling corporate contributions could be achieved, an added $2.5 billion would be available—hopefully not for charity, but for investment in urban development and jobs.

While an alphabet of investment tools is already available (CDCs, LISC, ICVF, LDCs, MESBICs, NRC, EDA Revolving Loan Funds, etc.), an urban development bank can have the pulling power to capture federal and corporate investment in a stable, organized way, building in the mix of needed incentives. It can counterbalance some of the federally fostered (or condoned) incentives that now place cities at such a competitive disadvantage in attracting investment.

SUPPORT FOR EXISTING URBAN DEVELOPMENT FINANCING TOOLS

Before discussing the bank concept in greater detail, the existing urban development tools—urban development action grants, Economic Development Administration grants, and community development block grants—should be examined. These programs are highly effective in stimulating development and employment. Without them, the already excessive unemployment and poverty levels would be further exacerbated, and urban areas and their citizens would become increasingly dependent on the federal government and all U.S. taxpayers, since self-help opportunities would be diminished.

Urban Development Action Grants (UDAGs)

In these days when urban programs are often lumped together as failures, the U.S. Department of Housing and Urban Development's UDAGs are clearly a success. As stated in the President's 1984 National Urban Policy Report:

> The UDAG program is a good example of a Federal program that embodies a number of key components of the Administration's urban policy: the program seeks to maximize local government and private sector control and dis

creation, and complements private sector efforts. It is targeted to distressed areas, and it results in permanent job creation through business creation.[12]

UDAGs are targeted to communities experiencing sluggish population growth or declines, large per capita income disparities, large numbers of persons in poverty, and an older housing stock in poor condition. All communities must meet criteria of distress; 64 percent of all awards to large cities go to the top third of distressed communities. UDAGs are among the most targeted of all programs to communities in need.

The nearly 2,000 UDAG projects funded to date (since fiscal year 1978) have resulted in an expenditure of nearly $3 billion. These funds are expended on the "but for" principle; that is, a UDAG is awarded in those cases where private investments would not be sufficiently profitable but for the availability of UDAG financial help. Often an economically distressed area is a higher investment risk than is a more affluent area, and UDAGs bridge the gap between an unacceptable risk and one worth taking.

UDAGs, therefore, leverage significantly higher levels of investments than their initial cost. Over the history of UDAGs, each UDAG dollar, on the average, has been combined with 5.7 private dollars in packaging a deal to bring a commercial, industrial, housing, or mixed-use project to an economically distressed area. The $3 billion in UDAG expenditures since 1978 have stimulated $21.8 billion in total investment, including $17.2 billion in private financing and $1.2 billion in state and local public financing.

These projects have created 405,000 permanent jobs, 55 percent of which are held by low- and moderate-income people. Additionally, 311,000 construction jobs have been created by UDAGs.

Minorities have filled 38 percent of all UDAG-created jobs, because of special efforts communities have made to target those jobs to minorities and also because projects funded by UDAGs are in areas where minorities are more likely to reside. However, only 7 percent of the dollar value of contracts awarded in UDAG-financed projects went to minority firms—a deficiency in UDAG implementation that should be corrected. This 7 percent figure could and should, at a minimum, be doubled or tripled.

Of all projects awarded, 36 percent funded industrial projects, and in recent years (1982–1983), 43 percent of the projects funded such industrial projects as metal fabrication and machinery, equipment manufacturing, synthetics, paper products, textiles, wholesale trade, and food processing. Since 1978, 38 percent of UDAGs leveraged such commercial projects as retail and office space, hotels, downtown commercial complexes, and neighborhood nursing homes. Another 15 percent helped fund housing projects; 88,000 housing units have been created, nearly 40 percent of which were targeted to low- and moderate-income citizens. The remaining 11 percent of UDAGs funded a variety of mixed uses.

Finally, it should be noted that UDAG projects have generated an additional $471 million in income, property, and other local tax revenues.[13]

The scale of UDAGs is, of course, much less than assistance granted to energy suppliers, the transportation industry, exporters, and other sectors and also considerably less than the business support granted to firms in relatively affluent, low-unemployment areas. Nonetheless, the payoff from the limited funds provided in UDAGs is one of the nation's best success stories—one that in many ways serves as a model for expansion of this concept.

However, UDAG funding has dropped sharply in recent years. The $440 million appropriated for 1985 was $235 million or 35 percent less than the 1981 level. The effects of inflation make this decline even sharper—nearly $320 million since 1981. Moreover, the federal budget for fiscal 1986 proposed to terminate the UDAG program altogether, "as part of the government-wide effort to cut back local economic development subsidy programs."[14] Mayors have urged restoration of, and ultimately an increase in, this highly successful program. In 1986 budget deliberations, the UDAG program was funded at 75 percent of the 1985 level, with 2 percent increases projected for 1987 and 1988.

Community Development Block Grants (CDBGs)

CDBGs differ from UDAGs in several key respects. First, CDBGs are an entitlement program, where eligible communities receive grants, funded according to a statutorily mandated formula, without submitting competitive applications. Not all cities are successful in receiving an adequate share of UDAGs; citizens and businesspeople are dependent upon the aggressiveness and fortunes of local governments in seeking UDAGs. The CDBG program is much larger than the UDAG program—$3.1 billion in 1986 compared to $0.3 billion for UDAG. The CDBGs give wide discretion to local communities for expenditures of CDBG funds, whereas, under UDAGs, specific development projects are submitted to HUD for approval.

Moreover, CDBGs are the primary community development mechanism of the federal government. Each use of funds is usually smaller in scale than is the case with UDAGs and EDA grants (discussed below). The greatest use of CDBGs is for housing-related activities, especially private and public housing rehabilitation with emphasis on low- and moderate-income communities. CDBGs also fund public service jobs (up to 10 percent limit), a helpful feature when so many communities continue to experience heavy unemployment.

CDBGs often complement UDAGs in that they precede and stimulate economic development. CDBGs provide for public facilities and improvements (street, parks, water and sewer, parking, etc.) as the second-largest use of funds (after housing); provide for acquisition and clearance of real property; and fund local development corporations which stimulate the initiation, retention, or expansion of usually small neighborhood businesses. UDAGs, on the other hand, usually fund larger commercial and industrial projects.

CDBGs, similar to UDAGs, are targeted quite well to communities in need. The most distressed 10 percent of cities are projected to receive 3.7 times more in per capita funding than the least distressed 10 percent of the eligible communities. Low-income neighborhoods receive the vast majority of funds directly. They are therefore not dependent on "trickle down" effects of the grant.

Crucial needs such as shelters and other assistance to the homeless are funded by CDBGs—the homeless received $33.5 million in 1983—while under UDAG there is no particular incentive for such aid. As can be seen, these two HUD programs have distinct benefits and complement each other well.

The FY 1986 CDBG appropriated level of $3.12 billion has declined somewhat from 1979 levels of $3.75 billion—and, of course, has lost considerable ground to inflation since that time ($2.7 billion annually in real dollars). The FY 1983 appropriation added $1 billion to CDBG for the emergency jobs program, bringing the level that year to $4.5 billion. The CDBG jobs program supported approximately 171,600 persons in direct employment. This special CDBG appropriation was not continued in FY 1984, despite continuing high levels of unemployment in CDBG communities. At the president's request, Congress decreased CDBG funding by 10 percent for fiscal 1986, with small (2%) increases projected for 1987 and 1988.

Another factor influencing CDBG funding is the number of eligible communities—814 eligible in 1985 compared to 594 in 1975, a 37 percent increase. The growth of eligible communities, along with the declines in funding, of course, means less funding per distressed city.[14]

Economic Development Administration Grants

Similar to UDAGs, Economic Development Administration (EDA) grants offer moderate levels of funding to stimulate urban development. The $175 million for 1986 primarily assists urban areas in rebuilding their infrastructure, including access roads to industrial parks, rehabilitation of public facilities, utility provisions, port facilities, and water and sewer treatment systems. EDA assistance also establishes revolving loan funds at the local level, which provide financing to a variety of small and minority businesses.

Although Congress appropriates EDA grants at a low funding level, mayors view these funds as an essential development ingredient, along with UDAG and CDBG funds. EDA grants are usually targeted to the early stages of project implementation. About 80 percent of EDA funds are provided for infrastructure improvements. UDAGs, on the other hand, enable private ventures to proceed with industrial and commercial projects. The CDBGs, in contrast to both of the other tools, have a neighborhood improvement and housing focus.

The FY 1986 appropriated EDA level of $175 million is but 39 percent of the FY 1980 level of $451.6 million—a reduction of $276.6 million, or a $443 million reduction since FY 1980 in real (inflation-adjusted) dollars.

The executive branch proposed terminating EDA altogether in the FY 1983, 1984, 1985, and 1986 budget requests, but Congress has continued to provide some funding. In fiscal 1986 budget actions, Congress reduced EDA to 88 percent of 1985 levels, with 2 percent increases projected for 1987 and 1988. In view of the urgency of economic development and infrastructure deficiencies in urban centers, mayors advocate full funding of EDA grants.

Other Development Tools

Two other principal development tools for cities are Small Business Administration (SBA) programs and Industrial Development Bonds (IDBs). Neither of these tools is specifically targeted toward economically distressed urban centers; they are available throughout the nation.

SBA loan and loan guarantee programs provide credit, at favorable rates, to businesses that otherwise could not obtain credit, helping cities retain and attract these key sources of jobs and income. Although the president's FY 1986 budget proposed to terminate SBA, Congress retained SBA loan guarantees at 1985 levels, while cutting sharply the smaller direct loan program.

Under the IDB program, state and local governments assist private developers by acting as conduits for tax-exempt bonds to finance development that creates new jobs, stimulates business growth, and generates new tax revenues. The tax-exempt nature of this type of financing lowers the effective rate of interest to developers.

The annual revenue drain to the U.S. Treasury from the use of IDBs is said to be $3.5 billion. However, this estimate assumes that these projects would have gone forward without the availability of IDBs, at conventional financing rates. At the 1984 winter meeting of the U.S. Conference of Mayors, several mayors stated that the availability of IDBs, in case after case, has made the difference between a financially feasible development and one that could not be successful. This revenue loss estimate must also be lowered by additions to the income and revenue stream resulting from the new jobs and projects built as a result of the availability of IDBs.

Further restrictions have been proposed to limit the use of IDBs. However, mayors have sought defeat of such proposals, since the resultant dampening of economic development would significantly hinder efforts to rebuild urban economies.

UDAG, CDBG, and EDA Funding in Perspective

The proportion of federal support for U.S. business that is provided to distressed urban centers from UDAGs, CDBGs, and EDA grants is just 1.5 percent of the total. Needless to say, the excessive levels of structural unemployment and economic stagnation in dozens of urban centers are of such magnitude that current levels of federal economic development stimuli are not going to turn the conditions around. Nonetheless, it is essential to support the existing programs to fund the additions of industrial parks, shopping centers, rehabilitated housing, and upgraded infrastructure. The programs add several times their funding levels to the economic stream of communities that need help the most.

To make a tangible difference and bring urban centers to a higher level of self-sufficiency and well-being, a funding mechanism of significantly greater magnitude is essential. Mayors therefore offer as an option the implementation of an urban development bank.

Because of concerns that the bank may be a radical departure from traditional means of federal support or intervention, the following discussion places the bank proposal in the context of present means of federal assistance to U.S. businesses.

EXISTING FEDERAL SUBSIDIES FOR U.S. BUSINESSES

There is a variety of views on the need for an additional urban development investment stimulus. An urban development bank is often thought of as a means for excessive tampering with the marketplace, benefiting some at the expense of others.[15]

Realistically, however, the free enterprise days of Adam Smith have long disappeared. The federal government for decades has implemented economic policies that benefit some industries and regions, subsidized by others. When there is a massive maladjustment in the marketplace, it is fully within the U.S. tradition to come to the aid of those in need. In this way, we are able to achieve a healthy marketplace where as many sectors as possible are self-sufficient and prosperous—city and suburb, sunbelt and frostbelt alike.

Under free market theories the strong regions and industries emerge and dominate, phasing out the weaker ones as inefficient and useless. But such theories are only valid in a society that does not already have a long history of stimulating certain favored or struggling industries. The nation today is in the process of examining all federal investment strategies that favor one industry or sector over another, with a view toward reducing or eliminating many targeting tools. This tax reform process should prove beneficial to taxpayers and the economy. Urban centers seek a fair share of the investment stimulus mechanisms that remain from this process, so that competitive disadvantages are reduced.

Under free market theories citizens are asked to "vote with their feet," relocating to prosperous regions of the nation. However, from a practical standpoint, it is unrealistic to think that millions of unemployed citizens could be transported to stronger local economies, assured of adequate housing, retrained, and placed in jobs. The millions of unemployed and low-income citizens do not have the means to make the readjustment, nor would massive federal expenditures for such purposes be considered by taxpayers to constitute a prudent industrial policy. One cannot solve problems by transporting them from place to place.

Our urban centers have only recently—in the last three decades, for the most part—been in economic jeopardy, and they already have the infrastructure to support a well-functioning society and economy. The neighborhoods and communities, the streets, the power plants, the traffic control systems, the water and sewer systems, political and decisionmaking bodies, the public school systems, training institutions and universities, the crime control systems, the mental and physical health institutions, and many other forms of social and physical infrastructure are already in place in U.S. cities. It would be the height of inefficiency to attempt to duplicate them elsewhere in a few years to accommodate the millions of unemployed and the millions living in poverty.

The long-run cost of neglect can only mount over time. The present and future costs of public assistance, crime, incarceration, family dissolution, public housing, special education, job programs, drug abuse and alcoholism treatment, and so forth outweigh many times over the cost of providing an economic stimulus giving cities and their residents the means to help themselves.

A major new economic stimulus for economically distressed urban centers would help give cities the means of self-sufficiency. An urban development bank, credit corporation, or other such financing mechanism can funnel investment dollars to retain and attract businesses, upgrade machinery and equipment, create jobs, and rebuild infrastructure for communities that most need assistance. As the President's 1984 Urban Policy Report states: "What is important to the Administration in this atmosphere of resurgence and increasing competitiveness is to . . . help cities suffering from disinvestment and obsolete plant either to modernize or shift their economic bases according to local situations."

Existing Tax Benefits to U.S. Industries

The development bank concept is anything but a radical departure from past and existing economic stimuli and in fact is well within the U.S. policy mainstream.

Tax expenditures to U.S. businesses dwarf the cost of the proposed urban development bank concept. The Congressional Budget Office lists forty-three tax credits, deductions, and exemptions favoring U.S. businesses.[16] The value of these exemptions and write-offs is in the tens of billions of dollars, although the total benefit is difficult to derive because of the interactive nature of these tax expenditures. The nine largest of the forty-three tax expenditures designed for multisector benefit (that is, not targeted for any specific industrial sector) are listed in Table 3-1 and have a value of well over $50 billion.

Table 3-1. Nine Largest Examples of Tax Expenditures for Industrial Support, 1984 (*billions of dollars*).

Tax Expenditures	*1984 Revenue Loss*
Accelerated cost recovery system	$18.3
Preferential treatment of capital gains	16.4
Investment tax credit	15.7
Reduced tax rates on first $100,000 of corporate income	6.5
Exclusion of interest on state and local government industrial development bonds	3.5
Expensing of research and development expenditures	2.5
Safe harbor leasing provisions	1.9
Exclusion of interest on state and local pollution control bonds	1.5
Deferral of income of domestic international sales corporations (DISCs)	1.2

These tax expenditures benefit urban, suburban, and rural businesses. Nonetheless, those industries that are prospering to the extent that they can take advantage of investment tax credits, capital gains, accelerated depreciation on their plant and equipment acquisitions, and research and development are able to extend their competitive advantage over firms that cannot afford to expand in this manner—struggling firms in areas having economic difficulties. Those tax expenditures that give general subsidy to industry could be restructured, at a cost saving, to provide greater targeting of aid specifically to industries in economically distressed, high-unemployment areas.

As seen in Table 3-1, the aid to DISCs is targeted a little more specifically than most of the others, providing subsidy to corporations engaging in export sales. Similarly, tax benefits for IDBs enable state and local governments to select industries they prefer to receive tax exempt interest rates to aid in the construction of certain facilities. However, these tax expenditures are not especially targeted toward high-unemployment areas which need help most.

Still other tax expenditures are targeted more specifically to industries favored by the federal government. In the vernacular of our times, "winners and losers" are selected. Depletion allowances granted to fuel extraction industries amount to $2.1 billion a year, enabling qualifying firms to write off 15 percent of gross income in the case of oil and gas. "Expensing" of exploration and development costs for fuels subsidizes this industry by another $1.2 billion a year. (Expensing allows the exploration and development costs to be taken in the year incurred rather than spread over the useful life of the field or well, as is the usual accounting practice.) Expensing of certain capital expenditures is also allowed in agriculture, at a cost to taxpayers of $600 million a year. Accelerated depreciation of income-producing buildings is another industry-specific tax break, at a revenue loss of $1.2 billion a year. This tax break is often considered questionable, since buildings often appreciate in value rather than depreciate in an accelerated fashion. Financial institutions receive a $600 million annual subsidy as they are permitted to deduct excess bad debt reserves—that is, deductions above their actual bad debt experience—according to a special formula.[17]

Some of the industry-specific tax subsidies may be more desirable to U.S. taxpayers than others. For example, there is considerable consensus in rural and urban areas alike to support several of the current agriculture subsidies but much less agreement on the magnitude of support for energy suppliers. Nonetheless, it should be obvious to citizens and policymakers that aid to struggling industries with obsolete plant and equipment and laid-off workforces should rank at least as high in value as aid granted to businesses that are not as much in need of the enormous variety of assistance presently available to them.

Direct Expenditures

On top of the over $50 billion in tax expenditures, industries also receive $13.7 billion in direct outlays. Direct farm support payments in the form of farm product purchases at higher than market value, as well as deficiency payments to farmers to make up the difference between the price they receive and a target price, amounted to $6.1 billion in 1984. Additionally, federal outlays for agriculture research and services (livestock and plant reproduction, soil improvement research, etc.) amounted to another $1.2 billion.

Research and development subsidies to nuclear and fossil fuel energy suppliers amounted to $1.8 billion in 1984. Federal support for research and technology development in the aeronautical industry amounted to another $700 million. Outlays to the water transportation industry for operating subsidies as well as research and development totaled $500 million. Direct outlays to the mining industry amounted to another $500 million. A wide variety of other means of direct expenditures to business provide an additional $1.4 billion a year to the synthetic fuels industry, the public broadcasting corporation, crop insurance, and so forth.[18]

Again, these expenditures are conscious public decisions to help some industries and not others—"tampering in the marketplace" and "picking winners and losers." Mayors argue that urban industries are at least as much in need as the most worthy of the above expenditures, and more in need than most. These subsidies may be restructured, at a substantial cost savings to taxpayers, to include the urban industries in greatest need.

Loan and Loan Guarantees

In addition to the over $50 billion a year in tax subsidies and $13.7 billion in direct federal expenditures to industries, another $20.9 billion in loans and $17.7 billion in loan guarantees are provided to various targeted U.S. industries. These loan and guarantee programs are nearly identical to the proposed urban development bank concept.

Rural programs account for the majority of this type of assistance. The Rural Electrification Administration has provided loans to rural cooperatives for capital investment, often at a rate of 5 percent a year for thirty-five years. The loans are usually for electricity-generating facilities and nuclear plants at a $4.5 billion cost per year.

The Commodity Credit Corporation (CCC) provided $7.4 billion in loans and another $3 billion in loan guarantees in 1984. The loan is for the value of the crop, and the CCC therefore provides price support to farmers (that is, the farmers have the option of selling the crop at a higher price on the open market or delivering the crop to the government and not repaying the loan). The CCC also provides loan guarantees to foreign buyers who import U.S. farm products.

The Agricultural Credit Insurance Fund provided $4.6 billion in favorable rate loans and $1.3 billion in loan guarantees for farm ownership and operating expenses, soil and water conservation or development, irrigation or drainage projects, and disaster loans.

The Export-Import Bank (Eximbank) promotes U.S. exports by providing below market rate loans and loan guarantees to foreign purchasers of U.S. goods. Eximbank loans were $2.5 billion in 1984. Loan guarantees were $9 billion in 1984. The interest rates are among the lowest on the market, and the risks inherent in export financing are minimized. Much of the financing goes toward export of aircraft and electrical power plant and equipment.

The Small Business Administration provides credit to small businesses that otherwise would be unable to obtain financing. New loans have been $1.5 billion per year. Loan guarantees have been $2.9 billion a year.

In addition to the above five financing programs, at least eleven other loan and loan guarantee programs provide favorable financing for aircraft purchases, ship financing, railroad improvement, health maintenance organization assistance, fisheries, pollution control, overseas investment, and the like.[19]

Several of the direct loan programs, including the Export-Import Bank, small business assistance, and agricultural credit, were proposed to be eliminated or substantially reduced in the president's proposed 1986 budget.

Total Federal Support for U.S. Business

The total of over $50 billion in tax expenditures, $13.7 billion in direct expenditures to industries, $20.9 billion in loans, and $17.7 billion in loan guarantees results in at least $100 billion in financial assistance flowing to U.S. businesses each year. The vast majority of this financial assistance is not targeted to revitalization of local economies in need of stimulus. Because struggling firms in economically distressed areas are not in a position to engage in the expansion needed to participate in many of these tax and financing breaks, the level of assistance to firms in urban areas is likely to be disproportionately low.

Of course, some of this $100 billion *is* targeted specifically to distressed areas—and usually urban areas. The Congressional Budget Office estimates that $170 million of EDA loan guarantees are targeted to assistance of U.S. businesses, another $291 million of EDA grants are so targeted, plus about $1 billion in UDAGs and CDBGs for business assistance. This total of $1.5 billion a year—a mere 1.5 percent of the more than $100 billion in total overall financial assistance to business—cannot possibly turn around the economies of urban areas. The agricultural industry was saved with precisely the kinds of financing now proposed by mayors. Similarly, urban areas can achieve a much needed boost of prosperity and employment with the relatively modest new financial assistance program discussed in this chapter.

EVOLUTION OF THE NATIONAL URBAN DEVELOPMENT BANK POLICY

We have demonstrated, above, that the bank proposal is in consonance with existing forms of aid to U.S. businesses. Now we will discuss how the bank proposal conforms to traditional, historical modes of U.S. economic action.

After conceptual development by the U.S. Conference of Mayors from 1970 to 1978, the President's National Urban Policy Report of 1978 called for "the creation of a National Development Bank, which would encourage business to locate or expand in economically distressed urban and rural areas."[20] The objective of the bank as set forth in that report is "to lower operating costs in urban areas [and] provide long-term, low-cost financing which, in conjunction with expanded grant programs administered by HUD and EDA, will reduce a firm's financing costs."

Under this 1978 proposal, businesses needing assistance to locate or remain in distressed economic areas would receive: (1) HUD and EDA grants which are coordinated with related bank actions for land assembly, site preparation, rehabilitation, and equipment; (2) loan guarantees which would total $11 billion over a three-year period; and (3) low-interest loans at rates as low as 2.5 percent. Private financing of at least 21 percent of the project's cost would be required to leverage greater investment dollars. The bank was conceived as a catalyst to jobs creation, and in fact "additional employment would be a key test of project eligibility."[21]

State and local government economic development entities, on behalf of chief elected officials, would approve all bank projects and would also guide most proposals to the bank, thereby easing fears of excessive federal dominance in local economic development decisionmaking. The bank was proposed as an interagency corporation governed by a board composed of the secretaries of HUD, Commerce, and Treasury.

The concept of a National Urban Development Bank has a long, bipartisan history. The War Finance Corporation (WFC), started in 1918 in the Wilson administration, had a $500 million fund from which to make loans to companies gearing up to produce uniforms, guns, and ammunition. The WFC was to be dismantled in 1921. However, because of the depression of 1921, President Warren G. Harding revived it, this time for the domestic purpose of lending $300 million in the early 1920s to farmers and rural banks.

The Reconstruction Finance Corporation (RFC), the model for the 1978 National Development Bank proposal and subsequent bills, was created in 1932 by President Herbert Hoover. In his memoirs Hoover cited the RFC first among his administration's accomplishments, stating: "The agency is credited with saving thousands of banks, railroads and businesses from failure during the 1930s."[22]

The RFC's initial capitalization was $500 million, with borrowing authority of $1.5 billion (which is about $5 billion and $15 billion, respectively, in today's dollars). During the RFC's lifetime of 1932 to 1954, the corporation disbursed over $33 billion in loans or investments to businesses, financial institutions, railroads, agricultural financing corporations, and public agencies.[23] The RFC spent $10.5 billion during the depression. All of these loans were repaid, and, moreover, the corporation earned a profit for U.S. taxpayers of $500 million.[24]

According to Representative Joseph G. Minish, who has introduced National Development Bank legislation in recent years and chairs the subcommittee responsible for such legislation, "Corporations such as General Motors, National City Bank, Chase Bank, Bank of America and Southern Railroad are in existence today due in large part to the RFC." The RFC also invested millions with such corporations as Goodyear, U.S. Rubber, B.F. Goodrich, Firestone, General Tire, Dupont, Standard Oil, and Shell Union Oil.[25]

The RFC's public projects included water projects in southern California, mass transit in Cleveland, the Pennsylvania Turnpike, the San Francisco Bay Bridge, and work on the Brooklyn Bridge. The RFC led directly to the creation of other federal financing agencies: the Export-Import Bank, the Commodity Credit Corporation, the Federal National Mortgage Association (FNMA), and the Rural Electrification Administration.[26]

During World War II, the RFC's powers were broadened to buy factories and mills and lease them to private companies for weapons manufacture. It brought strategic materials and stockpiled them. The RFC also created new industry to make synthetic rubber.[27] Its investments in wartime subsidiaries totaled $20 billion.[28]

More recently, Congress approved, on a case-by-case basis, up to $125 million in federal loan guarantees to the Lockheed Aircraft Corporation in 1971 and $1.5 billion in federal loan guarantees for the Chrysler Corporation. It also approved loan guarantees to New York City in the late 1970s.[29] Additionally, $2 billion was recently invested by the United States in Mexican banks, which have been in serious difficulty and which hold substantial U.S. corporate investments.[30]

FEDERAL POLICIES AFFECTING URBAN WELL-BEING

Ever since these federal financing corporations and loan programs were formed several decades ago, the question has been raised as to whether an intervention in free market forces would hinder the efficiency of the marketplace. In other words, if cities are declining, would not it be best simply to let them fall?

As the President's National Urban Policy Report of 1978 indicated, federal policies already implemented over the years have already intervened in free market forces to the detriment of cities, creating an artificial imbalance. For example, the report states:

> The most powerful direct Federal action that has contributed to metropolitan decentralization and central city decline, the opening up of non-metropolitan America, and the regional dispersal of population and economic activity has been the construction of the interstate highway system.[31]

Residents and businesses are no longer tied to a central city location, and many firms state a preference for suburban labor markets. Retail shopping centers are also made possible by our nation's subsidized accommodation to the automobile. The beltways wrapped around cities created what the 1978 report called multinucleated metropolitan development patterns. Mass transit systems also shortened travel time, making suburban locations more practical for residents and businesses.

America's tax policies have also been powerful inducements to suburban growth. As reported by the Urban Institute, the tax system has favored low-density sprawl over compact development, accelerated the rate of decentralization, favored investments in housing over other economic development, particularly favored single-family owner-occupied housing over multifamily rental apartments, and favored new construction over maintenance and repair of existing structures.[32] For example, tax deductions for interest payments and property taxes have favored higher priced, low-density construction of single-family homes. Renters, found disproportionately in urban areas, have been disadvantaged.

The 1978 National Urban Policy Report also noted that since the Korean War, there has been a "substantial shift in the patterns of [federal] procurement and the location of installations and federal payroll in favor of the Southern and Western regions and away from the older industrial areas of the North and Midwest."[33] This trend has accelerated because of increased emphasis on defense expenditures, which have a western and sunbelt orientation. California receives over 20 percent of defense expenditures, and seven of the top eleven states receiving defense dollars (accounting for over two-thirds of defense expenditures) are located in the West.[34]

The 1978 report also notes that, "over the past thirty years, national housing goals have been translated into the construction of new housing. Relatively little effort was given to conserve existing housing stock."[35] The report noted that millions of buyers have taken advantage of FHA/VA home mortgage programs, and by creating a new suburban market, the federal government has provided an "inadvertant incentive to the abandonment of housing and neighborhoods in central cities."

These are but a few of the explicit and implicit federal policies that have tended to hinder, beyond natural market forces, central city prosperity. Moreover, housing and job discrimination contributes an additional major economic factor favoring suburb over city. Because cities house the vast majority of minority populations who have been victimized over the years by job and housing discrimination, taxes are higher, poverty rates are higher, per-person service costs are higher, and the need for subsidies is greater in cities than in suburban communities. Therefore, residents and businesses who wish to escape paying for the burdens of poverty have an additional incentive to locate outside central cities.

In summary, the United States has had a full history of aiding businesses (e.g., energy and transportation industries) and regions (e.g., farming sectors) in times when an economic stimulus is needed. The nation also has adopted or condoned policies that have tended, in recent decades, to work to the disadvantage of urban areas. A National Urban Development Bank is needed to balance the nation's economic growth, restore health to regions of heavy unemployment, and spark needed investments to return the nation's industries, high tech and otherwise, to their best competitive positions worldwide.

THE BANK AS AN INVESTMENT STRATEGY

Table 3-2 compared capital formation in six developed nations in terms of gross investment and net fixed investments for the last decade.

As stated in the president's report, "no other major industrial nation devotes as small a fraction of total output to new investment as does the United States." Net fixed investment, which measures the change in total capital stock (plant and equipment) in the United States, is 56 percent of Germany's rate as a percentage of the GNP and 34 percent of the Japanese rate. The report also indicates that the rate of U.S. nonresidential fixed investment as a proportion of the GNP declined by 27.5 percent between the late 1960s and the late 1970s.[36]

The president's report also indicates that there is a "strong positive relationship" between a nation's investment and productivity rates. Table 3-2 indicates

Table 3-2. Capital Formation in Six Developed Nations, 1971-1980.

	Gross Investment as Percentage of GNP	*Net Fixed Investment as Percentage of GNP*	*Growth Rate of Output per Hour in Manufacturing*
France	24.2	12.2	4.8%
Germany	23.7	11.8	4.9
Italy	22.4	10.7	4.9
Japan	34.0	19.5	7.4
U.K.	19.2	8.1	2.9
U.S.	19.1	6.6	2.5

Source: *Economic Report of the President* (Washington, D.C.: U.S. Government Printing Office, February 1983), p. 81.

Table 3-3. Productivity Growth Rate in the United States, 1948-1981.

Year	*Growth Rate*
1948-1967	3.1%
1967-1973	2.3
1973-1981	0.8

Source: *Economic Report of the President* (Washington, D.C.: U.S. Government Printing Office, 1983), p. 83.

that the United States has the lowest investment performance and the lowest growth rate of productivity (as measured by growth rate of output per hour in manufacturing, last column), and Japan has the highest in both categories.

U.S. productivity growth has decelerated in recent times, as can be seen in Table 3-3. Had the United States been able to sustain the 1948-1967 productivity growth rate of 3.1 percent a year through today, our output per capita would be about 26 percent higher.

Moreover, the AFL-CIO notes that during the 1970s the U.S. *share* of the world market for producing manufactured goods declined 23 percent. It is often contended that manufacturing industries in developed nations are declining as a general worldwide phenomenon; however, manufacturing in the United States is declining disproportionately. This deindustrialization has resulted in the loss of at least 2 million jobs, according to the AFL-CIO. As the AFL-CIO has stated, "We cannot write off major industries in this country without paying for it dearly in the future. Nor can whole cities and regions of America be allowed to decay, without serious social and economic consequences."[37]

Capacity utilization in manufacturing, mining, and utilities stood at about 80 percent as of August 1985, five to eight percentage points less than in the previous two periods of economic expansion (1972-73 and the late 1970s).

The inability of outdated plant and equipment to increase productivity and restrain costs accounts for at least part of this decline.[38]

The president's economic report notes that public policies in the United States compared with other industrialized nations may be root causes of deficient investment levels here. For example, recent federal deficits have reduced net private investment to less than half its historical level. The high levels of unemployment in the United States in recent years contribute to the deficit and help hinder investment; the U.S. Conference of Mayors estimates that each percentage point of unemployment contributes from $20 to $26 billion in the federal deficit.

Moreover, tax policies favor consumption over savings and, hence, investment. Consumer interest payments are tax deductible, so that government helps finance consumption. Meanwhile, taxation of savings income has often left a negative real after-tax return to U.S. citizens on their savings.

While recent Economic Recovery Tax Act revisions have a favorable impact on savings, the huge federal deficits continue to thwart investment potential. A positive investment stimulus, via a development bank, would help reverse this trend.

Senator Robert C. Byrd (D-W.Va.), who introduced legislation similar to a development bank, states: "We can no longer allow other nations to outpace the United States in developing new and innovative technologies. We must ensure that American businesses have the capital they desperately need to maintain their competitive position." Byrd also viewed a development bank (or investment corporation) as a means that "explicitly commits the public sector to work cooperatively with the private sector [through state and local governments] to preserve high-paying growth industries and attack the problem of geographically unbalanced growth." The bank or corporation would "address the problems of regionally concentrated, long-term unemployment by encouraging the location of new industry in areas affected by chronic joblessness."[39]

It should be noted that correcting economic imbalance does not involve favoring one region over another as much as it means ensuring the economic well-being of the nation as a whole. As industries abandon traditional labor and production markets, they create the need for inefficiently duplicating costly infrastructure and capital plant. By using and improving upon the plant we have, we should increase our nation's productive efficiency. Firms will continue to seek new production centers, but our nation cannot accommodate unbalanced and abrupt shifts of the magnitude forecasted.

Unbalanced regional growth leaves behind an immobile and unskilled labor market which is not likely to be assimilated into tomorrow's economy without corrective actions. Continuation of current trends will lead to maintenance of growing dependent populations segregated by race and income, with state and local governments unable to provide jobs, income maintenance, housing, health, social services, and other necessities. Aggressive, well-targeted federal policies are essential to redirect these trends before the costs of taking action are doubled, tripled, or worse.

Felix Rohatyn, chairman of the Municipal Assistance Corporation (of New York City) supports a development bank, primarily because "American industries have been failing badly." He argues that, "a 'hands off' government cannot . . . keep inflation down, deal with our regional and industrial problems, our chronic poverty and education problems, or reduce interest rates. The objectives can only be achieved by governments actively involved in a process of cooperation with business and labor."[40]

Rohatyn sees the development bank as instrumental in achieving what he views as the nation's two main goals: first, to provide a functioning economy, with stable growth and emphasis on the creation of private sector jobs, and second, to have all elements of our society and all regions of the country participate in that growth as fully as possible.

INFRASTRUCTURE

Today there is near-universal consensus that our nation's, and especially our cities', infrastructure is in a critical state of disrepair. Cities and states do not have the financial capability to remedy the backlog of infrastructure needs. In a survey by the U.S. Conference of Mayors and National League of Cities, it was found that of 809 cities surveyed, over 40 percent stated they needed state or federal aid to finance repair of sewage collection, stormwater collection and drainage, and recreational facilities, while well over 50 percent required such outside assistance for rehabilitation of wastewater treatment, streets and roads, bridges, overpasses, and viaducts. Of those cities that provide public transportation, nearly nine times as many cities require at least 50 percent outside aid for rehabilitation of facilities and rolling stock as cities that can finance the majority of these costs themselves.[41]

Infrastructure expert Pat Choate states that "the quality of life of all citizens is now threatened because of public works decline."[42] Choate supports the development bank as a means of "finding the money to rebuild America."[43] Choate calls infrastructure repair, replacement, and maintenance "the single most expensive task now before the American people," with a total cost of $2.5 to $3 trillion in public works investment needed by 1995. Others place staggering pricetags on this task as well. For example, the Morgan Guaranty Trust Company of New York placed the infrastructure repair costs at $500 billion over three years. The Urban Institute says that maintenance costs alone will amount to $860 billion over the next fifteen years, because of years of neglect to existing infrastructure thus far.[44]

Various newspapers, newsweeklies and business magazines have cited what the Municipal Finance Officers of America called the "growing litany of horror stories of crumbling highways, rusty bridges, leaking water supplies, unsafe dams, obsolete port facilities, aging public buildings and overcrowded prisons."[45]

Below are but a few highlights:

- The Urban Institute reports that over a third of cities surveyed are losing 10 percent or more of their water because of deteriorated pipes. About 40 percent of Boston's water use is unaccounted for, much of which is due to pipeline leaks and breaks. New York City loses 100 million gallons of water a day because of leaks in old water mains.
- The Environmental Protection Agency estimates that 13,600 or 21 percent of U.S. water systems do not meet safe drinking standards.
- Urban water systems are especially deteriorated, with a pricetag of $75 to $110 billion facing them over the next decade.
- About half of U.S. communities have wastewater treatment systems operating at full capacity and cannot support further industrial or residential growth. Wastewater treatment costs amount to $119 billion to meet needs by the year 2000.
- It will cost $31 billion over the next five years to meet existing water pollution control standards.
- According to estimates of the Federal Highway Administration and U.S. Department of Transportation (DOT), $33 billion in repairs are needed on interstate highways, with $500 billion required on other roads over the next decade.
- About half of the nation's 557,516 bridges are considered by the Federal Highway Administration to be structurally deficient or obsolete, with a pricetage of $48 billion.
- According to DOT, 67 percent of all mass transit track should be upgraded. The total mass transit capital improvements pricetag, as estimated by the American Public Transit Association, is $37 billion over the next decade.
- About 3,000 of the nation's 3,500 prisons must be rebuilt, expanded, or substantially rehabilitated over the next decade, at a cost of $8 billion.
- The capital needs of AMTRAK are projected at $4 billion for the rest of the century.[46]

The nation arrived at its critical infrastructure deficiency by a variety of routes. First, the nation shifted in the mid-sixties away from infrastructure expenditures programs and then, more recently, to defense expenditures. Inflationary costs caused many projects to be postponed, and the subsequent recession—the longest and deepest in forty years—left cities and states with few revenues to attack the backlog of infrastructure needs.

Second, the high interest rates of recent years have pushed many public investment projects beyond the range of affordability.

Third, after decades of government growth, where the local, state, and federal governments increased taxes to finance their government expansion (as well as infrastructure) needs, the United States seems to have neared its taxing limit. Neither taxpayers nor our economy seem willing or able to tolerate further incursions into disposable income. Voters reject bond issues and impose tax and spending limits, and candidates are elected on budget-balancing promises.

Fourth, population shifts of middle and upper-middle income citizens away from cities have further eroded the tax base out of which repairs and maintenance to the existing infrastructure are funded. In a recent U.S. Conference of Mayors' survey, 61 out of 100 cities have had to lay off employees. The natural tendency of municipal governments is to avoid as many layoffs as possible—that is, to protect people before protecting infrastructure.

Fifth, the nature of federal capital assistance has the effect of encouraging new construction, while postponing maintenance and repair of existing capital assets. Most of federal matching grant construction funding is for new construction, so those projects are favored over regular maintenance projects where no federal funding is forthcoming. Moreover, various federal standards and requirements force the expenditure of limited capital funds to meet stringent water pollution and drinking water standards, noise abatement regulations, air pollution legislation, federal laws for the handicapped, and so forth. These relatively new requirements mean that fewer funds remain for more traditional infrastructure repair and maintenance than in years past.[47]

Sixth, our political system is structured in small two- or four-year administrations for elected officials—conducive to postponing long-run responsibilities in favor of short-run needs when economic conditions are especially severe.

Compounding all of these factors is the extraordinary reduction in federal funds to state and local governments. Such federal assistance has been reduced by $25 billion over the last two years, with further cuts designed to reduce such assistance to the lowest level since 1977. In 1979 federal aid to state and local governments constituted 11 percent of the federal budget. The present administration's plan is to reduce that proportion to 5 percent by 1987.[48]

Without this assistance, state and local governments usually devote resources to maintaining operating services as best they can, postponing longer run infrastructure needs.

The Economic Recovery Tax Act was an additional setback to long-term financing. The accelerated depreciation of tangible properties, liberalized use of tax-deferred retirement instruments, and new investment instruments such as the all-savers certificate have reduced the attractiveness of tax-exempt municipal bonds. These changes keep municipal bond interest higher than otherwise, placing them beyond the range of feasibility for many cities and states for all but the most urgent of capital projects.[49]

An examination of the impact of all of these factors shows that public works investments by federal, state, and local governments have been reduced in real dollars from $34 billion in 1965 to $24 billion in 1980, a reduction of 30 percent. Public works investments constituted 4.1 percent of the GNP in 1965; that proportion had shrunk to 1.7 percent by 1980.

State and local government public works investments have particularly declined, by 34 percent, in constant dollars, since 1968. These investments accounted for $170 per person in 1968, but by 1981 that figure had fallen to just $101. In 1960 state and local governments spent 27.1 percent of their budgets on infrastructure; by 1980 they were spending only 15.4 percent.[50]

On the federal side, we see a marked deemphasis of infrastructure investments in recent years. In the mid-1960s, 44 percent of total federal aid to state and local governments went for public works, but by 1980 this figure had declined to 25 percent.

Even though the federal government has deemphasized infrastructure investments, the state and local governments nonetheless are depending upon the federal government more than ever before to meet their infrastructure needs. In 1957 federal assistance accounted for 10 percent of state and local government outlays for public improvements. Today the federal government accounts for 40 percent of these outlays.[51]

Much of what is invested by the federal government in public works today goes for national defense purposes. These defense-related public works investments have grown from 1.7 percent of the GNP in 1978 to 2.5 percent by 1983—from $35 billion to $86 billion. Meanwhile, nondefense investments, which accounted for 3.9 percent of the GNP in 1978, accounted for just 2.5 percent by 1983.[52] The federal government is now investing as much in defense public works as all other infrastructure combined.

It is clear that national leadership is essential to reverse the disinvestment in our nation's capital stock. The federal government has abruptly changed its spending policies away from infrastructure, and state and local governments have not been able to adjust so far and have few hopes of doing so.

An infrastructure bank or infrastructure division of the National Urban Development Bank would provide the low-cost financing essential to reduce the backlog. A consolidated infrastructure block grant would provide assistance beyond loans and loan guarantees, for those projects where added stimulus is necessary.

Infrastructure rehabilitation would also go a long way toward reemploying Americans now out of work. Infrastructure funding would not simply boost public sector employment. In fact, 66 percent of cities surveyed by the U.S. Conference of Mayors and the National Urban League of Cities indicated that, if they received new funding and financing, the jobs created would be totally in the private sector; another 32 percent indicated that a combination of private and public would be used. Only 2 percent of the cities surveyed perform infrastructure rehabilitation by themselves.[53] See Chapter 5 for a discussion of the job creation potential of public works funding.

As Representative James Oberstar stated in an address to the U.S. Conference of Mayors:

> If our communities can't grow, if industry can't move its goods, expand its plants and employ more people because the public facilities of our cities can't sustain such growth, there will be less money in the Federal till, less in state treasuries, and less in the private balance sheets. Replacement of that public capital will have to be extracted from an increasingly distressed economy. . . .
>
> Infrastructure and economic development are tightly intertwined; it's time we put them together. It's time to make our cities productive, so that their businesses and industries can reach full productivity again.[54]

CONCLUSIONS

Fortunately, as stated by Felix Rohatyn, America's problems of excess industrial capacity and infrastructure backlogs provide the key to economic recovery: "The United States is probably the only country in the world today whose biggest problems may also provide its biggest opportunities."[55]

The development bank stands in contrast to government programs that are essential in providing temporary help to disadvantaged cities and persons but which divert resources away from economic growth opportunities. The bank builds the nation's production and jobs base, builds work skills, stimulates the economy, counters inflation by boosting aggregate supply, and rehabilitates infrastructure for a strong economic future.

NOTES TO CHAPTER 3

1. Amitai Etzioni, Statement on H.R. 638 before the Subcommittee on General Oversight and Renegotiation of the House Banking Committee, March 10, 1983, p. 23.
2. Governor Thomas Kean, Statement on H.R. 638 before the Subcommittee on General Oversight and Renegotiation of the House Banking Committee, March 9, 1983, p. 8.
3. Dunn and Bradstreet (D&B), *Failure Record, 1982–83* (New York: D&B, 1984), Table 1.
4. Senator Ernest F. Hollings, Statement introducing S.3110, Congressional Record—Senate, p. S15239.
5. U.S. Department of Housing and Urban Development, *The President's 1978 National Urban Policy Report* (Washington, D.C.: U.S. Government Printing Office, 1978), p. 137.

6. Frank Guarini, Testimony on H.R. 14 before the Subcommittee on General Oversight and Renegotiation of the House Banking Committee, September 15, 1982, p. 48.
7. See, for example, The President's Task Force on Private Sector Initiatives, *Investing in America: Initiatives for Community and Economic Development* (Washington, D.C.: The Task Force, December 1982); The President's Task Force, "Corporate Community Involvement" (Washington, D.C.: Partnerships Data Net, 1982); Yankelovich, Skelley and White Inc. (Y, S&W), *Corporate Giving* (Philadelphia, Pa.: Y, S&W, 1982); Committee for Economic Development (CED), *Public-Private Partnership: An Opportunity for Urban Communities* (New York: CED, 1982); R. Scott Fosler and Renee A. Berger, *Public-Private Partnership in American Cities: Seven Case Studies* (Lexington, Mass.: Lexington Books, 1982); and computer printouts on various types of development from Partnership Data Net, Inc. (1111 N. 19th Street, Suite 500, Arlington, Virg. 22209).
8. President's Task Force, *Investing in America*, pp. 20–27, 36–39, 91–95, 105–6.
9. Committee for Economic Development, *Public-Private Partnerships*, p. 95.
10. The President's Task Force, "Corporate Community Involvement," p. 7.
11. Committee for Economic Development, *Public-Private Partnerships*, p. 89.
12. U.S. Department of Housing and Urban Development, *The President's 1978 National Urban Policy Report*, p. 75.
13. The above information on UDAGs was derived from conversations with staff of the U.S. Department of Housing and Urban Development.
14. Executive Office of the President, Office of Management and Budget, *Budget of the U.S. Government, Fiscal Year 1986* (Washington, D.C.: U.S. Government Printing Office, 1985), p. 5-80.
15. For a discussion of a variety of development mechanisms, with pro and con arguments, refer to Congressional Budget Office (CBO), *The Industrial Policy Debate* (Washington, D.C.: CBO, December 1983).
16. Congressional Budget Office (CBO), *Federal Support of U.S. Business* (Washington, D.C.: CBO, January 1984), pp. 92–95.
17. Ibid., pp. 17–24, 34–38.
18. Ibid., pp. 24–29, 99–100.
19. Ibid., pp. 29–34, 96–98.
20. U.S. Department of Housing and Urban Development, *The President's 1978 National Urban Policy Report*, p. 137.
21. Ibid.
22. Senator Daniel P. Moynihan, Statement for hearing on H.R. 14 before the Subcommittee on General Oversight and Renegotiation of the House Committee on Banking, September 15, 1982, pp. 2–3.
23. Felix G. Rohatyn, Chairman, Municipal Assistance Corporation (of New York City), Statement for hearing on H.R. 14 before the Subcommittee on General Oversight and Renegotiation of the House Committee on Banking, September 15, 1982, pp. 3–4.
24. Moynihan, p. 4.

25. Representative Joseph G. Minish, Statement for hearing on H.R. 638 before the Subcommittee on General Oversight and Renegotiation of the House Banking, March 9, 1983, p. 2.
26. Rohatyn, p. 4.
27. Moynihan, p. 4.
28. Rohatyn, p. 4.
29. Moynihan, pp. 5–6.
30. Ibid., p. 2.
31. U.S. Department of Housing and Urban Development, *The President's 1978 National Urban Policy Report*, p. 101.
32. Ibid., citing an Urban Institute study, p. 105.
33. Ibid., p. 106.
34. Jacques S. Gansler, *The Defense Industry* (Cambridge, Mass.: The MIT Press, 1980), p. 46.
35. U.S. Department of Housing and Urban Development, *The President's 1978 National Urban Policy Report*, p. 110.
36. *Economic Report of the President* (Washington, D.C.: U.S. Government Printing Office, February 1983), p. 78.
37. Henry B. Schechter, Statement for hearing on H.R. 14 before the Subcommittee on General Oversight and Renegotiation of the House Committee on Banking, September 15, 1982, p. 3.
38. Federal Reserve System, "Capacity Utilization: Manufacturing, Mining, Utilities and Industrial Materials" (Washington, D.C.: The Federal Reserve, September 16, 1985), p. 2.
39. Senator Robert C. Byrd, Statement for hearing on H.R. 638 before the Subcommittee on General Oversight and Renegotiation of the House Committee on Banking, Finance and Urban Affairs, March 9, 1983, pp. 5–7.
40. Felix Rohatyn, Address to U.S. Conference of Mayors, Congressional Record—Senate, December 16,1982, p. S15243.
41. U.S. Conference of Mayors (USCM) and National League of Cities (NLC), "Capital Budgeting and Infrastructure in American Cities: An Initial Assessment" (Washington, D.C., NLC and USCM, April 1983), pp. 34–35.
42. Pat Choate, Senior Policy Analyst for TRW, Inc., Statement for hearing on H.R. 6591 before the Subcommittee on Economic Development, House Committee on Public Works and Transportation, September 14, 1982, p. 1.
43. Pat Choate, Statement of hearing on H.R. 638 before the Subcommittee on General Oversight and Renegotiation of the House Banking Committee, March 9, 1983, pp. 2–3.
44. The Government Finance Research Center, Municipal Finance Officers of America (MFOA), "Draft Working Paper on Financing Infrastructure for Economic Development," (Washington, D.C.: MFOA, February 1983), p. I–9.
45. Ibid., p. I–3.
46. Ibid., pp. I-7 – I-8
47. Ibid., p. IV-5.

48. U.S. Conference of Mayors (USCM), "The Federal Budget and the Cities" (Washington, D.C.: USCM, February 1984), p. vi.
49. Government Finance Research Center, p. IV-7.
50. Ibid., p. I-11.
51. Ibid., pp. I-11 – I-12.
52. Kenneth M. Duberstein, Letter dated May 13, 1982 to Representative Robert W. Edgar, reprinted in hearing testimony on H.R. 6591, September 14, 1982, pp. 29–30.
53. U.S. Conference of Mayors and National League of Cities, p. 61.
54. Representative James L. Oberstar, Remarks to U.S. Conference of Mayors (Washington, D.C.: USCM, January 27, 1983), pp. 5–6.
55. Rohatyn, Hearings on H.R. 14, p. 21.

4 TARGETING FISCAL ASSISTANCE TO ECONOMICALLY DISTRESSED URBAN CENTERS

Tax burdens are much heavier on citizens in economically distressed cities than on citizens in wealthier jurisdictions (see Chapter 2). Because of the pervasiveness of poverty and other socioeconomic problems, resources are often insufficient in these cities to meet statutory requirements of those in need and, at the same time, to balance budgets. As the tax base of middle income citizens and businesses seeks to escape the high tax rates and other urban pressures, urban governments react to revenue shortfalls by reducing services and laying off employees. However, even drastic budget reduction measures eventually will fall short of filling the fiscal gaps, and further tax increases are needed to balance budgets. This in turn drives away other taxpaying residents and businesses, in an all-too-familiar story.

Under present fiscal arrangements urban governments have an unfair share of the nation's responsibility to cope with poverty and related conditions. Similarly, affluent towns and counties just outside of an urban center have a disproportionately light share of the tax and budget burdens, which gives them an artificial competitive edge in attracting residents and businesses.

The destructiveness and inequity of this odd intergovernmental fiscal structure should be obvious to all citizens. Urban governments can barely hope to treat the symptoms of urban deterioration, much less the root causes. Meanwhile, suburbs have the resources to develop top quality school systems, lavish recreational centers, industrial parks, high tech centers and other improvements to attract industry, efficient police forces with the latest equipment, and tax rates that undercut substantially those imposed in urban centers.

Suburban residents may indeed gain in the short term from this inequitable arrangement. However, in the interests of strong central cities, which provide the reason for suburban existence, some reordering should be considered. Mayors therefore propose greater fiscal balance in our intergovernmental structure.

The two proposals designed to produce improved intergovernmental fiscal balance are (1) the retention and strengthening of general revenue sharing, and (2) a targeted fiscal assistance measure that aids particularly distressed cities.

General revenue sharing (GRS), initiated in 1973, is for 1986 a $4.2 billion program of fiscal assistance, allocated to local jurisdictions by a three-factor (population, tax effort, relative income) formula. For several years, GRS has declined in terms of real dollar allocations and was slated for termination altogether in the executive branch's proposed federal budget for fiscal 1986. Congress retained GRS in its 1986 budget deliberations; however, the program is currently scheduled for elimination in 1987. The states were removed from the program in 1981, with the cities remaining as GRS recipients. Mayors have consistently supported the GRS program as a key ingredient in the intergovernmental partnership.

The proposal to be discussed below for targeted fiscal assistance is similar to "countercyclical fiscal assistance" measures, such as the one in effect from 1976 to 1978. However, this proposal recognizes that urban economic problems extend beyond recessions; they are primarily structural in nature.

In this proposal the unemployment rate is offered as a proxy for a wide range of economic distress indicators, to provide for the added targeting of funds. The targeted assistance measure would trigger in any time that unemployment is higher than a certain level; for example, 6 percent nationally. Funding is $500 per unemployed person nationally, for a current cost of approximately $4.2 billion. This cost would be reduced annually as unemployment continues to drop, and the measure bears no cost once national unemployment drops below 6 percent.

The mayors are not proposing a specific formula other than urging that the vast majority of funds be distributed to local governments on the basis of need. Some brief guidance on possible formulas is provided in "The Targeting Formula" section of this chapter.

The targeted fiscal assistance funds should not be construed as a substitute for a jobs creation program. Targeted fiscal assistance primarily is intended to aid heavily distressed local governments in maintaining their service levels and avoiding deficits, further tax increases, and layoffs. The targeted fiscal assistance funds provide a relatively small measure of compensation to urban centers for treating a large share of the social and economic problems in the United States.

GENERAL REVENUE SHARING

In the President's 1984 National Urban Policy Report, general revenue sharing headed the list of "aid programs focusing on declining cities' needs" which have been maintained by the administration. GRS was said to "enable cities to direct those relatively unrestricted funds to areas of pressing local need." In producing this list of federal commitments to cities, the report states: "The Administration recognizes that neither the general economic recovery nor the increasing capacity and willingness of State and local governments and their residents to help themselves will solve the problem of all cities."[1] In view of this philosophy, the executive branch's proposal to end GRS, beginning in fiscal year 1986, came "as a shock to mayors who believed that the Administration would stand behind this program," in the words of U.S. Conference of Mayors' President Ernest Morial, mayor of New Orleans.[2]

Benefits of GRS

GRS has gained overwhelming success and popularity among U.S. cities. For example, a Rochester, N.Y. councilmember stated that "GRS is of greater benefit to all cities than any other federal program."[3]

The program is clearly an administrative success, requiring less than 2 percent overhead. Fewer than 100 federal employees administer GRS, the largest federal grant program, allocating $4.2 billion a year to 39,000 units of government.[4] Local governments continue this efficiency, using less than 1 percent of GRS receipts for administrative costs associated with GRS.[5]

There is also considerable agreement that large and small cities alike make good use of GRS funds. For the larger cities, and especially those most in need, GRS has been what the Northeast-Midwest Congressional Coalition calls "a lifeline for financially strapped communities."[6] Clearly, the funds have enabled cities to maintain essential services as much as possible and to help avoid additional layoffs or self-destructive tax increases.

For the smaller towns and cities, GRS is the *only* federal grant received by 62 percent of communities with populations under 10,000. Revenue sharing amounts to 15 percent of those towns' budgets and enables such activities as purchasing fire helmets, uniforms, and schoolbooks for children of welfare families and installing culverts.[7] GRS can prevent property tax increases of up to 25 percent in many communities and as much as 50 percent in the smaller communities.[8] States also spent funds productively when they were GRS recipients, mostly for education, social services for the disadvantaged and disabled, and construction projects.[9] GRS is one of those rare programs that receive widespread support from large and small jurisdictions alike.

Fiscal Conditions of Cities

An improved fiscal condition of the average city is often cited as a reason to reduce or eliminate GRS. For example, the president's proposed fiscal 1986 budget cites "improvements in the revenue-generating ability of local tax sys-terms" as a reason why "local governments have become less dependent on general revenue sharing."[10]

The key to understanding the need for GRS, and targeted fiscal assistance in general, is not whether a city is able to achieve a balanced budget. Many cities have balanced their budgets over time through heavy tax increases and severe service cutbacks to the extent that tax burdens are substantially higher and service levels much lower than is the case in more affluent jurisdictions. A balanced budget is no indication of a city's ability to provide parity in tax and service levels. Rather, targeted assistance helps a city provide a social and economic climate that is conducive to reducing the enormous economic and social disparities that presently exist between urban and suburban residents (see Chapter 2). Without such assistance the disparities of poverty, education, business location, employment, taxation, housing, and so forth can only widen further, even if the municipal budget is balanced.

Some cities do have healthy fiscal conditions; others do not. Assistance that is well targeted will reach cities with the greatest fiscal need.

A 1985 survey of cities' fiscal conditions found that in 53 percent of the 150 cities responding, general fund revenues were expected to outpace inflation in the coming year, thus lending some mild support to the fiscal 1986 budget's contention about local revenue strength. However, this nationwide average masks a number of fiscal difficulties. In the Midwest, general fund revenue growth was expected to be slower than inflation in 65 percent of the cities in 1985—a year of strong economic growth—and slower also in 56 percent of northeastern cities.[11] Moreover, within each of the regional averages, there are numerous cities in severe fiscal difficulties.

Property taxes are expected to grow more slowly than inflation in 51 percent of cities (and 71 percent of midwestern cities). Sales taxes are projected to grow more slowly than inflation in 43 percent of cities (and in 50 percent of cities in the West and Midwest). Business taxes are expected to grow more slowly than inflation in 61 percent of cities (including 79 percent of the cities in the Midwest and 78 percent on the Northeast).[12]

Turning to the expenditures side, most cities (72 percent) project general fund expenditures, at current service levels, to grow faster than inflation.[13] The "answer," as always, to the expenditure-revenue gap is to cut back services further and raise taxes—self-defeating but unavoidable (there are no other real choices) policy decisions which have been repeated year after year for two to three decades in many cities. Reductions in GRS compound these structural fiscal problems.

Impact of Reduced GRS

In real dollar terms, general revenue sharing has been reduced considerably since its inception, so that GRS receipts today amount to 25 cents for each dollar distributed in 1973 (see Figure 4-1).

Figure 4-1. General Revenue Sharing Allocations in Current and Constant Dollars.

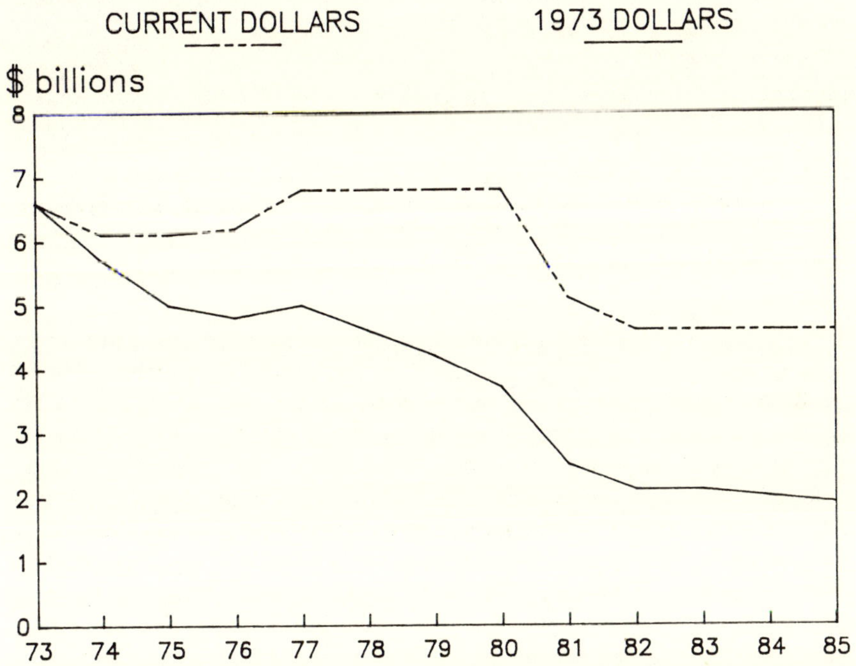

Note: States were removed from General Revenue Sharing in 1981.
Source: U.S. Office of Management and Budget, *Historical Tables for the President's Fiscal Year 1986 Budget* (Washington, D.C.: U.S. Government Printing Office, 1985), Table 5-6.

These real dollar reductions have largely been gradual, enabling urban budgets to adjust to real dollar declines, some cities adjusting better than others. What would be the impact of total elimination of GRS? A 1985 survey by the U.S. Conference of Mayors found that 97 percent of the 157 cities surveyed would reduce services, with oft-delayed capital improvements and public safety cited as the most likely areas of budget reduction. Additionally, 68 percent stated that a revenue increase would be needed.[14]

Comparison of Fiscal Strength: Federal Government and Cities

Perhaps the question should be raised as to which government entity is in greater need of assistance. If the federal government is in greater economic distress than cities, it is proper to terminate GRS.

Table 4-1. Federal Revenue Growth, 1985-1990.

	Percentage Revenue Growth	*Inflation*
1985-86	7.7%	4.3%
1986-87	8.6	4.2
1987-88	10.3	3.9
1988-89	8.4	3.6
1989-90	7.6	3.3

Source: Office of Management and Budget (OMB), *President's FY '86 Proposed Budget*, pp. 3-15, and *Historical Tables*, Table 1.2 (Washington, D.C.: U.S. Government Printing Office, 1985).

In Chapter 2 it was seen that the socioeconomic characteristics of urban residents (the extent of poverty, income disparities, population drains, business formation, unemployment rates, tax burdens) are far more severe than in the nation as a whole. The economic well-being of any society forms the basis for the well-being of the government entity.

Revenues are rising faster from federal sources than from city sources. It was indicated above that in only about half of the cities were revenues rising faster than inflation. Turning to federal receipts in the 1980-1985 period, inflation grew 31.4 percent, while receipts grew 42.5 percent, even considering the large federal tax cuts. Therefore, the federal revenue base appears relatively strong. Table 4-1 shows federal revenue projections in the years ahead. As can be seen from Table 4-1, federal revenues are expected easily to outpace inflation, even given legislative restraints on individual income tax growth and assuming continuation of the variety of special corporate tax deductions and credits.

Federal spending during fiscal 1980-85 increased 62.3 percent; inflation amounted to 31.4 percent. Federal spending rates also outpaced the gross national product, which grew 50.2 percent during that period. Even considering the austere proposed 1986 federal budget, spending would increase 64.8 percent in 1986 over 1980, faster than inflation (36.9%) and GNP (63%) over the same period.[15]

The point here is that the federal government faces relatively few inherent structural fiscal difficulties when compared to cities. The cause of the federal deficit (approximately $175 billion in fiscal 1986) is not a weak revenue base, as is the fiscal problem in cities. Rather, the primary cause was the *choice* to adopt an enormous tax reduction in 1981 (the Economic Recovery Tax Act of 1981), which has an impact of $210.8 billion in 1986.[16] The reductions were implemented without the concomitant intent to restrain increases in military expenditures in recent years.[17] The deficit could have been controlled if federal policymakers had elected to (1) control the rate of increases of military expenditures or (2) fund those steep increases by not reducing taxes quite so sharply.

Table 4-2. Growth in Defense Expenditures 1980-1985.

Fiscal Year	*Annual Percentage Growth*
1980-81	17.5%
1981-82	17.7
1982-83	13.3
1983-84	8.3
1984-85	11.6
Average Annual Percentage Growth 1980-1985	13.7%

The fastest growing item in the federal budget in 1980-85 was interest payments on the federal debt, increasing 148 percent, nearly five times faster than inflation. Assistance to state and local governments and payments to individuals, often cited as reasons for the deficit, actually declined in their share of the federal budget, dropping from a combined 57.1 percent in 1980 to a 51 percent share in 1985.

GRS amounts to less than one-half of 1 percent of the federal budget. It would take relatively little reordering of federal priorities to fund GRS, a program needed by cities because of fiscal difficulties resulting from far more adverse socioeconomic characteristics of the population (and, consequently, a weaker tax base) than is found in the nation at large.

Maintaining and Strengthening GRS

The concept of a strong revenue raiser, the federal government, sharing a small fraction of its receipts with weak revenue raisers, the cities, is recognized by mayors as a key element of the intergovernmental partnership. Mayors urge that GRS be maintained and strengthened over time. Should federal policymakers concur, a few areas for potential strengthening over time may be considered.

GRS as Percentage of Federal Income Tax Revenue. As Savannah Mayor John P. Rousakis has urged in his testimony on behalf of the U.S. Conference of Mayors, GRS overall funding levels should ultimately be fixed as a percentage of federal income tax revenue. This policy conforms to the original concept of revenue sharing and enables local governments to share with the federal government in future revenue growth. It prevents substantial real dollar decreases in GRS, as experienced over the past several years.[18]

Lifting the GRS Cap. Presently, GRS allocations to local jurisdictions are subject to a maximum per capita amount equal to 145 percent of the per capita allocation within the entire state. The U.S. General Accounting Office (GAO) supports increasing this 145 percent cap to 175 percent to improve GRS distribution to the nation's most fiscally distressed cities. The GAO indicates that New York City could expect a GRS increase of 10 percent if the cap were lifted, as one example of the effect of this provision on a major urban center.[19]

Detiering the GRS Formula. Currently, GRS funds to local jurisdictions are distributed in four tiers: to states, to county areas, by type of local government, and then to local governments within government type (city or township). According to the GAO, "the targeting of revenue sharing funds to those governmental units which on average contain the low-income population of the Nation would be enhanced significantly by eliminating the tiering procedure and applying the basic 3-factor formula directly to all units of local government within each state."[20] This measure could also be considered.

TARGETED FISCAL ASSISTANCE

In the long run a targeted fiscal assistance proposal that adds substantial funds to GRS is needed if the most distressed cities are to have a chance to provide a climate that can improve the adverse socioeconomic characteristics cited in Chapter 2.

Although the political mood at present likely cannot produce such a targeted fiscal assistance program, it will be presented nonetheless as a means to help turn around adverse urban economic conditions.

The Need for Targeted Fiscal Assistance

Long-term, structural economic decline has not been experienced in the United States outside of rural areas except in recent times. Earlier forms of targeted assistance appeared in such forms as the Appalachian Regional Commission and Tennessee Valley Authority.

In recent decades central city decline, in the form of loss of jobs, population, and sales, has depressed city revenues. As cities reduce employment levels through layoffs, raise taxes, and reduce services to adjust to deteriorating local economic conditions, a second wave of outmigration is forced, as residents and employers flee from worsening conditions. Meanwhile, the costs of city services are not reduced as population and employers leave, since those left behind—immobile, low-income populations—are increasingly jobless and dependent upon the local government. Moreover, the city's capital stock, constructed with a dense population in mind, now has its fixed costs spread over fewer employers and residents. Therefore, the per capita costs of local government increase substantially and swiftly in a times of economic decline.[21]

The basis of targeted fiscal assistance is to enable local governments to help maintain service levels, avoid employee layoffs, and avoid tax increases to prevent or reduce the continuing waves of outmigration and decline in central cities.

Countercyclical assistance, which was in effect from July 1976 through September 1978, recognized that local governments experienced particular difficulties during recessionary periods. Now, however, there is increasing recognition among those concerned about urban well-being that targeted fiscal assistance is essential to prevent or reduce long-term deterioration that extends beyond the definitions of a national recession. The Congressional Budget Office (CBO) staff noted in 1978 that, even though the recession was ending, unemployment rates were still high, then about 6 percent. The CBO warned prophetically that removing antirecession funds would risk a worsening of structural problems which remained in many areas even during economic recovery.[22]

Today, as Dr. Richard Nathan of Princeton points out, "the intergovernmental industry, which grew and prospered in the sixties and seventies, is in a state of shock."[23] Each reason for this state of shock is traumatizing by itself. Taken together, the results can be devastating.

First, the nation's worst economic downturn since the Great Depression crushed many urban governments' abilities to maintain services. The economic recovery did not restore that ability to prerecession levels in those urban centers which still must contend with 20 percent and higher poverty rates and heavy unemployment.

Second, the cumulative effects of thirty years of pervasive middle and upper-middle income class population loss, along with employer outmigration, has placed many urban governments in a position of simply trying not to retreat too fast in their service capabilities—instead of taking positive action to turn the trends around.

Third, on top of the effects of the recession and longer term economic decline have come substantial reductions in recent years in federal housing, employment and training, education for the economically disadvantaged, social services, nutrition, crime control, mass transit, and other key programs.

Fourth, local governments which have depended on GRS and targeted fiscal assistance have seen their GRS allocations cut in half by inflation and countercyclical funds removed altogether. They cannot develop their tax base sufficiently to treat the symptoms and causes of their structural problems.

Mayor Gibson of Newark indicated in 1979 that, with the antirecession fiscal assistance his city received in the late seventies, Newark was able to "stabilize taxes, deliver quality services, fill most of the vital positions in city government, engender the confidence of the business community, reverse the residential exodus, and revitalize entire neighborhoods." He added that "all this achievement is liable to go down the drain" if his city were to lose targeted fiscal assistance, which amounted to 10 percent of Newark's operating budget. The subsequent loss of funds meant a layoff of 441 municipal employees, 200 of whom were police officers, and the elimination of several recreation, drug treatment, and street-cleaning programs.[24] The U.S. Treasury Department echoed Mayor Gibson's remarks in congressional testimony, noting that the loss of targeted fiscal assistance meant layoffs or major tax increases in city after city.[25] These were actions that cities knew would inevitably be self-defeating; however, cities had no choice but to adopt them.

Federal aid to treat urban problems has been significantly reduced across the nation in recent years (see Chapter 1) but has been especially reduced in the areas with the most severe socioeconomic conditions. For FY 1982 the national average per capita reduction in domestic programs was $138. However, in New England the reductions were $145 per capita; in the Middle Atlantic region, $149; in the East-North Central, $146; and in the West-North Central, $151. In contrast, the West-South Central region experienced a $119 per capita reduction.[26] Therefore, a region such as the East-North Central, with 12.5 percent unemployment in 1982, received a 23 percent greater reduction in federal grant assistance than did the West-South Central, with 7.5 percent unemployment. The same relative proportions of federal funds reductions and unemployment rates apply today. Moreover, the Pacific region, which also has received lower than average reductions in domestic spending, is receiving far more than double the increase in defense expenditures than is received by any other region.[27]

There is yet another factor that targets federal funds away from regions most in need. Local governments in the Northeast and Midwest lost $53.6 million in GRS between FY 1982 and FY 1983 due to the composition of the GRS formula.[28] Jurisdictions in states that lose population or experience slow population growth lose GRS funds. As the GRS and other funds decrease, so does the jurisdiction's ability to treat the problems associated with stagnant or sluggish economies.

Moreover, there is no indication that states are willing to carry out the massive urban redevelopment needs now that the federal government has deemphasized its urban efforts. Just as "states' rights" never worked in ensuring equal opportunities for all citizens, so the states cannot be expected to compensate for urban fiscal inequities and initiate major new actions.

It is in this context of local tax increases, slow urban economic growth, heavy urban unemployment, and reductions in federal grant assistance that the federal government is seeking to remove itself from its responsibilities to cities. As stated in the President's Urban Policy Report of 1982: "The Reagan Administration intends to devolve the maximum feasible responsibility for urban matters to states and through them to their local governments, and to limit Federal Government responsibilities to those matters which a clear national interest is at stake."[29]

Mayors seek a reevaluation of this policy. The cities and states with the heaviest social and economic burdens are the same jurisdictions that are most heavily taxed. Increasing taxes further to combat the urban problems only provides minimal short-term relief, since employers and residents who are discouraged by such policies and who have mobility will seek a friendlier situation. The populations left behind are increasingly and intensively segregated economically and cannot be readily assimilated into mainstream economies elsewhere.

Benefits of Targeted Fiscal Assistance

Mayors have long endorsed targeted fiscal assistance to counter the long-term effects of structural economic problems. Even in times of general economic well-being, urban centers routinely experience economic conditions that if found nationally would be considered a depression.

In supporting targeted fiscal assistance, mayors have viewed the program as being fundamentally different from GRS. For example, Syracuse Mayor Lee Alexander, testifying in favor of targeted assistance on behalf of the U.S. Conference of Mayors in 1978, said, "We hope that in an effort to broaden support to ensure implementation of the program, the Administration and Congress do not make the program too inclusive and one of general assistance. For that is the purpose of another important program—General Revenue Sharing."[30] Similarly, St. Louis Mayor James Conway stated that "supplemental Fiscal Assistance should be directed at the substantially fewer governments with problems too severe to be adequately addressed by the ordinary assistance provided through General Revenue Sharing."[31]

At a 1976 hearing—when unemployment was 7.5 percent nationally—Mayor Moon Landrieu of New Orleans pointed out that, under countercyclical fiscal assistance, 75 percent of local government allocations went to jurisdictions with unemployment greater than 8 percent, compared to 43 percent for GRS. Moreover, only 1 percent of countercyclical funds went to jurisdictions having an unemployment rate of 5.5 percent or less compared to 23 percent of GRS funds.[32]

The heavier the unemployment, the more effective targeted fiscal assistance will be in creating jobs. In an area having unemployment greater than 8 percent, nearly 90 percent of the funds will have a direct jobs impact.[33]

Targeted fiscal assistance is primarily intended to provide aid to local governments in areas experiencing economic problems. It is not primarily intended as a jobs creation program, but it does have that effect. A survey of the Senate Subcommittee on Intergovernmental Relations found that countercyclical assistance created 87,000 jobs for each $1 billion spent and ranks with the most effective jobs programs enacted by Congress.[34]

A $4.2 billion targeted fiscal assistance program would reduce unemployment by about six-tenths of 1 percent. Thus, while targeted fiscal assistance can effectively supplement other jobs strategies, it cannot replace those strategies.

Use of Unemployment Data as a Proxy for Fiscal Distress

The Urban Institute has found that unemployment rates are correlated quite well to various factors of fiscal stress in cities. As unemployment increases over an extended period, cities are likely to experience budgetary deficits, population losses, and swift increases in per capita spending for the variety of municipal services.[35] Therefore, if the goal is to target funds to local governments most in need of resources, unemployment rates should prove successful as a primary targeting factor in the formula.

The Treasury Department has agreed, noting that the ten "highest fiscal strain" cities receive substantially higher per capita allocations than less strained cities under an unemployment-based fiscal assistance formula.[36] Moreover, a 1983 survey for the Congressional Joint Economic Committee noted that cities with unemployment rates of less than 7.5 percent anticipate significant increases in their municipal workforces, while cities having greater unemployment rates than 7.5 percent project workforce decreases[37]—yet another indication that a formula based on unemployment targets funds to local governments where they are most needed.

Certainly, other measures could be used as a basis for targeting aid to areas experiencing serious long-term decline. For example, changes in employment levels, rates of change in population, and rate of growth in per capita income could all be added to the formula, with considerable justification, to target funds as specifically as possible.[38] However, unemployment rates are chosen as the first-level proxy for fiscal stress to keep the formula from becoming complex and because the measure meets targeting standards.

The Targeting Formula

Since many urban centers are widely recognized as experiencing fiscal distress, regardless of business cycle fluctuations, U.S. mayors proposed permanent authorization of a targeted fiscal assistance program. The assistance would be based primarily upon unemployment rates as a proxy for fiscal distress. The program would trigger in when national unemployment is at or greater than a certain level—6 percent for example.

It will be recalled that the Employment Act of 1946 mandated federal responsibility for promoting employment, and the Full Employment Act of 1978 ("Humphrey-Hawkins") set a 4 percent overall employment rate as the full employment goal of the nation. Structural unemployment problems have magnified since then to the extent that 6 percent unemployment is now considered "full employment" by many economists.

Funding is established at $500 per unemployed person in the nation, with funds flowing to states and local jurisdictions to aid them in overcoming fiscal distress. Therefore, the funding at present unemployment levels is about $4.2 billion. The funding level would diminish, of course, as unemployment decreases, and be reduced to zero as unemployment once again falls below 6 percent.

Mayors offer no specific formula for targeting fiscal assistance in this proposal. Nonetheless, a logical starting point in developing the formula would be the standard three-part general revenue sharing formula (without the "145 percent cap" and with no "guaranteed minimum"), targeted further by the extent of unemployment in the jurisdiction.[39]

A city such as Gary, Indiana with an 18.3 percent unemployment rate (July 1985) would receive considerable assistance; Rochester, N.Y., on the other hand, with a 7.2 percent rate, would still be eligible for assistance but would receive less from the unemployment adjustment factor.

Unemployment rates are considered reliable only down to county level and, for the most part, cities of 50,000 population or greater.[40] Therefore, all jurisdictions of less than 50,000 in population would use the county unemployment rate in computing their allocation.[41] Cities over 50,000 in population could submit their own unemployment rate for purposes of receiving targeted assistance. As an added safeguard to ensure accuracy of data, these larger cities would be required to follow well-established methodology in computing the rates and have those rates certified by the Bureau of Labor Statistics. Failing receipt of such certification, the county unemployment rate would be used.

Despite the difficulties inherent in using city unemployment data, these data should nonetheless be used to produce a genuine targeting effect. Usually, unemployment rates of urban centers are significantly higher than the county data, which include the more affluent suburban areas having relatively low unemployment.

Summary

The result of this proposal would be to provide funding to local governments to enable them to avoid self-defeating service cutbacks and tax increases, to avoid employee layoffs, and in many cases to initiate economic development and other programs that enhance the well-being of their communities. Along with general revenue sharing, this program would improve the opportunities for distressed cities to compete in the marketplace with wealthier communities for retention and attraction of employers and residents.

NOTES TO CHAPTER 4

1. U.S. Department of Housing and Urban Development (HUD), *The President's National Urban Policy Report, 1984* (Washington, D.C.: HUD, May 1984), p. 13.

2. U.S. Conference of Mayors (USCM), *The Impact on America's Cities of the Administration's Federal Budget for Fiscal Year 1986* (Washington, D.C.: USCM, March 1985), p. 1.
3. Councilmember Chris Lindley, Testimony on revenue sharing allocations before the Subcommittee on Intergovernmental Relations, Senate Committee on Governmental Affairs, April 6, 1983, p. 5.
4. Mayor Jake Godbold of Jacksonville on behalf of the U.S. Conference of Mayors before the Subcommittee on Intergovernmental Relations, House Government Operations Committee, March 17, 1983, p. 1.
5. Office of Management and Budget (OMB), *Budget of U.S. Government, FY 1986* (Washington, D.C.: U.S. Government Printing Office, 1985), pp. 5-151.
6. Representative Frank Horton, Testimony on general revenue sharing before the Senate Intergovernmental Relations Subcommittee, April 6, 1983, p. 89.
7. Barton D. Russell, National Association of Towns and Townships, before the House Subcommittee on Intergovernmental Relations, March 16, 1983, pp. 5, 14.
8. Horton, p. 2.
9. Governor Richard A. Snelling before the House Subcommittee on Intergovernmental Relations, March 17, 1983, pp. 6, 7.
10. Office of Management and Budget, *Budget of U.S. Government, FY 1986*, p. 5-151.
11. National League of Cities (NLC), *City Fiscal Conditions and Outlook for FY '85* (Washington, D.C.: NLC, March 1985), p. 27.
12. Ibid., pp. 27–33.
13. Ibid., p. 27.
14. U.S. Conference of Mayors, p. 6.
15. Office of Management and Budget, *Historical Tables, Budget of the U.S. Government, FY 1986* (Washington, D.C.: U.S. Government Printing Office, 1985), Table 1.2.
16. Office of Management and Budget, *Budget of U.S. Government, FY 1986*, p. 4-4.
17. Office of Management and Budget, *Historical Tables*, Table 6.1.
18. Mayor John Rousakis, Testimony before Senate Intergovernmental Relations Subcommittee, April 6, 1983, p. 4.
19. Arthur R. Goldbeck, U.S.G.A.O., Testimony before Senate Intergovernmental Relations Subcommittee, April 5, 1983, p. 8.
20. Comptroller General of the United States, "Removing Tiering from the Revenue Sharing Formula would Eliminate Payment Inequities to Local Governments" (Washington, D.C.: U.S. Government Accounting Office, April 15, 1982), pp. iii–iv.
21. Comptroller General of the United States, "Anti-recession Assistance—An Evaluation" (Washington, D.C.: U.S. Government Accounting Office, November 29, 1977), pp. 15–16.
22. Congressional Budget Office, "Phasing Down Anti-recession Programs: Fiscal Year 1979 Budget Issues" (Washington, D.C.: U.S. Government Printing Office, November 1978), p. 21.

23. Richard P. Nathan, Princeton University, Testimony before Senate Subcommittee on Intergovernmental Relations, April 5, 1983, p. 2.
24. Mayor Kenneth A. Gibson, Testimony before Senate Revenue Sharing Subcommittee, March 13, 1979, pp. 1, 5.
25. Robert Carswell, Hearing on H.R. 3198 and 2698, House Intergovernmental Relations Subcommittee, June 27, 1979, p. 56.
26. John L. Palmer and Isabel V. Sawhill, eds., *The Reagan Experiment* (Washington, D.C.: Urban Institute Press, 1982), p. 448.
27. Ibid., p. 450.
28. Horton, p. 5.
29. U.S. Department of Housing and Urban Development, *The President's National Urban Policy Report* (Washington, D.C.: U.S. Government Printing Office, July 1982), p. 57.
30. Mayor Lee Alexander, Testimony on H.R. 12293, House Subcommittee on Intergovernmental Relations, May 4, 1978, p. 71.
31. Mayor James Conway, Testimony on H.R. 12293, House Subcommittee on Intergovernmental Relations, May 4, 1978, p. 71.
32. Mayor Moon Landrieu, Testimony on H.R. 3730 before the House Subcommittee on Intergovernmental Relations, March 8, 1977, p. 237.
33. Ibid., p. 234.
34. Ibid.
35. George E. Peterson, Urban Institute, Testimony on H.R. 3730, House Intergovernmental Relations Subcommittee, March 1, 1977, p. 14a.
36. Robert Carswell, p. 58.
37. Joint Economic Committee, Table 21.
38. See discussion on H.R. 12293, House Intergovernmental Relations Subcommittee, May 4, 1978, pp. 5–23.
39. Restrictions could also be considered for "tax enclaves"; that is, areas having an exceptionally heavy tax base because of intensive industry location. In this way the "tax effort" factor of the three-factor general revenue sharing formula does not become excessive.
40. House Intergovernmental Relations Subcommittee, Hearings on H.R. 12293, May 4, 1978, p. 113. Also see hearings on H.R. 3198 and H.R. 2698, June 27, 1979, pp. 62–74; and U.S. Advisory Commission on Intergovernmental Relations, "Countercyclical Aid and Economic Stabilization" (Washington, D.C.: U.S. Government Printing Office, 1978), p. 47.
41. If the jurisdiction happens to be located in two counties, then simply use the unemployment rate in the county in which the largest portion of the jurisdiction's population resides.

5 A NATIONAL EMPLOYMENT AND TRAINING POLICY

The nation would never consider planning for national defense by simply waiting to see what weapon systems are developed by other nations and then taking reactive measures. National defense policies and contingency plans are always in place and frequently fine tuned. Similarly, the economy is not simply allowed to evolve; the Federal Reserve Board, the Treasury Department, and the Council of Economic Advisers monitor early indicators of change and put into effect monetary and fiscal policies to achieve desired effects.

Yet when it comes to employment and training policies, the nation's level of planning is at the most rudimentary of stages. The civil rights movement has led to the creation of new job training and work experience programs, although these programs have been cut in half in recent years. More recently, the women's rights movement has lead to an increased national awareness of the need for progress. Legislation such as the Humphrey-Hawkins Act of 1978 has set full employment of 4 percent as a federal priority and responsibility. These gains, however, are hollow unless they can be substantiated by a thorough, comprehensive private and public sector response to the nation's structural unemployment and underemployment problems.

In this chapter mayors call for the development of a national employment and training policy. This policy should be developed in full partnership with U.S. business and labor, the sources of our nation's productivity and job base.

Presently, the federal-state-local roles in attacking unemployment are ambiguous. Consequently, no level of government is assuming responsibility for treating the causes or symptoms of the problems. The national policy proposed by mayors will clarify these roles.

Similarly, the income and employment gaps among the races are widening over time. While minorities are losing ground, with depression-level unemployment in many parts of the nation, there is no national plan that even pretends to address the problem.

As a nation we lack knowledge of where technological trends are taking us, what our long- and short-run education and training needs are, and what training program curricula and designs work best for dislocated workers and the economically disadvantaged. We need to seek systematically employers' assessments of job openings and training needs, and include U.S. business in the training program designs, so that program graduates may be placed in private sector jobs. We need to examine our incentive systems to ensure that businesses are motivated to include the economically disadvantaged in their training and hiring plans.

While the national employment and training plan is being developed, immediate needs must be met to achieve an additional 1 percent decline in the unemployment rate. Funding for the current Job Training Partnership Act should ultimately be set at least as high as under the previous job and training program legislation (CETA–the Comprehensive Employment and Training Act). Funding economic development projects and infrastructure repair is a particularly effective way to create jobs in areas that need them the most, at a low cost per job created, and to accomplish essential urban development objectives at the same time.

Finally, the nation's monetary and fiscal policies should be developed with full employment as a top priority; the well-being of American families should not be sacrificed as national policymakers achieve broader economic goals.

THE COSTS OF UNEMPLOYMENT

U.S. mayors are deeply concerned about the more than 8 million Americans who are currently out of work, the millions more who have dropped out of the labor force altogether in discouragement over not finding work, and the added millions who could eventually lose their jobs as a result of continuing economic fluctuations and dramatically changing labor market needs. It is sobering to note that it was the difficult problem of unemployment and its impact upon the nation that caused mayors to join together more than fifty years ago to form the U.S. Conference of Mayors.

As of September 1985 the unemployment rate was 7.1 percent; this overall rate masks serious economic imbalances:

- Minority unemployment stands at depression levels. The 15.3 percent rate for blacks continues to be more than double the white rate.
- The rate for black teens is 38 percent.

- An unemployment rate in the 7 percent plus range, during times of economic recovery and expansion, is among the highest structural unemployment levels in recent U.S. history. During the 1950s unemployment averaged 4.2 percent; during the 1960s, 4.8 percent; during the 1970s, 6.2 percent. During the first four years of the 1980s the rate averaged 8.5 percent. Each recession and economic recovery has left the nation progressively worse off.
- The unemployment rate of today—during a period of economic recovery and expansion—actually exceeds the unemployment rate at the troughs of most of our recent recessions.
- By adding in Bureau of Labor Statistics' data for discouraged workers and those underemployed (primarily those forced to settle for part-time work), the unemployment rate is over 13 percent.[1]
- Economic recoveries are increasingly selective and not general. Cities in particular remain in or close to double-digit unemployment levels, even as the nation's rate recovers. (See Chapter 2.)

Table 5-1. U.S. Civilian Unemployment, Selected Characteristics, 1978, 1980, 1982, and September 1985 (*in thousands*).

	1978	*1980*	*1982*	*September 1985*
Total Unemployed	6,202	7,637	10,678	8,274
Unemployment Rate	6.1%	7.1%	9.7%	7.1%
Females	3,061	3,370	4,499	3,854
Rate	7.2%	7.4%	9.4%	7.5%
Males	3,142	4,267	6,179	4,421
Rate	5.3%	6.9%	9.9%	6.7%
Youths (16–19 years)	1,583	1,669	1,977	1,394
Rate	16.4%	17.8%	23.2%	17.8%
Blacks	1,330	1,533	2,142	1,892
Rate	12.8%	14.3%	18.9%	15.3%
Black teens (16–19 years)	360	343	396	327
Rate	38.7%	38.5%	48.0%	38.3%
White	4,698	5,884	8,241	6,094
Rate	5.2%	6.3%	8.6%	6.1%
White teens (16–19 years)	1,189	1,291	1,534	1,025
Rate	13.9%	15.5%	20.4%	15.1%

Sources: U.S. Department of Labor, *Employment and Earnings, 1982*; U.S. Department of Labor, *Employment and Training Report of the President, 1982*; and recent Bureau of Labor Statistics news releases.

There is no way to overstate the problems relating to unemployment. For the individual who cannot find work, unemployment poses problems not only for physical survival but for mental well-being. When so many urban residents are out of work, the impact is nothing short of devastating. The demoralizing effects of unemployment can be felt by an entire city or even by an entire state or nation. Progress has always been based on optimism, on a belief that dedication and hard work will lead to a better life. When millions of people lose hope, that cannot help but reduce the collective optimism upon which a city, state, or nation bases its growth and development.

There are, of course, other more measurable effects of unemployment. The loss in wages reduces taxable income at all levels of government and makes it very difficult for those governments to maintain their services. Also, those lost wages and the resulting reduction in buying power hurt businesses. This, of course, not only results in additional reductions in tax revenues for governments but often forces businesses to lay off workers or to go under altogether. At the national level, each 1 percent of unemployment translates into a \$20 to \$26 billion addition to the federal deficit, putting a further drain on our economy.

The Urban Institute estimated the costs of unemployment from 1980 to 1983. Had unemployment remained at 6 percent during that time, the economy would have produced an additional \$654 million in goods and services. This translates into an after-tax income loss of \$3,837 per household in the United States. The cumulative loss between 1980 and 1986 (projected) from this excessive unemployment is \$5,879 per household. Of the billions of dollars of lost income, most (59%) of the loss is borne by workers; however, corporate profits account for a significant share (25%), as do farmers and small businesses (13%). The Urban Institute estimates that 60 percent of these costs could have been eliminated had the nation pursued fiscal and monetary policies that brought inflation down more gradually.[2]

Unemployment insurance provides some relief to the unemployed individuals, but, overall, in times of high unemployment the impact of such insurance could be as much negative as positive. First, such payments do little to address the individual and collective morale problems created by unemployment. In fact, in a society that values work, such payments may actually exacerbate those problems. Second, such payments are intended only to allow an individual and his or her family to survive. They rarely are sufficient to allow the recipients to regain any significant purchasing power. Thus, neither governments nor businesses are helped. The cycle remains unbroken though millions of dollars are expended. Additionally, the unemployment insurance systems in several states have been on the verge of bankruptcy as outlays have far exceeded income.

There are other problems that relate directly to unemployment. Unemployed people necessarily place a burden on local government social services at a time when there are insufficient funds to support those services. Crime and vandalism increase as people seek ways to survive or to vent their frustrations; alcoholism, drug abuse, and family break-ups all remain at high levels during times of heavy unemployment.

Such problems occur during any period of high unemployment. Today the problems are worsened by the fact that the nation is in the beginnings of a technological upheaval that has not been equaled since the Industrial Revolution. The uncertainty created by unemployment is complicated by the long-term uncertainty created by these basic technological and economic changes.

EMPLOYMENT OF MINORITIES, WOMEN

Up to this point the discussion has focused primarily on the general problem of high unemployment. However, three other specific issues must be addressed:

- the high rate of unemployment among minorities;
- the high rate of unemployment among youth; and
- differences in earnings between white males, females, and minorities.

Unemployment among the nation's minorities is disproportionately high, a reflection of the continuing problem of racial discrimination. Black unemployment has remained well into double digits for an extended period of time, and black youth unemployment remains over 40 percent in most cities. Hispanic unemployment falls just a few percentage points behind. The official unemployment rates do not include the millions who have dropped out of the labor market altogether, in discouragement over not finding work. Minorities must overcome not only the economic and technological problems that others must face but also the reluctance of employers to hire them.

The high rate of unemployment among youths is a harbinger of future problems. In September 1985 the unemployment rate among workers sixteen to nineteen years of age was 17.8 percent. Among black youths the rate was 38.3 percent.

Youths entering the adult work world with little job experience and no skills training will have little success in obtaining employment. The problem of finding and holding employment with little prior training seems to be growing worse over time. For example, in the late 1960s, 53 percent of black high school graduates who were not in college had jobs, as did 48 percent of the school dropouts. However, in the 1980–82 period, only 32 percent of black high school graduates not in college were working and only 16 percent of the dropouts held jobs.[3] If these problems are not addressed now, they will have to be addressed later at a significantly higher cost.

Differences in earnings that reflect sex or racial discrimination continue to show up in wage statistics. Although some progress has been made with regard

Figure 5-1. Trends in Black Families, 1960-1983.

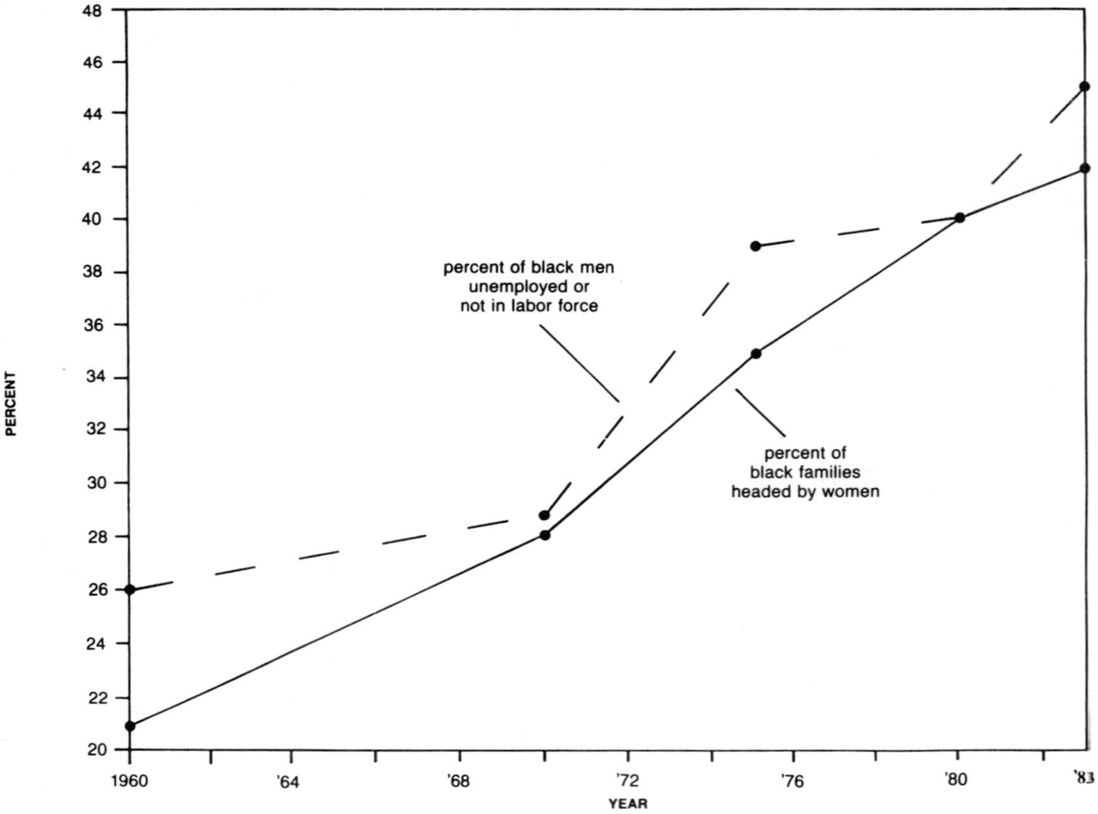

Source: The Center for the Study of Social Policy, "The 'Flip-Side' of Black Families Headed by Women: The Economic Status of Black Men" (Washington, D.C.: The Center for the Study of Social Policy, 1984), p. 11.

Figure 5-2. Youth Unemployment Rates by Age and Race, United States 1954 to 1984.

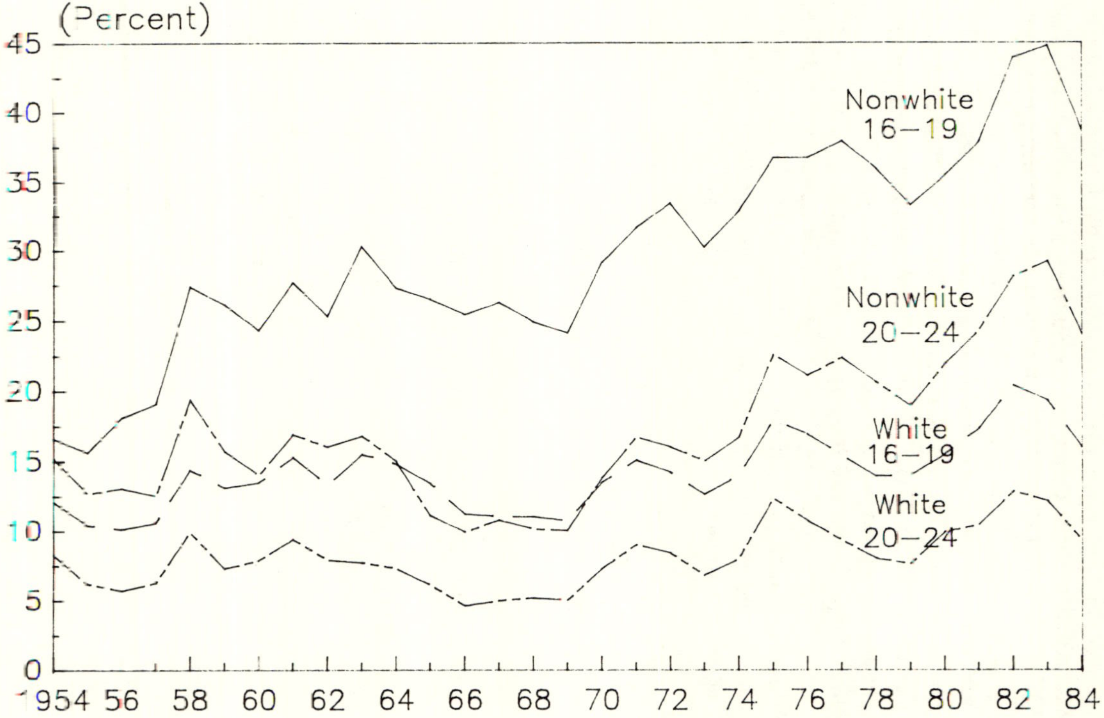

Source: U.S. Department of Labor, Bureau of Labor Statistics (BLS), *Databook, Current Population Survey*, Vol 1 (Washington, D.C.: BLS, 1982), pp. 503–508, 518–524; *Employment and Earnings* (Washington, D.C.: BLS, January 1984 and 85), Tables 3 and 4.

to the principle of equal work for equal pay, many problems still need to be overcome.

In other chapters of this urban policy report, we note the trends and problems of female-headed households and the enormous social and economic costs to treat those problems. In 1982, while 78 percent of all working-age white men were employed, only 54 percent of all working-age black men had jobs, according to methodology of the Center for the Study of Social Policy. The center observes: "If 46 percent of all black men are jobless—either unemployed, not looking for work, in correctional facilities or unaccounted for—it is little wonder that an increasing number of black women are raising families alone." The erosion of the black family, the center observes, is not a "mystical cultural trend," but a "palpable economic event." Figure 5-1 indicates that the upward trend in black male unemployment nearly exactly parallels the growth in female-headed households.[4] Employment and training programs must be developed with a new urgency, attracting and retaining both men and women participants. The Bureau of Labor Statistics indicates that these interracial gaps are huge in times of economic recovery and expansion as well. As of the third quarter 1985, 74 percent of working-age (16 to 64) white men had jobs, compared to just 62 percent of working-age black men.[5]

As can be seen from Figure 5-2, youth unemployment has been increasing for all races over the last few decades. However, the growth rate has been especially sharp among minority youth; the gaps between the races are rapidly widening.

THE ROLE OF THE FEDERAL GOVERNMENT

It is easy to justify the involvement of the federal government in reducing unemployment problems. Certainly, employment is basic to the health and welfare of U.S. citizens and, consequently, can be viewed as a constitutional responsibility of the federal government. The federal government has played a principal role in every major economic or technological transition that this nation has faced. It has also been responsible for many of the changes that have occurred to equal employment opportunities.

The federal government has also played a role addressing unemployment. It was the federal government that established land grant colleges to meet the educational needs of a changing labor force. It was the federal, state, and local governments that built the highway and railway systems to meet the demands of an expanding nation. It was the federal government that provided emergency jobs programs during the Great Depression to keep people going until the economy regained its strength. Since the depression the federal government has provided financial assistance packages to help foundering companies to stimulate business growth and expansion. It has provided employment and training programs designed to help ensure that all segments of the population have access to the training opportunities necessary to secure employment.

The programs of the 1930s, including creation of the Employment Service, the Works Progress Administration, and the Civilian Conservation Corps, demonstrated that the federal government recognized that it has a responsibility to address employment problems. With the passage of the Economic Opportunity Act and the Manpower Development Training Act in the 1960s, the federal government recognized its responsibility to address the special needs of economically disadvantaged and minority citizens who face overwhelming barriers to employment. The Comprehensive Employment and Training Act (CETA) in the 1970s and the Job Training Partnership Act (JTPA) in the 1980s reaffirmed the federal responsibility.

Moreover, the Employment Act of 1946 mandated federal responsibility for promoting employment, and the Full Employment Act of 1978 (Humphrey-Hawkins) set a 4 percent overall unemployment rate as the full-employment goal of the nation. The latter act required the development of a comprehensive and consistent national policy to achieve annual quantitative employment goals.

With all of these efforts, however, unemployment remains a major problem. Significantly, the consensus among some national policymakers seems to be that the programs developed by the federal government have had little impact. At best, critics claim, the programs seem to have minimized additional damage without really effecting solutions.

Much of the criticism of federal employment and training programs has been unjustified. Land grant colleges have played an undeniable role in providing higher education to millions of people. The depression employment programs at least helped people get through a difficult time and established the principle that government and employers have a responsibility to provide assistance to those who have lost their jobs. Finally, although recent employment and training programs, such as CETA and Public Service Employment, received harsh criticism, they actually provided immediate relief to millions of unemployed people and trained millions more in marketable skills. These programs should not be painted as "failures" because they did not immediately remove all the barriers to employment (lack of education, low job skills, race and sex discrimination) that were built over decades.

As prominent human resource analysts have indicated: "The number enrolled in employment and training programs were always too low, compared to the numbers inflicted by unemployment and poverty, to have offset demographic trends, worldwide inflation, energy crises, international competition, and domestic microeconomic forces."[7]

Does JTPA Work?

Today's debates on the efficiency of employment and training programs usually sound like antiphonal choruses: "Jobs programs don't work," followed by, "Oh yes they do." Perhaps it would be better not to consider whether or not the job programs work but simply consider the numbers.

Classroom training has been measured to produce a 10 percent increase in earning power for program participants over a control group. Public service employment produces a 7 percent increase in earning power, on average. On-the-job training in the private sector produces a 16 percent earnings power increase for the enrollees. The Jobs Corps, which provides skills training to the economically disadvantaged in residential settings, returns $1.39 in increased earnings for each dollar invested. Typically, ninety hours of basic skills instruction produces a 1.5-year achievement gain in reading and 1 year in math. Job search assistance has demonstrated the ability to increase by 50 percent or more the job-finding rates of the unemployed.[6]

In the first nine months of the Job Training Partnership Act, from October 1983 through June 1984, there were 615,500 participants during the year, with 390,100 completing the program and 275,400 still on board at the end of the program year. Moreover, 96,100 were enrolled in the dislocated worker program. Of those completing the training programs, 62 percent were placed into jobs at an average wage of $4.58 per hour. The cost per placement was $3,485.

JTPA seems to be well targeted, youth constituting 39 percent of enrollees and high school dropouts 26 percent of the enrollees in its first year (1984–85). Half were women. Blacks constituted 32 percent of enrollees, Hispanics 12 percent, and other minorities 4 percent. Economically disadvantaged citizens constituted 94 percent of all enrollees, and public assistance recipients were 41 percent of the total. Citizens who were public assistance recipients when they enrolled were nearly as successful in obtaining a job at the end of the training program as were those who were not public assistance recipients (59 percent versus 68 percent). The wages of the job obtained were nearly as high for the welfare recipients as for the nonrecipients ($4.44 versus $4.58). However, wages obtained by blacks ($4.43) were lower than Hispanics ($4.52) and whites ($4.59).

On-the-job training participants were most successful in obtaining employment (80 percent of those finishing the program), followed by 72 percent for those receiving job search assistance and 57 percent for those receiving classroom training.[8]

Therefore, the above data provide the extent to which the program "works." The numbers receiving employment at the end of training—about 242,000—is quite low when compared to the more than 8 million who are out of work at any given time and the many others who are discouraged workers. Nonetheless, the program reaches the people it is intended to reach, and it has a placement rate that is at least adequate and perhaps even good. It would be desirable to lower the cost per placement, although the program has met its stated objectives in that regard as well.

THE NEED FOR A NATIONAL POLICY

Not all of the criticism of jobs programs has been unfair. Perhaps the federal government has been most vulnerable to the charge that it has no national employment and training policy. Federal legislation relating to employment and training has primarily been reactive to problems that have already caused personal and national damage. They have addressed specific issues rather than the interrelated network of forces that impact upon the economy and unemployment. Public Service Employment, for instance, provided jobs for unemployed people (chiefly in the public sector), but it was not coupled with comprehensive effort to eliminate the problems that caused the unemployment in the first place. Further, the programs that were created were usually not large enough to have a significant impact upon the specific issues they were designed to address. Turning again to Public Service Employment, it is clear that during the height of federal funding for that program the total impact was such that the unemployment rate was reduced by no more than one percentage point.

Another problem with federal programs has been their reactive nature. There has been little effort to establish a policy to prepare for economic changes or to plan for or direct those changes. Government at any level has not reached out to the private sector sufficiently to include U.S. businesses as full partners in determining training needs and in designing training programs to facilitate placing graduates of the programs into private sector employment. As a result, federal legislation has resulted in little more than a hodgepodge of programs, only loosely related each to the other, with no comprehensive approach that relates economic trends to labor market needs. For this reason, mayors urge the U.S. Congress to embark on a major effort to develop a comprehensive employment and training policy that addresses the following:

- The determination of the appropriate role of the various levels of government and of the nongovernmental sectors;
- The provision of immediate relief to unemployed Americans;
- The rehabilitation of the urban infrastructure;
- Determination of long- and short-term education and training needs with the degree of sophistication necessary to meet technological and labor market objectives;
- Development of measures for protecting workers during periods of economic downturns or technological change; and

- Development of measures for ensuring equal opportunities for the structurally unemployed, including, as a minimum:

    minorities;
    women;
    the economically disadvantaged;
    the handicapped;
    youth;
    senior citizens;
    migrant workers;
    aliens and refugees; and
    offenders and ex-offenders.

Granted, the federal government has created programs that, on an individual basis, address several of the above issues. However, there has been no approach ensuring that each individual program was tied in some way to an overall design to build economic growth or minimize damage to the economic system during periods of disruption. Such a national policy relating previously disparate issues to overall goals and objectives would not solve all unemployment problems. It would, however, provide direction for the nation—direction that could be followed by state and local governments as well as by the private sector.

THE ELEMENTS OF A NATIONAL EMPLOYMENT POLICY

The remainder of this chapter discusses the issues and policy actions that should be included in a national employment and training policy.

Determining the Responsibilities of the Public and Private Sectors

Within Congress there are numerous differences of opinion regarding the proper role of the various levels of government and of the private sector in resolving economic problems. Congressional resistance to subsidized employment programs, for example, is often more a reflection of differing philosophies regarding federalism than a concern for the cost of such programs.

Mayors feel strongly that the federal government must play a major role in resolving economic problems and in planning for economic growth. Obviously, the very creation of a national policy must be carried out at the federal level. However, mayors also recognize that the state and local levels of government, as well as the nongovernmental sectors of society, must assume substantial responsibility.

U.S. mayors recommend:

- that the president and Congress initiate a national discussion to examine the roles of the various sectors in resolving economic problems and planning for economic growth;
- that, in the course of the national discussion, Congress set forth basic responsibilities of the federal, state, and local governments as well as the nongovernmental sectors of the society;
- that, in determining roles and responsibilities, Congress recognize that the federal government is the only instrument developed to date to collect and distribute resources equitably among low- and high-unemployment areas, so that all have opportunities to achieve full employment; and
- that, once responsibilities are established, Congress take the lead role in turning those responsibilities into effective measures that address economic issues comprehensively. That lead role should include not only federal initiatives but assistance to the other actors in the fulfillment of their responsibilities.

Divergent congressional philosophies, applied variously to individual legislative initiatives, contribute to the disparate nature of our national employment and training programs. A national division of responsibility, which attempts to compromise the philosophical differences and which is in place and applied consistently to the resolution of problems and development of programs, would do much to organize the national policy.

Meeting Immediate Needs

Jobs—even federally subsidized jobs—are preferable to unemployment checks and welfare payments. Job creation programs are a positive step toward alleviating immediate unemployment problems. Further, wage earners have purchasing power. With jobs, the cycle is broken.

Contrary to much congressional opinion, CETA's Public Service Employment program did what it was designed to do. Considering the programmatic and fiscal changes that the CETA system underwent, the program worked quite well. The problems encountered with Public Service Employment were not inherent in the program; they were the result of the nation's ineffectiveness in changing the underlying economic problems that created the unemployment that brought about the creation of the jobs program in the first place.

Certainly, no one hopes to make that mistake again. With this in mind, mayors make three recommendations:

- The Congress of the United States should enact permanent targeted fiscal assistance legislation that is triggered nationally when the unemployment rate is higher than 6 percent (see Chapter 4 for a complete discussion of this proposal). This legislation will funnel assistance to state and local governments that are experiencing heavy unemployment in their areas. The funds will help these levels of governments provide a wide variety of services that are necessary in times of high unemployment.

- At the same time, a more direct jobs creation and training program is essential to put people back to work in times of heavy unemployment. This program should be funded at a level to reduce unemployment, at a minimum, by 1 percent. Mayors would like to see a substantial private sector emphasis in this job creation and training program, with incentives for businesses to retain the individuals they train as permanent employees at the conclusion of their training or work experience period.
- Congress should take care to ensure that any targeted fiscal assistance and direct job creation programs are part of a comprehensive plan to reduce economic problems. Unemployment is a symptom. If steps to effect a cure are not taken simultaneously with treatment of the symptom, the illness will not be eliminated. Therefore, employment programs should be implemented in conjunction with other efforts designed to stimulate economic growth, including small-business development programs, infrastructure development projects, employer hiring incentives, and training programs based on reliable labor market projections.

Economic development initiatives in cities, in particular, are proven job creators. In Chapter 3 the number of jobs added by a variety of federal economic development programs is provided. Invariably, the results are impressive. The General Accounting Office (GAO) has estimated in a two-year econometric analysis that between 1974 and 1978 every $500,000 additional federal economic development expenditure produced 216 jobs—an average of $2,315 per job. This cost is considerably less than that found in many other types of job creation and training programs. Moreover, the effectiveness of economic development grants was most pronounced in the fifteen lowest employment growth states, where each $500,000 in additional grants produced 407 jobs, at an average cost of $1,229 per job created.[9]

Maintaining and Improving Unemployment Insurance

Even when jobs creation programs are implemented, no one can expect the federal government to put everyone back to work. For that reason, unemployment insurance must be maintained. However, mayors recommend that Congress examine ways to make unemployment insurance programs do more than maintain individuals. There are several avenues to explore. For instance unemployment insurance funds, with added federal subsidy (e.g., from current federal jobs programs or the measures proposed above), could be used to pay for retraining of dislocated workers. Such a fund could also be used to provide training subsidies to employers who agree to hire additional workers.

The concept of the Individual Training Account (ITA) also has considerable merit. Employees and employers contribute to a training fund analogous to the Individual Retirement Account, drawing out funds, without penalty, when retraining is needed.[10]

Proposals are worth exploring that provide funds for retraining from a small fee on imports. These funds would help workers who have lost their jobs because of increased foreign imports. A 1 percent fee would raise about $350 million for retraining.

Also, jobs search assistance could be provided to each unemployed worker at an average cost of $100 to $200 per unemployed person. Although this assistance could prove costly (about $400 million if one-third of all unemployment insurance (UI) recipients received the assistance), it should also be recognized that UI benefits, now averaging $125 per week, would be trimmed. The concept of the unemployment voucher, where an employer could share in the value of an unemployed person's remaining UI benefits via some form of partial tax credit to the employer, could also be considered as an incentive to an employer to hire an unemployed person.[11]

Perhaps the easiest change would be to eliminate the current disincentive to attend school. Currently, people who are in school are not considered to be in the labor force. Therefore, an individual receiving unemployment benefits who enters school generally loses those benefits. Mayors urge that unemployed people be encouraged to seek retraining, when necessary, rather than be penalized for returning to school.

All states and major local governments should be encouraged or required ro automate their applicant files (including educational levels, training course completion, work experience, areas of job interests, and other indications of skills) as well as automate their job banks, to facilitate matching of available jobs with those looking for work. With federal guidelines assuring compatibility of hardware and software, a national job matching system can be implemented. Federal funding can assist in implementation of these systems. All employers should be encouraged to list their job openings in the job bank.

Rehabilitating the Urban Infrastructure

Numerous newspapers and magazines have documented the plight of America's urban infrastructure and the nation's highways and bridges quite well. State and local taxes are insufficient for state and local governments to solve these problems on their own. Resource shortages resulting from tax limitations have been exacerbated, of course, by the reductions in revenues created by high unemployment.

For this reason, mayors urge the federal government to provide assistance to state and local governments to rebuild the infrastructure. The disrepair not only deteriorates the quality of life but seriously impedes business growth and development.

Mayors strongly support such programs as the Community Development Block Grant and the Urban Development Action Grant as means of rebuilding the infrastructure. In the GAO analysis discussed above, public works grants (primarily from the Economic Development Administration) were the most effective producers of jobs, creating 51 percent more jobs, at a 34 percent lower cost per job, for each $500,000 spent, when compared to other economic development grants.[12] However, other approaches could be added. For instance, an infrastructure jobs program, funded through a national urban development bank or other vehicle, would meet immediate employment needs while helping cities rebuild the base upon which economic growth depends. (Additional details are provided in Chapter 3.)

Developing a Data Base

The development of targeted fiscal assistance and direct jobs creation programs, the connection of the UI system with training opportunities, and the rehabilitation of the urban infrastructure are immediate needs. The problems are clearly identified and should be addressed. However, the national employment and training policy should be predictive and anticipatory rather than reactive. Our employment policies should take advantage of new trends rather than be defeated by them.

In times of economic change, the effectiveness of the public and private response is often influenced by how knowledgeable are those responsible for determining solutions. It is imperative that national policy decisions and the approaches derived from those decisions are based on an information base that validly and reliably reflects pertinent social and economic factors. At a minimum, the federal government should develop data collection procedures that yield sophisticated information on economic and technological trends, employment trends, skill training needs, an assessment of what training program designs work best, current and projected labor market needs, an assessment of the labor supply, an assessment of private and public sector technological and response capability, and an assessment of resources needed to meet labor market requirements. Such a data base can only be gained through close partnership with U.S. employers.

Current data collection activities, such as those undertaken by the Bureau of Labor Statistics, fall far short of the level of sophistication necessary to assess adequately current needs and projected trends. Current data collection methodologies are driven by budget restrictions and past informational needs rather than by today's national needs.

The types of data required for short- and long-term needs projections will cost more than Congress has ever indicated it is willing to pay. However, it is impossible to develop a solution if the problem is never clearly identified.

As a first step—one that can be implemented immediately—major employers could be asked by the U.S. Department of Labor what types of job openings they project, what training programs would be useful to them and their industry, what skills development should be included in these training programs, and what training opportunities in particular could be designed for low-income people and other workers that could lead to jobs in their company or industry. This first step appears basic, but it is well beyond the level of private-public cooperation attempted thus far in the United States.

Developing a Sound Training Infrastructure

Currently, most of the money for traditional vocational education comes from states rather than from the federal government. The current status of the U.S. vocational and skill-training system reflects the same problems that are found in the urban infrastructure. That is, many vocational and skill-training systems are faced with deteriorated equipment and antiquated curricula.

Most states are not in a position to carry out a major overhaul of their training infrastructure. First, the cost involved in determining the needs, obtaining the equipment, and revising the curricula to meet those needs would be prohibitive. Second, the lack of a national policy that has hindered the effectiveness of employment and training programs makes it difficult to make valid and reliable plans from which the training infrastructure could be designed.

Consideration should be given to amending the Vocational Education Act to provide for:

- research and development activities to improve labor market projection techniques;
- additional technical and financial assistance to states for the purpose of redesigning curricula; and
- additional funds (in the form of grants or guaranteed loans) for the purchase of state of the art training equipment in those skill areas projected to be in future demand.

Moreover, an occupational orientation should be designed and implemented, to a far greater extent than at present, into the nation's public school system.

A national employment and training policy should address future needs; however, current economic and technological changes have created the problem of dislocation among today's workers that must be addressed immediately. During the past few years Congress has enacted a hodgepodge of twenty-two separate programs to address the problems of workers in various types of employment, including everything from the auto to the redwood industries. These programs have provided little more than financial assistance to out-of-work laborers who have been more or less permanently dislocated from their jobs. They have not addressed the need to prevent future dislocations by anticipating labor market changes and developing retraining programs.

The Job Training Partnership Act includes the first attempt to focus attention to the general problem of job dislocation. It provides financial support to states to develop retraining programs that are relevant to the changes in their economies. This program is an important first step, but it is insufficient for three reasons. First, the funding level is too low to allow most states to have a major impact upon the problem of dislocation. Second, the money is based on state unemployment rates and is not necessarily targeted to the local communities that have the greatest dislocation problems. There are many situations in which the state has a relatively small problem but specific localities have large numbers of dislocated workers. Third, there is entirely too little information on the extent of the dislocation problem and, consequently, no way to develop a rational policy regarding the resolution of that problem. Each state and service delivery area within the state is given the "freedom" to assess for itself the extent of the problem, the types of new jobs for which to train dislocated workers, and the design of training programs in those skill areas. There are isolated success stories, but most states are groping in the dark and have few clues about what directions to take. In fact, states could only spend 37 percent of dislocated worker funds during the first year of JTPA, which led to a sharp decrease in congressional funding for the dislocated worker program in 1986. For these reasons, the following policies should be considered:

- Provision of additional funds to carry out labor market research to determine (1) the extent of the problems of dislocated workers, (2) how best to treat those problems, and (3) appropriate policies that will minimize future dislocations that result from technological and economic change;
- An increase of funding for the Dislocated Worker Program under JTPA as capability improves to spend funds effectively; and
- A change in the allocation formula for that program so that it is targeted to localities having the greater need rather than to states.

Ensuring Equal Opportunities for the Structurally Unemployed

Unemployment is generally viewed as a product either of economic fluctuations (cyclical) or of sociocultural barriers that exist regardless of the economy. The latter type is referred to as structural unemployment. Even in times of low unemployment certain groups display a disproportionately high unemployment rate and a disproportionately low average wage. A national policy must overcome the barriers that prevent these groups from open access to employment and training opportunities.

For purposes of discussion, this section focuses specific attention on several groups that have structural barriers to employment: minorities, women, aliens and refugees, youth, offenders, and ex-offenders. A more detailed policy statement is provided in Chapter 6. Employment policies for older Americans are proposed in Chapter 13.

Women and Minorities. Mayors believe that a national employment policy must include guarantees that minorities and women have equal access to employment and training activities and that minority- and women-owned businesses have equal access to any federal programs designed to assist business growth. Mayors believe that the concept of equal opportunity must include a commitment to erase the inequities that have developed as a result of racial and sex discrimination. This means that federal programs should include provisions specifically designed to meet the special problems of minorities and women, including:

- improved minority set asides for small business development programs;
- specific requirements for providing services to women and minorities in employment and training programs;
- strengthened affirmative action requirements for federal contractors, which help achieve the goal of workforces, at all salary levels, that are representative of the race and sex composition in the firm's population area;
- affirmative action requirements for recipients of any federally sponsored business development incentive, including loans, loan guarantees, and tax credits; and
- programs designed to stimulate economic growth in communities having concentrations of minorities.

Economically Disadvantaged Americans. Just as minorities and women have been the victims of racial and sexual discrimination, so have low-income people of all races been trapped by limited access to the education, training, and employment opportunities that are necessary to improve their economic status. For that reason, mayors recommend that the national employment and training policy specifically address the problems created by poverty that inhibit successful training or employment experiences. These include a wide range of factors, such as:

- the need to provide financial support to economically disadvantaged people who otherwise would be unable to undertake training, such support to include funds for transportation, child care, training equipment, and tuition;
- the need for nutritional and health care prior to and during training;
- the need for educational remediation; and
- the need for introductory work experiences to acquaint the chronically unemployed person with the world of work.

Such policy should address the need for special education, training, and employment programs targeted to the economically disadvantaged.

Mayors believe that current JTPA funding levels are inadequate to make sufficient impact upon the problem of unemployment among economically disadvantaged people. At a minimum, the funding level should be equal to the funding level of the CETA program, which ended in FY 1983. Moreover, the JTPA allocation formula is not sufficiently targeted to the eligible economically disadvantaged population. A formula that gives added weight to poverty rates of states and jurisdictions within states would better achieve the act's goals.

Funding must not be sharply reduced at a time when structural unemployment in our nation is the highest in recent history. Currently, the JTPA provides job and training opportunities to just 3.7 percent of the eligible, economically disadvantaged population, as surveyed by a consultant to the National Commission for Employment Policy. Only 1 to 3 percent of the eligible population are served in the large urban areas.[13] Federal funding for employment and training has declined from $14 billion in 1977 to $9.6 billion by 1980 to $5.1 billion in 1985. The private sector is not compensating for these public deficiencies; the private sector spends an average of $300 in training costs per worker compared to $3,000 per worker in capital investment.[14] In addition, the mayors urge Congress to consider the possibility of creating special incentives to encourage the private sector to invest its own money in projects serving the same population as is served by the Job Training Partnership Act. For example, the federal government could fund a share of all private sector training programs for the targeted population.

Moreover, mayors recognize the value of protected employment opportunities for people who have structural barriers to employment. When employers provide the necessary employment exposure and training opportunities designed to introduce the participant to the requirements of the work world, the employers should be at least partially compensated, usually by way of participant wage subsidies. Otherwise, it is more cost efficient for the employer to hire workers from the "traditional" sources, who are considered "job-ready," that is, those who are from educational and employment experience backgrounds that ease their transition into the new job.

Prior experience with the structural employment program funded under CETA demonstrated that private sector subsidy programs must be designed in such a way that they:

- provide meaningful employment opportunities that reflect the unsubsidized job market;
- include career exploration activities that assist the participant in assessing interests, determining abilities, and deciding upon training needs;
- assist the participant in finding a subsidized job or securing the necessary remedial education or skill training; and
- assist the participant in finding an unsubsidized job.

Refugees and Aliens. In recent years there has been a tremendous increase in the number of aliens and refugees primarily from Hispanic nations and Southeast Asia. The aliens and refugees themselves have their own set of structural barriers to employment, such as language difficulties and low job skills. In addition, they create employment problems as they compete for limited education and training dollars and limited job opportunities.

Mayors recommend that a national employment and training policy address the problems that aliens and refugees face as well as the problems created by their increased number. City services have been strained by the influx of aliens and refugees. In some cities the competition between noncitizens and citizens for employment, training, and service opportunities has created tension that must be relieved.

Mayors strongly support the tradition of the United States as a land of opportunity for non-American newcomers. At the same time, the mayors cannot support any measure that, in providing employment and training opportunities to aliens and refugees, deprives cyclically and structurally unemployed U.S. citizens of those same opportunities. Therefore, a national employment and training policy must address problems related to aliens and refugees and establish guidelines for developing programs that meet their needs without straining the services available to cyclically or structurally unemployed Americans. Services provided to aliens and refugees should be in addition to those provided to citizens.

Youth. Youth unemployment is a particularly difficult problem. Most youths are unprepared for employment. Minority and economically disadvantaged youths quite often have had little access to the world of work and have little help in learning the ropes for obtaining employment. Consequently, unemployment is especially high among youths and highest among minority youths.

Opponents of employment and training programs for youth argue that the problem is temporary and that youth do not really have to work and that if they just wait until they are adults they will be able to find employment. This argument is fallacious for at least two reasons. First, many economically disadvantaged youths need to work. They need the money to continue their education and to help support their families. Employment for them is as much a necessity as it is for adults.

Second, a youth that is not prepared for the work world will have little chance for employment as an adult. This is especially true for minority and economically disadvantaged youths, whose economic status often prevents them from learning employer expectations, exploring career opportunities, and obtaining job training. It is also true for school dropouts and other troubled youths, regardless of their economic status.

Mayors support the creation of employment and training programs that are designed specifically to meet the special training needs of youths. The programs created under CETA—Young Adult Conservation Corps, Youth Community Conservation Improvement Program, and the Youth Employment and Training Program—generated excellent program models that can be improved on. Such programs should be large enough to provide all youths facing employment barriers access to needed education, training, and employment opportunities.

Offenders, Ex-Offenders. Mayors recommend that the national employment and training policy address the special problems faced by and created by offenders and ex-offenders. Numerous studies have demonstrated a relationship between unemployment, structural barriers to employment, and crime. Regardless of one's philosophy about the severity of punishment for crimes, it is clear that meaningful employment and training opportunities should be made available to offenders and ex-offenders. Such opportunities will help erase their structural barriers and reduce the crime rate. Further, the cost of training is far less than the $20,000-a-year cost of incarceration.

Assisting U.S. Business

A national employment and training policy should address needs of U.S. business in developing the labor market. Other elements of the mayors' urban policy address the broad issue of economic development. With regard to a national employment and training policy, mayors urge that such policy address:

- the use of urban development programs and tax incentives as a way to increase employment opportunities while stimulating business growth;
- the creation of targeted small business programs as an additional way to create business ownership and employment opportunities for minorities and women; and

- the use of capital infusion and tax incentives for business as a way to stimulate economic development in areas having concentrations of minorities and low-income people.

The Targeted Jobs Tax Credit (TJTC) is an initial step toward the development of an effective tax incentive. This program, implemented in 1977, provides partial reimbursement—50 percent the first year, 25 percent the second—to business for wages paid to the economically disadvantaged. The TJTC is said to be ineffective by those seeking to terminate it. Perhaps the chief concern is that it is becoming too successful, leading to a large tax drain from the federal treasury. Corporations hired 563,381 persons through this program into private sector jobs in 1984, up from 202,198 in 1982—a 179 percent increase in just two years—with a minimum of 650,000 forecast for 1985. Although the tax losses of the program are rapidly growing, it is still projected by the president to cost a relatively modest $340 million for 1985.

Bolder concepts, such as some of the tax incentives set forth in the various urban enterprise zone proposals, are necessary to stimulate new jobs, especially if such incentives are coupled with capital infusion programs to assist business development. For example, the National Urban Development Bank (see Chapter 3) can provide the capital that is essential to make possible location in an urban enterprise zone.

If a worker's expected productivity is lower than the wage rate for a given job, then the person will likely not be hired. A wage subsidy, however, would close that gap. A fifty-fifty wage subsidy program in Minnesota, covering the first six months of employment (after which the company agrees to retain the worker for at least a year in an unsubsidized job) has produced extraordinary results. Half of the placements were either receiving or eligible for public assistance. Moreover, 70 percent of the jobs were in the private sector, and 63 percent of employers indicated they would not have expanded their workforce without the subsidy.[15]

This model has potential for future national implementation, particularly with a strong program of persuasion to U.S. business to hire eligible persons. The direct wage subsidy program overcomes criticisms of TJTC in that (1) employers receive immediate cash payments rather than waiting at least a year for the filing and processing of the tax return, and (2) all employers benefit, not just those who are making a profit (and who would stand to benefit from a tax credit).

A NATIONAL EMPLOYMENT AND TRAINING POLICY—FINAL WORD

All of the major recommendations in this chapter are predicated upon the creation of a national employment and training policy. Until such a policy is developed, employment and training programs will continue to be reactive and fragmented. Consequently, their impact will be severely limited. Mayors welcome the opportunity to join with Congress, the administration, states, counties, the private sector, labor organizations, and other interested groups in the establishment of a comprehensive policy based on two assumptions:

- That every American should have the opportunity to seek and obtain employment that makes maximum use of talent and ability; and
- That the ultimate goal of such policy will be to reduce the negative impact of economic and technological upheaval by anticipating such change and preparing the labor market prior to those changes.

NOTES TO CHAPTER 5

1. *Employment and Training Reporter* 16, no. 19 (January 1985): 573; and *Employment and Training Reporter* 16, no. 30 (April 1985): 921.
2. James L. Palmer and Isabel V. Sawhill, eds., *The Reagan Record An Assessment of America's Changing Domestic Priorities* (Cambridge, Mass.: Ballinger Publishing Company, 1984), pp. 82–84.
3. Center for National Policy Review, Catholic University School of Law, *Job Watch Alert*, August 13, 1984, p. 2, citing the findings of Andrew Sum of Northeastern University.
4. Center for the Study of Social Policy, "The 'Flip-Side' of Black Families Headed by Women: The Economic Status of Black Men" (Washington, D.C.: Center for the Study of Social Policy, April 1984), pp. 8–11.
5. Data by phone from Bureau of Labor Statistics, November 1985. The Center for the Study of Social Policy and BLS used different methodology to compute the percent of working age men holding jobs. The center added a factor for uncounted urban residents in census data.
6. Sar A. Leviton and Garth Mangum, "A Quarter Century of Employment and Training Policy," *Jobs for the Future* (Washington, D.C.: Center for National Policy, May 1984), p. 43.
7. Ibid., pp. 43–44, citing research by Robert Taggert.
8. U.S. Department of Labor (DOL), "Job Training Partnership Act Transition Year Performance" (Washington, D.C.: DOL, December 1984), various tables.
9. Government Accounting Office (GAO), *Federal Economic Development Assistance Programs: An Economic Analysis of Their Employment Effects* (Washington, D.C.: GAO, August 16, 1984), pp. 33–43.
10. Pat Choate, "Retooling the American Workforce: Toward a National Training Strategy" (Washington, D.C.: Northeast-Midwest Institute, 1982), pp. 40–42.
11. Congressional Budget Office (CBO), *Promoting Employment and Maintaining Incomes with Unemployment Insurance* (Washington, D.C.: CBO, March 1985), pp. 51, 64–65.

12. Government Accounting Office, p. 39.
13. Gary Walker et al., "An Independent Sector Assessment of the Job Training Partnership Act" (Washington, D.C.: National Commission for Employment Policy, March 1984), p. 102.
14. Pat Choate, p. 4.
15. Asha Rangan, "MEED Means Business, Private Employers Assess the State Jobs Programs" (Minneapolis: The Minneapolis Foundation, December 1984), p. 5 and appendixes.

6 EQUAL OPPORTUNITIES FOR ALL AMERICANS

Fairness in employment for Americans of all races and both sexes has the smallest of pricetags and the largest of benefits for the entire society. A national commitment to achieve economic and social justice for all Americans would do more for cities and their residents than any other policy, at any cost, that national leaders could adopt.

Our nation's major urban centers have long been the home of the richest diversity of people, a characteristic that constitutes the greatest strength of cities and the best hope for the future. Nonetheless, the decades and centuries of race discrimination have impacted on cities to a far greater extent than in their surrounding suburbs, which have only a fraction of the poverty and unemployment problems with which to contend. While cities must keep tax rates high to provide the vast array of services upon which those excluded from the economic mainstream must depend, the more affluent jurisdictions have the means to fund educational and other services that further widen the disparities.

Had this basic inequity not developed in our society, perhaps none of the proposals contained in this book would be necessary. Certainly there would still be poverty, but without the added poverty and related conditions induced by racism and sexism, the treatment of urban problems would likely be well within manageable proportions with present levels of federal, state, and local resources. The actions recommended in this report are needed only because of past and present inaction.

In this chapter it will be shown that the ways to achieve progress need not be shrouded in complexities. For example, simply enforcing an effective level of affirmative action compliance among federal contractors would by itself go a long way toward fully integrating the U.S. workforce. What is primarily needed is national leadership to build and maintain a consensus that fairness in employment, housing, and other areas is an essential element of U.S. society.

The 1978 Urban Policy Report of the President states:

> The Federal government should initiate several anti-racism strategies:
>
> 1. The White House and Congress must continue to speak out against racism and take the lead in educating the public on racism's economic, social and physical costs.
> 2. The Federal government will take steps to strengthen enforcement of current equal opportunity and affirmative action laws.
> 3. The Federal government will enforce stronger equal opportunity and affirmative action guidelines [governing] current Federal aid programs.[1]

U.S. mayors seek national leadership in both the executive and legislative branches and in both major political parties in educating the public about the devastating effects of continued economic injustice and in educating the public on ways in which true progress can be achieved. Further, mayors seek national leadership in enforcing and strengthening affirmative action laws and policies.

"PROGRESS" OF RECENT YEARS

Equal opportunity seems low on the scale of priorities in public opinion polls, in the rhetoric of most political candidates, and in the agendas of the executive and legislative branches. Let us look at the record to date: Many people in the nation assume that progress in overcoming the barriers of discrimination is continuing at a rapid pace—in fact, at such a frenzied pace that "reverse discrimination" is threatening the economic security of the majority population. However, the facts indicate otherwise.

Income

In 1984 minority median family income, at $17,098 was just 61.8 percent of white median family income, at $25,757. In 1970 the minority-to-white income ratio was 63.7 percent.[2] Therefore, although we have seen individual gains, taken as a whole, the gap between the races is widening.

Blacks as a group have fared rather more poorly than other minorities. The median family income of blacks in 1984 was $15,432, or 55.7 percent of white median family income. In 1970 that same ratio was 61.3 percent.[3]

Since 1970 all population groups except whites have lost ground to inflation. The 1984 white median family income of $27,686 was a slight $305, or 1 percent increase over the 1970 white median family income of $27,381 in constant (inflation-adjusted) dollars. However, blacks lost considerable ground to inflation. Blacks' 1984 median family income level of $15,432 was $1,364 less—and over 8 percent less—than their 1970 constant dollar median family income level of $16,796.[4]

Taking an even longer view, between 1950 and 1980 black families gained $6,276 in constant (1980) dollars, from $6,398 to $12,674 in median family income. During the same period white families gained $9,662 in constant dollars, from $11,792 to $21,904.[5] Where is the "racial progress" that is so routinely assumed by much of the American public?

Unemployment and Underemployment

Unemployment rates among blacks are historically at least double those of whites and in recent years have remained at depression levels—more than 14 percent. Moreover, the ratio of black-to-white unemployment rates has been growing in recent years. Hispanic unemployment rates have averaged 1.6 times the white rate over the past several years. The minority teenage rate is 40 percent or higher in many cities. Additionally, blacks constitute a third of all discouraged workers (those who have dropped out of the labor force in discouragement over not obtaining a job and not counted among the unemployed), even though the black share of the labor force is just 10 percent.[6] Significantly, only 46.9 percent of black males, 58.3 percent of Hispanic males, 39.1 percent of black females, and 48.6 percent of Hispanic females who were in the labor force in 1980 were counted as "neither unemployed or underemployed" by the U.S. Commission on Civil Rights.[7] Underemployment includes part-time work (when full time work is desired), overeducation for the types of job held, intermittent employment, inequitable pay, and other kinds of marginal jobs.

The outlook for progress is uncertain. This is especially the case when one considers that 77.3 percent of all black males in private industry are in so-called blue collar (operatives, laborers, craft workers) occupations at a time when manufacturing-type employment has fallen to 20 percent of total jobs in recent years, with unfavorable prospects for manufacturing and laborer jobs regaining past shares of employment.[8] Moreover, federal funds to train and retrain citizens have been slashed by 63 percent since 1977.

Women and Poverty

Women as a group have gained some ground but not the startling gains one may expect when hearing discussions of the revolution of women in the workplace. In 1984 females had 64.2 percent of the median income levels of males, counting year-round full-time workers only. In 1960 that same figure was 60.6 percent. Moreover, fully employed black females earned only 56.5 percent as much as fully employed white males in 1984, and fully employed Hispanic females earned just 52.5 percent.[9] It is evident that the revolution in the workplace has yet to occur.

Within the overall data for women are some significant variations. For example, the number of unemployed white women declined by 22,000 between 1975 and 1984, and the unemployment rate for that group declined from 8.8 percent to 6.5 percent during those years. In contrast, the number of unemployed black women increased by 282,000, and the unemployment rates increased from 14.8 percent to 15.4 percent during those same years.[10] White women have an 11 percent median income advantage over black women and a 20 percent advantage with respect to Hispanic women. Nonetheless, every grouping of women, regardless of race, has a large income deficiency (of at least 37%) compared to white males.[11]

Of deep and growing concern are the poverty and unemployment levels in female-headed households, especially in black and Hispanic families. By 1984, 51.7 percent of black families with children present were headed by women, a significant increase from an already high 30.6 percent level in 1970. Women headed 25.5 percent of all Hispanic families with children in 1984; women headed 15.8 percent of white families with children in the same year.[12]

Children

Of greatest consequence is the profound statistic that 66.2 percent of all children in black female-headed households and 71 percent of all children in Hispanic female-headed households lived in poverty in 1984.[13] In 1979 the majority of blacks were born to single mothers—in all parts of the country, from Arkansas (54%) to Indiana (75%) to Wisconsin (63%) and New Jersey (60%).[14]

Moreover, 46.2 percent of all black children, of all types of families, husband and wife present and not, lived in poverty in 1984. This is a startling increase from 39.6 percent ten years earlier.[15] Among Hispanic children, 38.7 percent are growing up in poverty, up from 28.6 percent in 1974.[16] This picture of our children growing up in poverty is a chilling view of at least a good part of America's future. We seem to be squandering our chances to achieve the ideals upon which this nation was founded.

Education

Often one hears the argument that there really is no discrimination and that if people would build their training and education levels, then all else would follow. Again, let us review the facts. A black male high school *graduate* (twenty-five and over) had a lower median income in 1981 (latest data available) than a white male high school *dropout.*[17] Of all families headed by a black high school graduate, 26 percent lived in poverty; only 21 percent of families headed by a white with an elementary (less than eight years) school education lived in poverty.[18] Perhaps the most astonishing statistic is the fact that black male *college* graduates (twenty-five and over) had a lower median income in 1981 than white male *high school* graduates (twenty-five years and older).[19]

With the proportion of minorities finishing high school increasing significantly in recent years (e.g., during the 1970s the proportion of all blacks twenty-five and older who were high school graduates increased by 47%)[20] and with the numbers of minorities attending college growing at encouraging levels (a 93 percent increase among blacks from 1970 to 1980),[21] opportunity to end discrimination is at hand. The median school years completed is 12 for blacks and 12.5 for whites—a gap that has been closing rapidly in recent years.[22] What is lacking is the will among public and private sector leaders to encourage and effect social change.

THE BURDEN OF CITIES

All of the problems discussed above are especially severe in cities. The overall poverty rate in central cities in the United States in 1983 was 19.8 percent—one out of every five residents of cities, amounting to 12.9 million central city residents.[23] This is an average figure, including the more affluent and the poorer cities, the large and the small combined. Many of the older, high-density larger cities have poverty rates even higher.

Twenty-five percent of the white population live in cities; 58 percent of the black population and 50 percent of the Hispanic population live in cities.[24] Therefore, cities and their residents shoulder the burdens of discrimination disproportionately. Cities also have the most to gain should the nation build a sincere commitment to economic and social justice.

"WELFARE"

One way that public assistance or other such benefits can be described is as token payments to subsidize people who have been excluded from the mainstream of American life. Making these payments is considered easier, at least in the short run, than making the necessary structural adjustments to solve the basic problems.

This way of thinking has several problems. First, we can never unify our nation and take advantage of all the talents of our people by keeping millions in a state of dependency. Second, the long-term costs of this policy, which encourages blighted neighborhoods, crime, heavy government costs for incarceration, drug abuse, social services, and so on, are enormous. Third, government assistance programs are not as widely available as generally believed.

For example, unemployment compensation does not provide the support for the overwhelming majority (70%) of unemployed blacks. Over half (56%) of all poor black households receive no welfare assistance (AFDC or General Assistance). Of those black households that do receive welfare assistance, only half (51%) of those have Medicaid coverage.[25] Under the present system of justice, stifled opportunity among those in poverty is the rule, not the exception. The only real alternative is to create a more open society in which all may fully participate.

THE NEED FOR EQUAL OPPORTUNITY POLICIES

It is within this context that effective equal opportunity policies are essential, since, as stated by the U.S. Commission on Civil Rights, "without affirmative intervention, discriminatory processes may never end."[26]

Despite the long-standing and immediate need for action, the federal role in ensuring equal opportunity and affirmative action has been deemphasized in recent years. The federal government now requires proof of intent to discriminate before takint remedial action to improve the race and sex composition of an employer's workforce, instead of viewing patterns of inadequate representation of minorities and women as sufficient indications that remedial action is needed. Similarly, goals and timetables as a means of achieving fair representation in the workforce are often opposed. The argument offered is that those who tend to benefit from affirmative action are not necessarily the same ones who have been wronged in the past.

The budgets in the Office of Federal Contract Compliance Programs (OFCCP) and the Equal Employment Opportunity Commission were reduced, in inflation-adjusted dollars, by 24 percent and 10 percent, respectively, between 1981 and 1983, resulting in staff reductions of 34 percent and 12 percent, respectively. The staff of the Justice Department's Civil Rights Division also was reduced 13 percent. The federal government only imposed one debarment of a federal contractor (loss of contract or prohibition against future bidding) between 1981 and 1983. In employment discrimination cases the proportion of "no-cause" findings has increased by a third. Back-pay awards for discrimination were reduced by 72 percent between 1980 and 1984. In April 1985 the Justice Department requested 41 state, county, and city governments to retreat from affirmative action agreements involving hiring, promotions, and layoffs that were, in most cases, reached between the chief executives and employee groups or unions and monitored by the courts.

The Justice Department has filed only one school desegregation case in recent years. Class action suits in general are not favored, since the current practice is to seek remedies for only identifiable victims of discrimination, not population groups. And, of course, the Treasury Department was overruled by the Justice Department when Treasury sought to deny tax breaks to colleges having racially discriminatory admission practices.

Furthermore, presidential appointments in recent years of minorities and women have lagged considerably behind past levels. The previous administration had 50 percent more female appointments, more than double the minority appointments, and triple the black appointments, proportionately, than the present administration.[27] Two black federal judges were appointed in The Reagan first term, compared to thirty-seven under Carter.

The federal policies condone the brutal effects of centuries of past and present discrimination. Simply to declare that everyone is blessed with equality of opportunity does not make it so. To be successful, equal opportunity policies must appeal to the basic fairness of the American people, with the help of a massive educational campaign. As stated by the Civil Rights Commission, "measures that take race, sex and national origin into account intervene in a status quo that systematically disfavors minorities and women in order to provide them with increased opportunities."[28]

HISTORICAL BASIS FOR AFFIRMATIVE ACTION

Equitable sharing of employment opportunities is key to ensuring participation in the full range of societal benefits. By now, affirmative action policies have a strong historical precedence and only lack vigorous leadership and enforcement.

In 1971 the Supreme Court stated that the primary objective of the Civil Rights Act of 1964 (Title VII) was preventive—that is, that it was "to achieve equality of employment opportunities and remove barriers that have operated in the past to favor an identifiable group of white employees over other employees.[29]

Statutory efforts to outlaw discrimination in employment can be traced to federal policy enacted during World War II outlawing race discrimination by war contractors.[30] Since that time a series of executive orders has expanded and refined this principle for federal contractors.[31] In 1964 the Civil Rights Act was passed, prohibiting discrimination by all private employers; and in 1972 that act was extended to cover public employees as well.[32]

Beginning attempts to enforce these laws reveal that court awards of retroactive relief to identified victims of discrimination coupled with injunctions against future discrimination were insufficient to remove barriers to achieving equality of employment opportunities. To overcome long-standing practices and the effects of ingrained prejudices, the award of damages for past violations is simply not adequate. Future-looking awards were needed. Thus, courts and federal agencies began to require employers to take concrete steps, complete with goals and timetables, for measuring progress to ensure that members of a previously deprived class are hired and promoted without discrimination. Affirmative action plans provide goals or other numerical devices that give a means for accountability in implementing a court order or voluntary plan to eliminate discriminatory practices. A goal is a measure of the success of an employer's newly instituted system for making nondiscriminatory employment decisions and achieving the inherently intangible state of nondiscrimination.

Virtually all the federal courts of appeals have ordered or approved such goals and timetables of hiring and promotion when necessary to remedy proven discrimination.[33] They have done so out of a recognition that, where practices of discrimination are involved, specific goals are needed to ensure nondiscrimination in the future. The courts have also acted out of a realization that past discrimination based on race, sex, or other proscribed grounds has a continuing impact on people that cannot be erased overnight. Institutions that have used race-conscious policies to disadvantage minorities cannot remedy their wrong by converting immediately to "color blindness." As Justice Blackmun reminded us in his opinion in *Bakke* v. *Regents of California*, "In order to get beyond racism, we must first take account of race. There is no other way. And in order to treat some persons equally, we must treat them differently."[34]

Further, in weighing the remedies for job discrimination, the courts have found it effective to encourage voluntary affirmative opportunities for those who have suffered discrimination and exclusion. Thus, in *United Steel Workers of America* v. *Weber*,[35] the Supreme Court held that it is altogether appropriate and lawful for employers and labor unions voluntarily to adopt carefully structured and time-limited affirmative action plans, including numerical preferences, to ensure the inclusion of minorities in jobs and job-training programs previously closed to them.

The Court's reasons for ordering affirmative action plans are supported by clear evidence that affirmative action works. A U.S. Department of Labor (DOL) report studying the effects of affirmative action plans mandated by the Office of Federal Contract Compliance Programs shows that businesses with affirmative action plans during 1974 to 1980 were able to increase minority employment by 20 percent as compared to 12 percent for noncovered businesses and that the participation of women in the workforce increased 15 percent for the companies with plans as opposed to 2 percent for the noncovered workforce.[36] In a second study, completed in July 1983 by Jonathan S. Leonard of the University of California for DOL, the author reached similar conclusions as to the effectiveness of affirmative action.[37] Both studies reported increased employment of minority groups and increased upward mobility due to affirmative action requirements.

In addition to these two detailed, nationwide studies, enrollment statistics for higher education programs indicate the success of affirmative action plans in increasing the percentage of minority students, thereby better preparing these graduates for highly skilled employment. Hence, for example, the enrollment of black students in higher education programs has doubled in the past fifteen years. Affirmative action plans have allowed women to enter positions formerly viewed as men's work and have contributed to the beginnings of educating employers about the feasibility of integrating older and disabled workers into their businesses. Therefore, mayors believe it imperative that federal agency and court implementation and enforcement of affirmative action plans be strengthened.

POLICY RECOMMENDATIONS

A national commitment to equal opportunity must be supported with specific strategies to be successful. History should have taught us that evolution, by itself, is too fickle a friend to rely upon. Building specific goals for minority and female participation into our federally funded training efforts, developing investment strategies for minority business development, contracting only with firms having fair employment patterns, and ensuring that unions achieve their egalitarian ideals are all essential in producing an open society. Finally, a national strategy would include an implementation plan for massive educational effort (as called for in the President's 1978 National Urban Policy Report) to gain public and private sector employer support for achieving a well-balanced labor force. Recent presidents have seldom even mentioned human rights for Americans, although such leadership is among the most critical elements of an equal opportunity program. Implementation plans could include a sign-up campaign in which U.S. businesses state their firm commitment to achieving affirmative action goals, conditional to receipt of federal contracts.

Affirmative Employment and Training Efforts

No serious attempt can be made to achieve equality of employment opportunities until the employment training gap, caused by historical and current discrimination, is eliminated. The Job Training Partnership Act of 1982 (JTPA), provides us with an opportunity to move toward this goal. First, as indicated in Chapter 5, resources should be restored to previous employment and training levels. Moreover, performance standards should be developed that specifically measure improvement in the training and hiring of minorities, women, and the handicapped.

Funds were slashed under JTPA primarily because it was assumed that the private sector would fill the gaps left from reduced federal funding of job-training programs. Thus, a "partnership" could do more than a mere government program. However, there are no real incentives or mandates to ensure private sector participation, and there does not appear to be a landslide of volunteering by the private sector to remedy the training and employment gaps. To encourage evolution of this partnership, Executive Order #11246 (pertaining to federal contracting) could be amended to require federal contractors to participate in JTPA training programs. Moreover, incentives could be provided to business to design and fund such programs. Minorities, women, and the handicapped should also be assured of full participation in State Job Training Coordinating Councils and Private Industry Councils under JTPA.

Minority Business Development

Even if the nation did seek a progressive affirmative action employment policy, such an effort would go only part of the way. The American society can only be truly open to all when business ownership is shared among all population groups.

Between 1977 and 1982, the number of black-owned businesses increased by 47 percent, and gross annual receipts increased by 44 percent (more recent data on Hispanic-owned firms were not available as of this writing).[38] Black-owned firms now account for 2.7 percent of all sole proprietorships, partnerships, and small corporations (25 or fewer shareholders). This is a disproportionately low level; nonetheless, progress is evident.

Within the overall signs of progress are some serious concerns. First, the larger corporations are excluded from this survey by the U.S. Commerce Department because of complexities in determining whether a large corporation is minority-owned. Had such firms been included, the share of minority firms, already low at 2.7 percent, would be considerably lower since all but a very small fraction of large corporations are white-controlled.

Second, the Commerce Department indicates that some of the increase in the number of minority-owned firms is due to a change in data collection policies for 1982 data. Multiple Schedule C tax forms were counted as one firm in 1977 but as separate entities in 1982.[39]

Third, the minority firms are generally the smallest of enterprises. The 339,239 firms employed a total of just 165,765 employees in 1982 (an increase of less than 1% from 1977). In fact, 89 percent of minority-owned firms had no paid employees at all, other than the owners, in 1982.[40]

Fourth, minority-owned firms had under a 1 percent share of gross sales and receipts among all U.S. sole proprietorships, partnerships, and small corporations. While progress was widely reported in the 44 percent gain in gross receipts between 1977 and 1982, it should be recognized that in constant, inflation-adjusted dollars gross receipts actually declined by 10 percent during those years. Gross receipts of all firms declined by 3 percent in constant dollars during those years; thus, minority-owned firms fared less well than other U.S. businesses.[41]

Mayors support the use of federal, state, and local government procurement set-asides to improve the proportion of minority- and women-owned businesses. Today some federal legislation includes such targeting; however, this policy should be applied to all federal procurement (see Chapter 16, which develops this recommendation further). Sole sourcing of federal contracting usually goes to majority-owned firms. When a contract is sole sourced, a statement of availability of minority firms that could supply the same good or service should be completed prior to approval of that contract.

Goals and timetables for federal contracting to minority- and women-owned firms should be set at a sufficiently high level and closely monitored and enforced. Achievement of these goals could be improved if minority- and women-owned businesses are awarded additional points in bidding for federal contracts. Moreover, whenever economic development strategies are funded by the federal government, minority- and women-owned businesses should be built into private sector investment opportunities.

Contract Compliance Program

One should not be mystified as to the means of achieving equal employment opportunity, since the means to do so are in many ways already at hand. There are over 75,000 business establishments that are federal prime contractors, employing over 21 million people in the United States, and thousands more subcontractors. Thus, the federal contract compliance program, if strongly enforced, can by itself go a long way toward ensuring a fully integrated national workforce.

First and foremost, goals and timetables must be established, monitored, and enforced by the federal government for all federal contractors, to provide full representation of minorities and women at all wage and salary levels. Such a policy is the *only* way to hold businesses accountable. A business or government would not consider going into a fiscal year without a budget, only providing their managers with the admonition to try not to spend too much money. Similarly, simply requesting employers to be fair in their employment practices accomplishes little. Affirmative action goals and timetables are the only known way to achieving desired results.

When the affirmative action goals are set, they are often based on the availability of minorities and women in a given occupation in a certain labor market area. Such goals simply mirror existing patterns of discrimination. Goals can be raised closer to the proportion of minorities and women in the population of the region by taking into account the potential for training programs to qualify added numbers of minorities and women to obtain jobs and be promoted into higher paying positions. Negotiations with federal contractors of goals to include training opportunities is at times undertaken by the Office of Federal Contract

Compliance Programs, although the record is spotty in using this technique. Moreover, in construction, goals for women are often based on aggregate percentage goals rather than trade-by-trade goals. If goals are set for each trade, such a revised policy would prevent the clustering of women in the lowest pay and lowest skilled jobs (e.g., "flag wavers" or traffic directors at construction sites).

A 1984 study by the Department of Labor's Office of Federal Contract Compliance Programs (OFCCP) provides clear and conclusive evidence that affirmative action is an effective means of achieving a much fairer representation of minorities and women in federal contractor workforces. In that study the workforces of 49,000 federal contractors and 28,100 nonfederal contractors were examined in 1974 and again in 1980.

In 1974 federal contractor workforce compositions were the result of employment discrimination practices that antedated the establishment of effective compliance programs. The report states that, "typically, federal contractor establishments had the best-paying jobs, and competition for those jobs was most intense. It was also in those establishments that some of the most jealously guarded systems of preference for white males were prevalent. Where minorities were employed, they were found almost entirely in the so-called '3-H' jobs—hard, hot and heavy."[42] Women were concentrated in clerical or low-paying semiskilled jobs.

By 1980, after several years of affirmative action compliance efforts by the OFCCP with federal contractors, it was found that federal contractors had made substantially greater improvements in their workforce patterns than noncontractors. Minorities in "officials and managers" jobs increased 57 percent among contractor firms in 1980 over 1974, compared to 32 percent for noncontractors. For professionals, the difference was 57 percent against 11 percent; for technicians, 45 percent against 6 percent; for sales workers, 56 percent against 21 percent.[43]

Similarly, the growth of female employment among federal contractors substantially exceeded noncontractor increases over the same time period. For example, females in professional jobs increased 50 percent in federal contractor firms and 10 percent in noncontractor firms; the growth was 47 percent among officials and managers in contractor firms compared to 18 percent among noncontractors.[44]

Moreover, another study revealed that the gains are not temporary. Females and minorities have had a lower ratio of terminations relative to hires among federal contractors reviewed for affirmative action compliance when compared to other workers.[45] The "last hired-first fired" syndrome can be broken with effective monitoring and compliance efforts.

We have been able to find little data from OFCCP practices in recent years. Off-the-record interviews with a number of OFCCP staff reveal low morale and frustration resulting from what they describe as a deemphasis among some (but far from all) OFCCP and other federal policymakers in affirmative action efforts.

To ensure that goals and timetables are effective, means of enforcement are essential. In most cases federal leadership will be all that is needed to encourage firms to comply. In some cases, however, it may be necessary to impose as a penalty for persisting in maintaining unfairly represented workforces a loss of contract or loss of opportunity to bid on future contracts. Over the years, debarment has been a rarely used instrument in cases of persistent failure to comply with an affirmative action plan. Yet debarment is the most powerful and persuasive of all possible tools to achieve representative levels.

In recent years the executive branch has proposed an increase in the threshold for firms that should comply with federal contracting provisions to those having 250 or more employees and contracts of one million dollars or more. Such a policy would exclude 75 percent of all federal contractors, and mayors oppose such a policy change.

Certificates of Merit

One positive way to build a national consciousness in favor of equal employment practices is to grant certificates of merit to those firms that have achieved equal opportunity employment. The certificates would be granted to all firms that achieve representative levels of minorities, women, and the handicapped at all wage and salary levels in their workforces, whether the firms are federal contractors or not. Over time, stores and other businesses would display their certificate for potential shoppers and clients to view. In this way societal pressure would be applied to those businesses that do not display such a certificate.

Firms that hold certificates could receive added points in bidding for federal contracts. Moreover, firms could be required to have a certificate of merit in order to receive a sole-source contract from the federal government, except when national security or other extreme disadvantage is at stake. Since firms holding a certificate of merit would have earned the nation's confidence that they are fair employers, perhaps they could be exempted from much of the existing affirmative action reporting requirements. They could report on their workforce patterns every three years, for example, rather than annually. Finally, business incentives through the tax system or favorable investment assistance could be targeted to firms holding certificates of merit, whether or not those firms are federal contractors.

The certificates are an example of a device national leaders could employ to encourage a society that values fairness.

Trade Unions

A recent affirmative action study concludes that "despite its varied and, at times, intensive efforts to end discrimination in the construction industry over a period of close to two decades, the federal government has been largely frustrated by the complexities of regulating this industry."[46] The great majority of workers in the construction industries are hired by referrals through hiring halls controlled by unions. The OFCCP negotiates goals with employers but has had no direct leverage on the unions.

Overall, minorities made small gains in trade union membership during the 1970s, increasing from 15.1 percent in 1970 to 17.4 percent in 1979. Membership of minorities in some trades (e.g., electrical workers and carpenters) increased more than others (e.g., bricklayers, roofers) where there were either very small or no gains. Black membership in referral unions increased hardly at all, from 8.2 percent in 1970 to 8.4 percent in 1979.

The area where the largest improvements were recorded was in apprenticeship. Minorities increased from 10.6 percent of apprentices in 1970 to 19.3 percent in 1979, with blacks recording a fairly healthy increase, from 6 percent in 1970 to 9.6 percent in 1979.[47] Therefore, future membership among minorities in trade unions should improve.

Efforts should be intensified in negotiating preapprenticeship, apprenticeship, and membership agreements with trade unions, including ample training opportunities for minorities and women. Such agreements have been developed over the years, although participation by the unions continues to be inconsistent.

Possible Organizational Realignments and Civil Rights Block Grant

The organization of existing equal opportunity agencies could be examined for possible realignment to improve efficiency and perhaps reduce expenditures in the process by reducing duplication. For example, analysts could explore merging the Department of Labor Office of Federal Contract Compliance Programs into the Equal Employment Opportunity Commission. Both operations have as their primary mission achieving improved employment patterns. A merger could increase efficiency—as only one set of reports is filed, monitored, and enforced—and improve relations with businesses as demands upon their time for compliance are reduced.

The U.S. Civil Rights Commission, basically a publicly funded advocacy body with little authority, could be examined to enable it to become more independent from the political tides of the times. Its level of authority and effectiveness could be examined to give it the status and functions of a regulatory agency or to merge it with an operating agency. These are not mayoral recommendations at this point, but simply areas to explore.

Should a more centralized equal opportunity administration be decided upon, a civil rights block grant could be considered to provide funds to state and local equal opportunity efforts for complaint investigation activities; development of affirmative action (employment) and affirmative marketing (housing) programs; establishment or enhancement of state and local contract compliance programs, which require affirmative action compliance for a firm to become eligible to obtain contracts with state and local governments; establishment or enhancement of minority- and women-owned business development programs; and staff training and technical assistance.

To be eligible for receipt of these funds, state and local governments should have civil rights laws at least equivalent to federal civil rights statutes. That is, funds would not be disbursed to states or localities to enforce weak civil rights laws that have little promise of producing results.

Fair Housing Initiatives

Mayors support strengthening the Federal Fair Housing Law (Title III of the Civil Rights Act of 1968). At present, most complaints of housing discrimination are handled through voluntary conciliation. In fact, between 1980 and 1983 the federal government only filed six fair housing suits, an 87 percent reduction from the 1976-1979 period.[48] This deemphasis has occurred in a time when entire neighborhoods are being transformed from one race of residents to another, with numerous violations of fairness certainly occurring in the process.

The law can be strengthened through effective enforcement mechanisms, including a requirement that the Department of Justice initiate court action when the Department of Housing and Urban Development (HUD) refers housing discrimination complaints to them. Moreover, anyone receiving federal funds should be required to comply with all civil rights laws, including freedom from housing discrimination.

CONCLUSION

We see a number of indications that recent federal policies against affirmative action go well beyond the desires of the business community. For example, a *Business Week* editorial states that "few businesses are calling for watering down affirmative action. For most companies it has become a routine part of personnel management. [The U.S. Department of] Justice has mounted a crusade that nobody else seems ready to join."[49] With active and positive national leadership in favor of full representation of minorities and women in private and public workforces—instead of opposition to affirmative action—we can regain the momentum to solve the most serious and inequitable of all U.S. deficiencies

NOTES TO CHAPTER 6

1. U.S. Department of Housing and Urban Development, *The President's 1978 National Urban Policy Report* (Washington, D.C.: U.S. Government Printing Office, August 1978), p. 125.
2. U.S. Bureau of the Census, Current Population Reports, Series P-60, No. 149, *Money Income and Poverty Status of Families and Persons in the United States: 1984* (Advance data from the March 1985 Current Population Survey) (Washington, D.C.: U.S. Government Printing Office, 1985), p. 9.
3. Ibid.
4. Ibid.
5. James D. McGhee, *A Dream Denied: The Black Family in the Eighties* (Washington, D.C.: National Urban League, 1982), p. 31.
6. Full Employment Action Council (FEAC), "The Hidden Jobless" (Washington, D.C.: FEAC, April 1985), p. 2.
7. U.S. Commission on Civil Rights, *Unemployment and Underemployment among Blacks, Hispanics and Women*, Clearinghouse Publication 74 (Washington, D.C.: Commission on Civil Rights, November 1982), p. 5.
8. James D. McGhee, *Black Solidarity: The Tie that Binds* (Washington, D.C.: National Urban League, 1983), Table 13.
9. U.S. Bureau of the Census, *Money Income and Poverty Status: 1984*, pp. 13, 14; and U.S. Commission on Civil Rights, *A Growing Crisis: Disadvantaged Women and Their Children*, Clearinghouse Publication 78 (Washington, D.C.: U.S. Commission on Civil Rights, May 1983), p. 23.
10. U.S. Department of Labor, Bureau of Labor Statistics (BLS), *Employment and Earnings, January, 1985* (Washington, D.C.: BLS, 1985), pp. 156-158; and U.S. Bureau of the Census, *Current Population Survey, Data Book*, Vol. 1, Bulletin 2096 (Washington, D.C.: U.S. Government Printing Office, September 1982), Various tables.
11. U.S. Bureau of the Census, *Money Income and Poverty Status: 1984*, pp. 13-14.
12. U.S. Commission on Civil Rights, *A Growing Crisis*, p. 7, citing Census data; and U.S. Bureau of the Census, *Money Income and Poverty Status: 1984*, computed from pp. 28-29.
13. U.S. Bureau of the Census, *Money Income and Poverty Status: 1984*, p. 22.
14. Joint Center for Political Studies, *A Policy Framework for Racial Justice* (Washington, D.C.: Joint Center for Political Studies 1983), p. 10.
15. U.S. Bureau of the Census, *Money Income and Poverty Status: 1984*, p. 21.
16. Ibid.
17. U.S. Bureau of the Census, Current Population Reports, Series P-60, No. 137, *Money Income of Households, Families, and Persons in the United States: 1981* (Washington, D.C.: U.S. Government Printing Office, 1983), p. 159.

18. U.S. Commission on Civil Rights, *A Growing Crisis*, p. 37.
19. U.S. Bureau of the Census, *Money Income of Household, Families, and Persons: 1981*, p. 159.
20. Robert B. Hill, *Economic Policies and Black Progress: Myths and Realities* (Washington, D.C.: National Urban League, 1981), p. 6.
21. James D. McGhee, *Black Solidarity*, Table 6.
22. James D. McGhee, *A Dream Denied*, p. 23.
23. U.S. Bureau of the Census, *Money Income and Poverty Status: 1983*, p. 3.
24. U.S. Bureau of the Census, *Statistical Abstract of the U.S.: 1982-1983*, 103d ed. (Washington, D.C.: U.S. Government Printing Office, 1982), p. 15.
25. National Urban League, "The Myth of Income Cushions for Blacks" (Washington, D.C.: National Urban League, 1980), p. iv.
26. U.S. Commission on Civil Rights, *Affirmative Action in the 1980's: Dismantling the Process of Discrimination*, Clearinghouse Publication 70 (Washington, D.C.: Commission on Civil Rights, November 1981), p. 41.
27. John L. Palmer and Isabel V. Sawhill, eds., *The Reagan Record: An Assessment of America's Changing Domestic Priorities* (Cambridge, Mass.: Ballinger Publishing Company, 1984), pp. 204-8.
28. Commission on Civil Rights, *Affirmative Action in the 1980's*, p. 35.
29. Albemarle Paper Co. v. Moody, 422 U.S. 405, 417 (1975), citing Griggs v. Duke Power Co., 401 U.S. 424, 429-430 (1971).
30. The first executive orders expressing this policy were E.O. 8802, 6 F.R. 3109, 3 C.F.R., 1938-43 Comp. 957 (June 25, 1941) and E.O. 9001, 6 C.F.R. 6787, 3 C.F.R. 1938-43 Comp. 1054 (December 27, 1941).
31. A summary of executive orders since their origin is set forth in Contractors Assn. of Eastern Pennsylvania v. Secretary of Labor, 441 F.2d. 159, 168-170 (3rd Cir. 1971, cert. denied, 404 U.S. 854 (1971).
32. 42 U.S.C. 200e(1) et seq., as amended by the Equal Opportunity Act of 1972, Pub. L. No. 92-261, 86 Stat. 103.
33. Refer to U.S. Commission on Civil Rights, *Affirmative Action in the 1980's*, p. 22, footnote 60, which provides an extensive listing.
34. 438 U.S. 265, 307 (1978), separate opinion of Justice Blackmun.
35. 443 U.S. 193 (1979).
36. U.S. Department of Labor (DOL), Office of Federal Contractor Compliance Programs, "A Review of the Effect of Executive Order 11246 and the Federal Contract Compliance Program on the Employment Opportunities of Minorities and Women" (Washington, D.C.: DOL, January 6, 1983).
37. Jonathan S. Leonard, "The Impact of Affirmative Action," National Bureau of Economic Research and Institution of Industrial Relations and School of Business Administration, University of California at Berkeley, July 1983.
38. U.S. Bureau of the Census, *1982 Survey of Minority-Owned Business Enterprises: Black* (Washington, D.C.: U.S. Government Printing Office, 1985), Table 1.
39. Phone interview with U.S. Census Bureau staff member, October 1985.
40. U.S. Bureau of the Census, *1982 Survey*, Table 2.

41. Ibid., Table 1, and phone interview with U.S. Census Bureau staff member, October 1985.
42. U.S. Department of Labor (DOL), Office of Federal Contractor Compliance Programs, "Employment Patterns of Minorities and Women in Federal Contractor and Noncontractor Establishments, 1974-1980" (Washington, D.C.: DOL, June 1984), p. 26.
43. Ibid., p. 40.
44. Ibid., p. 48.
45. Herbert Hammerman, *A Decade of New Opportunity: Affirmative Action in the 1970s* (Washington, D.C.: The Potomac Institute, 1984), p. 43.
46. Ibid., p. 51.
47. Ibid., p. 57.
48. Palmer and Sawhill, p. 206.
49. *Business Week*, April 15, 1985, p. 174.

7 HOUSING AND COMMUNITY DEVELOPMENT

Since 1949 the nation has been committed legislatively to the goal of a decent home in a suitable living environment for every American. This goal was further quantified in 1968, when Congress adopted a goal of 26 million housing units—6 million of them for low-income people—over the following decade to meet the nation's housing needs.

Although this ambitious goal has not been met, great progress has been made in housing America's homeless and needy. Over 4 million households today enjoy direct housing assistance from the federal government, through such diverse programs as low-rent public housing, Section 8, and "existing housing certificates" using privately owned dwellings. Yet, according to the 1980 Census, another 7 million households nationwide are either living in substandard or overcrowded housing or are paying too much rent for the shelter they are in. Despite repeated national rededications to the goals established in 1949, the fact is our national progress has stalled. We even face the threat of losing ground already won.

Since 1980 few components of the federal budget have been slashed as deeply as housing—over 60 percent. Moreover, new construction and substantial rehabilitation of housing have been virtually eliminated as federal programs (see Figure 7-1). The result will only be felt in years to come, as the pipeline of commitments made in prior years dries up and no additional resources are made available to replace them.

Not only have lower income people lost ground in the housing field, but continuing high rates of real interest have foreclosed homeownership opportunities to all but a small percentage of the population. The housing industry has only

Figure 7-1. Low- and Moderate-Income Housing Net Units Assisted by the Federal Government, 1977-1985.

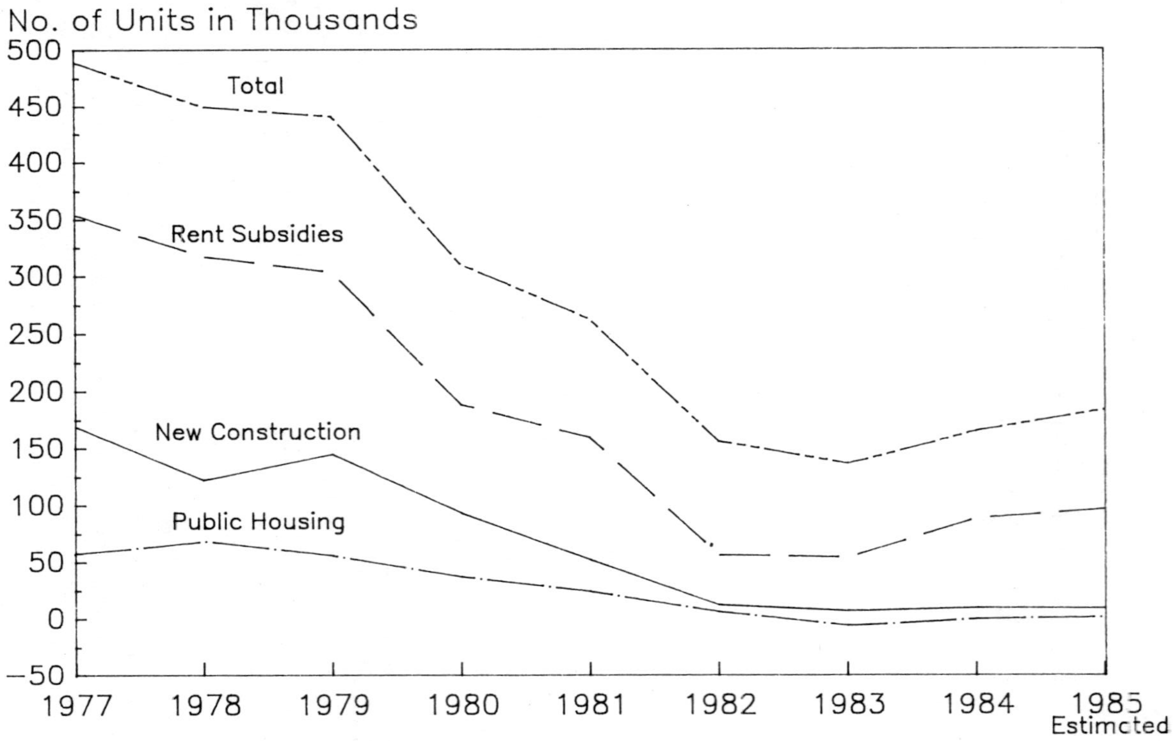

Source: Congressional Budget Office (CBO), "Tables of Net Additional Households Assisted, Housing Assistance Programs" (Washington, D.C.: CBO, February 21, 1985), Table 4.

just begun to recover from the most persistent and damaging recession in several decades. The implications of these shifts are not fully known. However, we must be concerned about this trend and what it implies for the generation now coming of age: continuing and increased difficulty in affording a home.

The nation must rededicate itself to the goal of a decent home in a suitable living environment for every American family. The need is undeniable. The resources needed to meet this goal will be substantial. Yet we must remember that these resources are being invested in a long-term, durable good that provides employment while being built or rehabilitated and shelter while maintained and which enhances the general environment in which it is located if it is managed sensibly and financed adequately.

All incomes of homeowners in the United States need continued assistance. Nonetheless, assistance granted previously to relatively affluent homeowners in the form of mortgage and interest deductions and other such tax expenditures—\$41.4 million in 1985—far outweighs the outlays for housing assistance to the lower income—\$10.6 million in 1985. Equity in our society demands that the vast differential in these two sums be rectified. A nation cannot prosper by providing generous subsidies to those who can afford to own their homes and denying assistance to those who cannot.

Another related aspect of the housing problem in cities is the need for continued support for overall community development investments. The Community Development Block Grant (CDBG), since 1974, and Urban Development Action Grant (UDAG) program, since 1977, have provided targeted, flexible assistance to localities to address neighborhood decline, infrastructure, and housing improvement. Despite its acknowledged success and popularity, however, grants to cities under CDBG have been declining slightly in absolute dollars since 1980 and substantially in real inflation-adjusted dollars. More importantly, the number of jurisdictions receiving entitlements through the program has expanded tremendously as a result of population growth. Cities are struggling to maintain services through this program in the face of these overall reductions. To further the overall objectives of a national urban housing and community development policy, the following recommendations should be adopted.

First, the federal government should maintain an "all-incomes" housing policy that emphasizes the needs of lower income persons especially. Federal housing policy should be founded on the following principles:

- Adequate funding to support existing federal low-income housing investments, particularly low-rent public housing;
- Support for new construction and substantial rehabilitation of subsidized housing where this is necessary to meet local needs; and
- Continuing commitment to increasing rental subsidies, with the goal of ensuring that every household eligible for assistance has the opportunity to receive it.

Second, policies should be adopted to ensure the continued availability of adequate capital for housing construction and rehabilitation in the private housing market.

Third, mayors advocate continued support for the CDBG and UDAG programs, with funding levels that at least compensate for the increase in cities eligible for assistance since 1980. These recommendations will be discussed in greater detail after a general discussion of federal subsidies for housing.

FEDERAL HOUSING ASSISTANCE IN PERSPECTIVE

Only a small proportion of households eligible for and needing assistance are now living in federally subsidized housing. About 16 percent of households below the poverty level and 21.6 percent of households classified by the Department of Housing and Urban Development (HUD) as "very low income" (below 50 percent of median family income) were receiving housing assistance in 1980.[1]

Housing assistance can be received directly by a low-income family through a HUD housing assistance program, or it can be received via "tax expenditures." Under the latter method, a homeowner pays less taxes because of mortgage interest and property tax deductions or deferral of capital gain subject to taxation. Either method—direct subsidy or tax expenditures—results in the same consequence, a drain from the treasury.

In Figure 7-2 it is shown that tax expenditures for homeowners continue to climb steadily over time, while annual budget authority for housing programs has dropped sharply in recent years.[2] The 1986 figures are as proposed by the executive branch and include the first year of a proposed two-year moratorium on additional assistance for low-income housing. Congress did not accept the president's proposed moratorium in its actions on the 1986 budget, but instead enacted a 7 percent reduction. The 1985 data provided in Figure 7-1 are the last year of congressionally approved amounts. In that year tax expenditures were worth $41.4 billion, compared to $10.8 billion in budget authority for federal housing programs (or $10.6 billion in projected federal outlays). Therefore, the value of tax expenditures is nearly quadruple the value of federal housing programs.

Only one-eighth of U.S. taxpayers with incomes below $10,000 receive federal housing assistance, via HUD programs or tax deductions. In contrast, four-fifths of households with incomes above $50,000 received federal assistance through the tax code. The average level of assistance per households earning below $10,000 in 1981 was $22.61 (including both $10.40 per month in federal housing subsidy and $12.21 per month in tax deductions); the average assistance to $50,000-plus households was $155.54 per month.[3] Therefore, the more

Figure 7-2. Federal Support for Housing, 1981-1986.

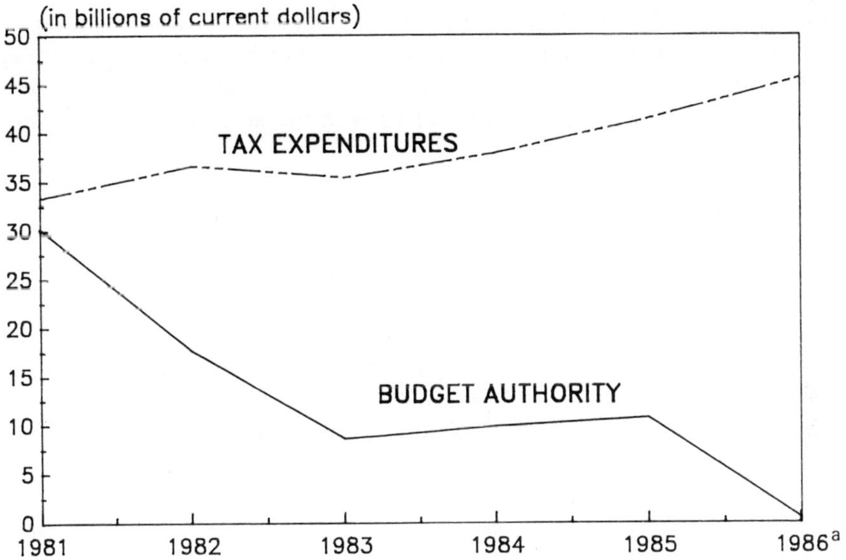

a. 1986 Budget Authority as proposed in the President's FY1986 budget.
Source: Cushing N. Dolbeare, "Federal Assistance: Who Needs It? Who Gets It" (Washington, D.C.: National League of Cities, 1985), pp. 31-41.

affluent received nearly seven times the level of assistance as the average under-$10,000-a-year family.

One-quarter of all federal housing assistance went to the 7 percent of all households with incomes above $50,000. In contrast, the 25 percent of U.S. households with incomes under $10,000 received one-eighth of federal housing assistance.[4]

Various plans have been advanced to remedy this imbalance. For example, tax deductions could be limited just to one's principal residence. This policy could have the added benefit of discouraging speculation in housing purchased as rental properties and would thereby tend to restrain housing prices somewhat. Others have suggested an upper limit on the value of a tax deduction for interest and property taxes (e.g., the equivalent of a $200,000 home). These policies would free substantial funds for lower income housing assistance.

The U.S. Conference of Mayors has never supported a reduction in housing assistance from the tax code to citizens, in recognition of the extraordinary financial difficulty citizens have in buying and maintaining a house. Nonetheless, mayors ask federal policymakers to remain aware of the considerably greater difficulties faced by lower income citizens in participating in the same tight and costly housing market. The President's Commission on Housing, in a 1981 report, found that three-fourths of all U.S. very low income households were living in substandard housing, paid more than they could afford for shelter, or both.[5] Therefore, serious housing problems are the rule rather than the exception among low-income Americans.

The following is an outline of potential actions that may be taken.

ADEQUATE FUNDING FOR PUBLIC HOUSING

Since 1937 the federal government has invested billions of dollars in the construction and rehabilitation of subsidized housing alone, under the administration of local public housing authorities (PHAs). This housing has come to serve as the "social safety net" in housing for millions of lower income Americans for whom alternatives do not exist in the private marketplace. Moreover, public housing is a significant part of the urban housing economy. In Atlanta, for instance, public housing constitutes 15 percent of the total housing stock. In Baltimore this figure is 10 percent; Philadelphia and Cleveland, 9 percent; and the District of Columbia, 7 percent. Three-quarters of the households in public housing are minorities, nearly half are elderly, and many are families with dependent children.

The preservation of this housing resource as affordable housing for low and moderate income people must be one of the very highest priorities of national urban policy. Public housing need not mean dilapidated, overcrowded, despair ridden, crime-infested high rises. Many cities have created attractive living environments with public housing funds, especially in recent years. Yet, neglect and underfunding over the years have contributed to a situation where many units are vacant, cannot be occupied, and need considerable work to meet accepted standards of decency. Many more need the timely reinvestment that would ensure their continued availability for another generation.

A recent survey of sixty-six cities by the U.S. Conference of Mayors indicated that $1.7 billion was needed in those cities to bring public housing units up to safety and other standards. However, the surveyed cities indicated that they would receive a total of $218 million to meet these needs, just 12 percent of the required amount.[6]

In June 1983 the Congressional Budget Office (CBO) observed in a report to Congress that roughly $10 billion would be needed to make necessary improvements, including energy-related ones, in public housing throughout the United States. The present modernization program was enacted in 1980 in response to the continued deterioration of the public housing stock. At that time Congress made it clear that the program should emphasize comprehensive modernization and that the local authorities should have a preeminent role in defining needs and setting goals. However, during the past few years, HUD has hindered comprehensive planning and PHA decisionmaking through repeated delays in releasing funds to the field.

Mayors call on Congress to fund the comprehensive modernization program at adequate levels—which, after the mayors' proposed budget freeze, could mean $2 billion per year in authorizations—until all work currently necessary to bring public housing units up to acceptable standards has been completed. Furthermore, mayors support a program emphasis of comprehensive modernization based on local assessments of the work that is necessary to ensure the continued availability of these units over the next twenty years.

A second area in which adequate support for existing public housing is required is operating subsidies. Since 1968 these federal payments have been necessary for housing authorities to cover the difference between rents paid by lower income tenants and the actual costs of operating the housing. Repeated attempts have been made over the years to cut back this subsidy, often without regard to the actual costs faced by authorities. Unpredictable funding levels and inadequate subsidies in the late 1970s made management of the inventory increasingly difficult and led to deferred maintenance and avoidable deterioration. The modernization program has been critical in reversing this trend. Congress has also grasped the essential link between adequate and dependable operating subsidies and the long-term preservation of public housing. Since 1980 it has provided full funding for operating subsidies.

However, HUD's research has identified a number of flaws in the formula that have tended to underfund large public housing authorities operating in distressed communities. The subsidy calculation has also proved unresponsive to changes in operating circumstances since 1975, when the formula was introduced. Congress has considered, but not passed, legislation in recent sessions that would correct for inequities in the original application of the formula as well as for changes during the past ten years that have affected costs.

Mayors call on Congress and the administration to provide operating subsidies to public housing through a formula allocation that realistically supports the operation of the units and, to the greatest extent possible, is based on the actual costs of operating them in a cost-effective manner.

SUBSIDIES FOR NEW CONSTRUCTION AND SUBSTANTIAL REHABILITATION

Great progress has been made in improving the stock of housing in the United States since 1934, but there are still areas of the country where an absolute shortage of housing presents major problems, especially for low and moderate income households. Although rental supplements are an effective way of providing housing assistance to many, they are no panacea. Moreover, many urban areas suffer from substantial deterioration in the existing housing stock. As demonstrated by HUD's own research on the matter, the use of housing certificates or vouchers provides practically no incentive for owners substantially to rehabilitate their properties. The production and rehabilitation of housing, particularly for lower income renters, must be a major part of a national urban policy.

In the Conference's recent survey of sixty-six cities, 77 percent of the cities reported an increase in low-income housing demand over the past year. Moreover, in over two-thirds of those cities, the increase was substantial, ranging from 25 to 100 percent.

In fact, demand for assisted housing is so out of scale with available housing resources that 61 percent of all cities surveyed have closed their waiting lists to households seeking assistance. The waiting period for assisted housing is about two years for eligible families in most cities, but it ranges up to a twenty-five-year wait in the most hard-pressed cities.[7] The survey demonstrated that those people on the waiting lists have a high likelihood of currently living in substandard housing, paying more than 50 percent of their income for rent, or both.

Rent subsidies alone cannot address the fundamental question of long-term housing supply. The most frequently cited reason for the shortage of housing available to lower income people is diminished levels of new construction. As seen in Figure 7-1, the number of new low- and moderate-income units added to the housing units has declined drastically, from 145,038 new units added as recently as 1979 to an estimated 8,717 in 1985. The effects of today's housing policies will be felt for years to come.

During the 1970s the total number of housing units available to the lowest income people (those earning $3,000 or less a year), where they could pay 30 percent of their income or less to rent, declined by 75 percent. During this decade housing prices for all income classes increased by 77 percentage points more than the general price index, putting home ownership and affordable rent out of the price range of millions.[8]

A primary way to build the housing supply is through rehabilitation of vacant units. In the recent U.S. Conference of Mayors' housing survey, sixty-six cities reported an average of 3,873 vacant units—a huge number of these blight-creating units when one considers that the average number of households in the surveyed cities is under 150,000. Concentration of public policy on rent subsidies cannot address the need for housing rehabilitation. In the lowest of income areas, the private market cannot recover rehabilitation expenditures; some level of public subsidy is necessary to stimulate private investment.

In November 1983 Congress adopted a Housing Development Action Grant (HoDAG) program and a rental rehabilitation program, funded at $315 and $300 million, respectively, for the two-year fiscal 1984-85 period. Mayors strongly support these concepts.

The HoDAG program is modeled on the highly successful UDAG program and may assist in the construction or substantial rehabilitation of up to 16,000 rental units over the two-year period. Grants are targeted to communities with severe shortages of decent rental housing without other reasonable alternatives.

Rental rehabilitation grants are distributed on a formula basis to states, urban counties, and cities to support the rehabilitation of rental properties. HUD makes available Section 8 certificates or vouchers or both to make the rehabilitation units affordable to lower income families. The rehabilitation subsidy is limited generally to 50 percent of costs, not to exceed $5,000 per unit.

Mayors support the concept of these initiatives but stress that the funding levels presently available are negligible when compared to the actual need for development subsidies. Mayors support the new construction and substantial rehabilitation of at least 100,000 units of rental housing for low and moderate income households per year. Although this goal is out of line with today's housing policies, it is well within the levels of new construction and substantial rehabilitation achieved in recent times (Figure 7-1). Using the programs enacted by the Congress in 1983 to meet this goal would require at least $5 billion in additional budget authority. In contrast, the HoDAG and rental rehabilitation programs are funded by Congress at only $75 million each for fiscal 1986, while the executive branch is urging recision of even these amounts.

In addition to general programs supporting construction and rehabilitation of housing, there will continue to be a need for the development of publicly owned housing to ensure that all households' needs can be met. In particular, experience over four decades has shown that private development is unlikely to provide units for very large low-income families. Suitable programs that will enable localities to ensure that such housing is provided are essential, since rent subsidies are largely ineffective in addressing this need.

Mayors support continued authorizations and appropriations for the conventional low-rent public housing program, with sufficient funds available to provide at least 5,000 units of development a year over the next ten years; this level assumes adoption of the other housing policy elements offered in this chapter. If these other policy elements are not fully adopted, then development of a minimum of 10,000 public housing units a year would be necessary. The number of new public housing units has declined from an average of 60,438 a year during 1977 to 1979 to 1,426 in 1985. Therefore, the mayors' goal of 5,000 to 10,000 new public housing units a year is relatively moderate.

MEETING HOUSING AFFORDABILITY NEEDS

Affordability is clearly the most pressing and widespread housing problem in the country today, particularly among lower income households. The President's 1980 National Urban Policy Report stated that,

> Housing affordability problems are severe for lower income households in central cities. Over 85 percent of renter households with annual incomes less

Table 7-1. Percentage of Households Paying More Than 25 Percent of Income for Rent, 1980.

Income Level	*Percentage*
Under $3,000	86.1
$3,000 to $6,999	80.7
$7,000 to $10,000	72.7

Source: Cushing N. Dolbeare, "Federal Assistance: Who Needs It? Who Gets It?" (Washington, D.C.: National League of Cities, 1985), p. 14.

than $5,000 paid more than one-quarter of their incomes for rent in 1977. About two-thirds of central city renter households with incomes of between $5,000 and $10,000 paid more than a quarter of their incomes for rent.

According to the 1980 Census, an estimated 61 percent of all renter households had incomes below 80 percent of median, and 40 percent had incomes below 50 percent of median. These two thresholds have been established by Congress as the measures of low income and very low income, respectively, in subsidized housing programs. According to the 1982 report of the President's Commission on Housing, fully 51 percent of the renter households with incomes below 50 percent of median paid more than 30 percent of their income for rent in 1977, and 22 percent of those with incomes between 50 percent and 80 percent of median did so. Moreover, a 1984 study indicates that 83 percent of long-term poor households that presently do not receive any housing subsidies pay more than 30 percent of their income for rent. Many of the units these households rent—40 percent—are deficient in their condition, by HUD definition.[9]

A 1985 study provides a more recent examination of households paying more than 25 percent of their incomes to rent. (See Table 7-1.) In fact, 62 percent of the lowest income households (under $3,000 per year) paid more than 60 percent of their incomes to rent. Moreover, 76 percent of the under-$3,000-a-year households and 66 percent of the $3,000-to-$7,000-income households paid more than 35 percent of their income to rent. In contrast, only 12 percent of renter households with annual incomes of $25,000 per year paid more than 25 percent of their income to rent, and just 3 percent paid more than 35 percent.[10]

Only 16 percent of renters with incomes below the poverty level in 1980 were living in subsidized housing.[11] Therefore, housing assistance provided to the low income falls far short of the need.

At 25 percent of income, a household with an income of $5,000 can afford only $104 in rent. There are twice as many households with incomes below $5,000 as there are affordable units in the present housing inventory.

According to the president's commission data, nearly 7 million renter households are eligible for housing assistance under the Section 8 rental subsidy programs using the existing housing stock. However, only about 37,500 households are receiving assistance from this program in 1985.

Additionally, under 40,000 families were served in 1985 through a new housing voucher program—a program that is eventually slated by HUD to replace the Section 8 Existing Housing Certificate Program. Although the programs are similar, they differ in a number of respects.

Voucher tenants will be allowed to pay more than 30 percent of income to secure a unit that itself may be let for more than the local fair market rent standard. Unlike Section 8, the voucher subsidy can be increased no more than two times during the five-year period. A tenant will be required to pay all rent increases not approved by the local housing authority or above the two approved increases. Tenants would pay the extra amounts by contributing more than 30 percent of adjusted income toward rent.

The results of the housing voucher demonstration are not yet available. The "demand experiment" of the Experimental Housing Allowance Program (EHAP), from which the voucher concept evolved, showed that vouchers will often not be effective for a number of groups: very large families, because not enough multibedroom units exist; single-parent families and minorities, because many private landlords will avoid renting to them; and people with special needs, such as the handicapped. EHAP has shown that a mix of programs is essential to meet the nation's housing needs. Although the voucher program may prove an important component of a comprehensive national housing policy, it should not be implemented at the expense of other, demonstrably effective programs such as new construction, substantial rehabilitation, low-rent public housing, and Section 8.

Mayors support the continuation of major federal rent subsidies through programs such as Section 8 existing certificates to make decent, safe, and sanitary housing affordable to lower income households. The nation should adopt a goal of providing rent subsidies to all households eligible to receive them—at least 7 million as of 1977—within a decade. At a minimum, 100,000 units of additional assistance should be made available annually, requiring at least $6.7 billion per year in fifteen-year budget authority. Again, this goal is a moderate one in view of the fact that the numbers of rental units subsidized just a few years ago were double and triple current levels (see Figure 7-1).

ADEQUATE FUNDING FOR COMMUNITY DEVELOPMENT BLOCK GRANTS

During the 1975-1982 period, the number of communities receiving entitlement grants through the Community Development Block Grant (CDBG) program increased by 23 percent. Yet the funds available for distribution to these communities increased by only $272 million, or 13 percent, over the same period.

According to the HUD 1983 Report to Congress on CDBG, in FY 1982 alone the combination of a greater number of recipients and congressionally adopted changes in distribution patterns meant that 75 percent of all entitlement grantees—principally metropolitan cities—had their grants reduced 10 to 17 percent from the previous year's level. Additional substantial changes have taken place, the number of cities and counties with entitlement status increasing from 732 in 1982 to 814 by 1985, further reducing funding levels for each eligible city.

These funding reductions have severely hampered cities' abilities to attack the underlying problems of urban distress. This affects city housing problems by exacerbating neighborhood decline and reducing cities' abilities to cope with blighting influences which affect the value of housing and private reinvestment decisions.

Mayors have supported a budget freeze at least through FY 1986. Beyond that, mayors support an increase in funding for the CDBG program at least to compensate for reductions in entitlement grants caused by increased participation in the program. Appropriate increases on an annual basis would account for inflation and expansion in program participation.

Another effort that has enhanced cities' overall economic health is the Urban Development Action Grant (UDAG) program. Despite cuts from $675 million in FY 1981 to only $330 million in FY 1986, this program continues to stimulate billions of dollars in private investment in new development in cities. The result has been substantial gains in employment and the tax base. Continued support for this program is essential during times of economic recovery, to ensure that cities are able to participate fully in this recovery.

The CDBG and UDAG programs are discussed in greater detail in Chapter 3.

POLICIES FOR THE HOMELESS

One striking effect of our nation's revised housing, employment, and social policies is what should be an alarming increase in homelessness in the United States.

In a 1984 survey of ten cities by the U.S. Conference of Mayors it was found that, despite lowered unemployment rates and the economic recovery:[12]

- In Boston the demand for emergency shelter increased by 50 percent between 1983 and 1984.
- Referrals to the Chicago Department of Human Services were up approximately 30 percent from 1982 to 1983. New shelters filled to capacity as soon as they opened.
- The demand for shelter in Denver increased by 20 percent during 1983.
- In Columbus requests for emergency assistance increased by 75 percent between October 1982 and October 1983 and continued to increase over the winter.

- From 1982 to 1984, the number of families sheltered by New York City almost tripled and the number of facilities used to house them quadrupled.
- Philadelphia has seen a sevenfold increase in placements of homeless persons since 1981.
- In Seattle the requests for assistance have more than doubled since 1980.
- Although neither Atlanta nor San Francisco can provide a specific indicator that quantifies the increase in homelessness, officials in both cities reported that the number of homeless people has increased dramatically.

All ten cities indicated that they raised about as much money locally from public and private resources as they could. They said they could not meet the need with local resources, and that additional funds and federal intervention were needed. For example:

- Boston said that there were 10,000 to 14,000 homeless people in the city and only 1,036 shelter beds for them;
- Chicago estimated 12,000 to 25,000 homeless persons, with 1,000 shelter beds; and
- Atlanta, Columbus, Denver, and Seattle reported that there were sleeping spaces for only one-third to one-half of the people who needed them.[13]

Homelessness is not just a city's problem; it is America's problem. Homeless people gravitate to cities from all areas. The report indicates that in most of the cities surveyed, transients constitute from 40 to 60 percent of the homeless people.[14] Cities did not create the national economic problems of joblessness, skyrocketing housing costs, or cuts in federal benefit programs; the responsibility is much broader.

Estimates of the total numbers of homeless people have ranged from 250,000 to 3 million. The lower figure was estimated by HUD and was considered far too low by many involved with homeless programs. Yet even under that most conservative estimate, less than 50 percent of the need can be met by existing shelter space, estimated by HUD at 110,000 spaces.[15]

A 1985 survey by the National Board, Emergency Food and Shelter Program found that 122 people are turned away per month in the average shelter, compared to 65 people per shelter per month a year earlier. Significantly, 65 percent of all shelters and 70 percent of shelters in the largest cities reported an increase in first-time users of shelters, despite the fact that the economic recovery and expansion were well underway at the time of this survey.[16]

With the help of federal emergency shelter funding, localities are attempting to keep up with the need. In fact, the board's 1985 survey indicates a 16 percent increase in the number of persons who were sheltered over the previous year. Still, the numbers turned away are apparently doubling.[17]

A House committee, after analyzing homeless conditions, states that "the federal government's response to the crisis has been inadequate. The few federal programs available to aid the homeless have been disappointing, or have simply been too small to have a significant impact." The committee details the federal government's pledges to provide food from military commissaries and shelter from surplus federal buildings and vacant houses under federal ownership. The committee notes that only a small handful of sites were made available.[18]

The Federal Emergency Management Agency's Emergency Food and Shelter Program is the only federal program designed to provide direct assistance to the homeless. This program operates on a temporary, year-to-year basis. Established in 1983 through the emergency jobs bill, the program has provided 27 million nights of shelter and 135 million meals (as of July 1985).[19] The $70 million in annual federal funding is combined with considerable local government and non-profit organization funding and in-kind contributions (structures, food distribution networks, supplies), enabling the establishment and maintenance of new shelters. Extended funding of an emergency food and shelter program with flexibility to meet the needs of local governments is essential.

Needless to add, the nation must address the causes of the homeless problem so that cities and citizens do not have to cope year after year with the same emergency situation.

CONCLUSIONS: PROVIDING EQUITY IN HOUSING ASSISTANCE

Low-income housing is one of the most difficult public policy areas for the average citizen to understand, which at least partially accounts for its general lack of public support. Middle and many upper income people are aware of the struggles they face in their daily lives to buy and maintain a home. These relatively affluent Americans should try to become aware that the struggle for affordable housing is many times greater for low-income families. Dwelling deficiencies and overcrowding, as well as rent payments that exceed affordability, are commonplace in low-income neighborhoods. These are conditions that would not be tolerated by the average American.

Only a fifth of the eligible low-income population is being served by housing assistance programs today. There are about 1 million fewer families being assisted today than under previous (1976–1980) policies, and two-thirds fewer households per year are being helped today compared to that earlier era.[20]

Some may argue that this drastic cutback of housing assistance is to be expected in these days of budgetary austerity and deficits. Housing, after all, is one of the most expensive of all commodities and cannot be easily subsidized. However, mayors reason with the general public to understand that federal tax policies direct $46 billion annually to middle and upper income households to subsidize housing costs through mortgage and property tax deductions. This level is many times greater than the subsidies granted to the low income.

Consider also that the cost of *one* MX missile equals the two-year cost of the entire HoDAG rental housing development program, discussed above, for all of the United States. The cost of *one* B-1 bomber equals the two-year cost of the entire rental housing rehabilitation program that was newly enacted by Congress for the 1984-85 period.

Mayors are receptive to new or improved ways of providing low-income housing assistance. Cities are not tied to present programs and are flexible about the policy proposals advocated in this chapter. However, much of the discussion about new and improved ways to finance low-income housing assistance is diversionary. There is no way an innovative program by itself can overcome drastic funding cutbacks in housing. A national commitment to housing assistance for low-income families—as well as to middle and upper income families—must be maintained while the discussion of various voucher, HoDAG, and public housing operating formulas proceeds.

Providing federal assistance to guarantee access to decent, safe, and sanitary housing is not cheap. The federal government invested about $35 billion in actual outlays between 1937 and 1980 to meet this goal. Meeting our current and future needs will require more substantial investments. The United States enters the coming decade with the largest population group in its history coming of age. Projections of household formations over the next decade include requirements for at least 20 million new housing units, net of demolitions. Even at the 1983 level of housing starts—just under 1.5 million—this baby boom generation will put unprecedented stress on the nation's housing resources. As this generation comes of age and moves into its own units, the pressure on lower income households least able to compete will be intense.

Yet, with some reshifting of priorities, the task is manageable. Even if all of the recommendations proposed in this chapter were adopted, the cost would still fall more than $4 billion, or 18 percent, short of the level of federal housing assistance in 1981. A decent home in a decent neighborhood is one of the most important prerequisites to equal opportunity. In comparison to subsidies already authorized and obligated every year for those more fortunate, these policy recommendations are not unreasonable.

NOTES TO CHAPTER 7

1. Cushing N. Dolbeare, "Federal Assistance: Who Needs It? Who Gets It?" (Washington, D.C.: National League of Cities, 1985), p. 21.
2. Ibid., p. 31.
3. Ibid., pp. 39, 41.
4. Ibid., p. 36.
5. Ibid., p. 19.
6. U.S. Conference of Mayors (USCM), "Housing Needs and Conditions in America's Cities: A Survey of the Nation's Principal Cities" (Washington, D.C.: USCM, June 1984), p. 14.
7. Ibid., pp. 7, 9.
8. Ibid., p. 3.

9. Harold Katsura and Raymond Struyk, *Shelter Supplements for Welfare Recipients* (Washington, D.C.: The Urban Institute, July 1984), p. 2.
10. Dolbeare, p. 14.
11. Ibid., p. 4.
12. U.S. Conference of Mayors (USCM), "Homelessness in America's Cities: Ten Case Studies" (Washington, D.C.: USCM, June 1984), p. 5.
13. Ibid., p. 8.
14. Ibid., p. 6.
15. U.S. Congress, House Committee on Government Operations, "The Federal Response to the Homeless Crisis," House Report 99–47 (Washington, D.C.: U.S. Government Printing Office, 1985), pp. 7–9.
16. National Board, Emergency Food and Shelter Program, "Study of Homelessness" (Washington, D.C.: National Board, March 1985), pp. 16, 18.
17. Ibid., p. 2.
18. Ibid., pp. 14–16.
19. Phone conversation with staff member of the National Board, Emergency Food and Shelter Program (Alexandria, Virg.) on October 7, 1985.
20. John L. Palmer and Isabel V. Sawhill, eds., *The Reagan Record: An Assessment of America's Changing Domestic Priorities* (Cambridge, Mass.: Ballinger Publishing Company, 1984), p. 372.

8 EDUCATION REFORM
A New Challenge for the Cities

Though our nation has celebrated the thirty-year anniversary of the landmark Supreme Court public school desegregation mandate in *Brown* v. *the Board of Education*, we still have separate and unequal school systems in many parts of our country. One of the most basic injustices in our society is that the children who need help the most attend public schools in communities that have the fewest resources. Children from affluent families already have a "head start." Their advantages are perpetuated through their attendance at well-financed school systems—systems with relatively low levels of children with educational or emotional handicaps that can drain resources. In recent times these trends have accelerated.

The federal government is the one intergovernmental entity that can redistribute resources for the benefit of all children. Yet recent decreases in federal educational resources have widened the educational gap of urban children. Adoption of such measures as tuition tax credits would further place urban school systems in jeopardy, diverting additional resources to private schools and accentuating segregation patterns.

Educational improvement is not just a question of dollars. Quality education can be achieved only through a partnership between parents, a healthy community, and a dedicated school system. Other chapters in this report recommend policies to build the family, neighborhoods, and urban economies. While building those key components, the urban school systems should not be neglected.

Several national reports have cited problems and deficiencies in the public schools and the urgent need to address them for a rapidly growing technological society and the demands of the future.[1] Mayors have long recognized that America's heritage of universal, free public education of the highest quality is essential to the health of our families, our industries, and our cities and that it has formed the foundation of our democratic traditions and institutions. Both public and private institutions–including federal, state, and local government; educators; organized labor; parents' groups; individual corporations; and business organizations–have a role to play in enabling our public school system to improve its standards and performance, now and in the future.

The mayors strongly urge all sectors of our society to act in partnership with our public school system in pursuit of educational excellence. Certain factors are critical as we explore ways to achieve excellense in our public schools:

- educational funding and the role of the federal government;
- equal access to educational opportunities; and
- preparation and training of youth and adults for the demands of the future.

Although state and local governments have the primary responsibility for education, the federal government must participate as a full partner in achieving educational goals. The federal government must meet its responsibilities to public education by (1) maintaining the U.S. Department of Education; (2) declaring a moratorium on all budget actions that negatively affect public schools; and (3) reversing the pattern of reduced education aid and instead producing greater support for nutrition, integration, preschool, vocational, postsecondary, compensatory, handicapped, and bilingual education funding.

Though educational funding would be frozen at current levels under the budget freeze resolution adopted by mayors (see Chapter 1), several actions can be taken now or can be considered during the freeze period for the future. Specifically, mayors call for:

- an active response to national reports on educational reform through effective cooperation among and coordination of all sectors of this nation;
- a moratorium on budget cuts in federal education programs;
- sufficient funding for Chapter 1 of the Education Consolidation and Improvement Act of 1981, to help ensure equal educational opportunity;
- maintenance of current regulations pertaining to the Education for All Handicapped Children Act of 1975 (P.L. 94-142) with sufficient funding to provide a free appropriate public education to all handicapped children as required under the law;
- continued support for the Vocational Education Act with sufficient funding so that young people, especially from low-income families, can meet the needs of the changing job market and a high technology workplace and acquire the basic skills necessary for survival and progress;

- sufficient funding to renew college education opportunities for those students who have been hampered by changes and budget cuts in student financial assistance programs;
- continued support for the Bilingual Education Act with sufficient funding so that limited or non-English-speaking students are not excluded from the mainstream of American society. The "sink or swim" method of education, without bilingual assistance, results in too many educational drownings;
- continued congressional funding of desegregation assistance legislation to provide equal educational opportunity for minority children and support for enforcement of desegregation laws; desegregation efforts have been diluted since the consolidation of Emergency School Aid Act into the Chapter 2 Block Grants;
- continued congressional funding of math and science education legislation to enable school systems to hone the skills of the future U.S. labor force and to increase the competitive ability of U.S. firms through adequate funding of local school districts;
- opposition to education vouchers that would promote segregation by race and income, create constitutional conflict between church and state, reduce services for economically disadvantaged students, and hurt the already struggling urban school system;
- opposition to tuition tax credits that would support elitist, segregated school systems while devastating public school systems;
- support of community education to open school facilities and provision of resources to all members of the community—the young and old alike—for social, cultural, recreational, and educational purposes.

Each of these recommendations is detailed below.

EDUCATION FUNDING AND THE ROLE OF THE FEDERAL GOVERNMENT

The current administration's quest to restore flexibility, diversity, and creativity to local governments while drastically paring away federal education programs has put many cities adrift in a sea of financial disaster. The Council of the Great City Schools—a coalition of thirty-five of the nation's largest urban school systems—reveals some startling statistics on federal education funding. In the 1984-85 school year the nation's major urban school districts received $967.4 million in federal funds from the U.S. Department of Education. In FY 1980 these same districts received about $1 billion from the U.S. Department of Education. The change between FY 1980 and FY 1984 amounts to a decline of 5.2 percent, or

25.9 percent in inflation-adjusted dollars. Most troublesome is the unequal distribution of the educational funding reductions. The urban school systems, with only 11 percent of the nation's enrollment, have absorbed one-third of all elementary and secondary education cuts since FY 1980.[2] As a result of this decrease in federal revenue, urban schools are increasingly unable to maintain quality education programs. Compensatory reading and mathematics programs, federally funded in the high schools, have been virtually eliminated. Voluntary desegregation efforts are being curtailed. Bilingual programs are being shut down. Vocational education efforts have not been able to keep pace with inflation or with new job-training demands.

COMPENSATORY EDUCATION PROGRAMS

Title I of the Elementary and Secondary Education Act of 1965 (ESEA) was enacted by Congress to expand and improve elementary and secondary education programs to meet the special needs of educationally disadvantaged children in low-income areas in public and private schools.

Chapter 1 of the Education Consolidation and Improvement Act of 1981 (ECIA) replaced Title I. ECIA was included in the Omnibus Budget Reconciliation Act of 1981, one of the most comprehensive and potentially far-reaching laws ever enacted. Under Chapter 1, local education agencies receive formula grants to serve educationally deprived children. Many students who participated in the program have improved their reading skills by as much as 71 percent and their math ability by as much as 74 percent, according to a study by the National Institute of Education (NIE).[3]

When Congress first authorized compensatory education over seventeen years ago, it did so because of the lack of adequate state and local resources or commitment. Because local communities must rely so heavily on local property taxes to run their schools, impoverished neighborhoods are obviously less capable of providing all the resources that schools and schoolchildren require. Chapter 1 currently provides each child served nearly $700 in educational services, representing an average increase of almost 35 percent over what these students normally receive from state and local sources. Chapter 1 is made available to schools that have traditionally served the greatest number of disadvantaged youth. What these dollars are buying has been documented by both government and independent studies, all of which testify to the success of Chapter 1 programs and their Title I predecessors. For the graduates of these programs the gains are long-lasting and meaningful. For Chapter 1 students, academic performance continues at a higher level with greater maturity and devotion, according to the National Advisory Council on the Education of the Disadvantaged.[4] In part, this success is explained by the quality of teaching available for Chapter 1 students. According to an NIE report to Congress, over 62 percent of compensatory education teachers are classified as specialists. Some 96 percent have training beyond a bachelor's degree, most having at least a master's degree.[5] By contrast, nearly one-third of all regularly assigned teachers have only a bachelor's degree or less. In addition to better trained teachers, Chapter 1 funds better programs. Of the 140 local programs recognized as "exemplary" by the Department of Education, 53 are Chapter 1 programs.

In recent years the assault on public education has been unrelenting. Disturbing statistics have documented increasingly insufficient homework demands, less thoughtful and critical reading expectations, fewer writing assignments, and substantially declining enrollment in basic courses.

Chapter 1 has been a model success story in combating these trends. As the competency of teachers is increasingly questioned, Chapter 1 teachers remain highly trained and devoted. At a time when education experts criticize excessive emphasis on electives, Chapter 1 continues to focus on the basics. Since parent apathy is a factor in poor student achievement, Chapter 1 has coordinated parent advisory councils and other parent involvement activities.

For the traditionally disadvantaged minority student, the program has a special significance. Of the estimated 5 million children receiving Chapter 1 services, nearly half come from minority families. Specifically, 34 percent of Chapter 1 students are black, compared with 19 percent of the total enrollment in the schools served; 10 percent are Spanish surnamed, compared with 5 percent of the total enrollment in the schools served.

While test scores have declined for most groups, for minorities they have risen. For black nine year olds, for example, average reading performance rose by a dramatic 9.9 percentage points between 1970 and 1980. Chapter 1 cannot take the *full* credit for this gain, but the National Assessment of Educational Progress cites Chapter 1 as a key factor.[6]

Included among the successful Chapter 1 techniques that have been adopted by the education mainstream are (1) the hiring of paraprofessional aides to help teachers, (2) the diagnostic testing of students at the beginning and end of each year, and (3) the more direct involvement of parents in monitoring the education of their children.

The task that Chapter 1 performs of overcoming the effects of poverty is an enormous one. Less than half of children from poverty-level families become high school graduates, while 77 percent of above-poverty children do graduate (1983 data). Only 8 percent of black children from poverty-level families and 14 percent of all impoverished children attain one year or more of college, compared to 34 percent of blacks and 38 percent of all children from above-poverty-level families.[7]

The structural barriers to educational attainment and a steady, well-paying job are enormous for the low-income population. Without a healthy commitment of Chapter 1 resources, those barriers are all the more formidable.

Additionally, 35 percent of all children from female-headed households drop out of high school before obtaining a degree, compared to 20 percent of children from two-parent households. Only 7 percent of children from female-headed households obtain a college degree, compared to 25 percent of children from two-parent households, an astounding differential.[8] Chapter 1 funds are well targeted to single-parent households as well.

More than 11 million disadvantaged children are eligible for Chapter 1 programs. Currently, only 45 percent are being served because of insufficient funds. The FY 1980 funding level for Chapter 1 (Title I) was $3.2 billion. The FY 1986 appropriation was $3.7 billion; $4.4 billion would have been needed in FY 1986 just to keep pace with inflation. A doubling of funds would be necessary to serve all eligible children.

EDUCATION BLOCK GRANT

Chapter 2 of the Education Consolidation and Improvement Act of 1981 consolidated about twenty-eight elementary and secondary programs into a single block grant to the states. It targeted assistance for three general purposes: (1) basic skills improvement, (2) educational improvement and support services, and (3) special projects. Both state and local boards must conform to these general categories, but there is no requirement that all be covered. Nor are there any guidelines about how to distribute funds among them. Some of the major programs folded into the block grant include: Teacher Centers, Teacher Corps, Emergency School Aid, Youth Employment, Training Grants to Institutions of Higher Education, Basic Skills Improvement and Education Proficiency, Pre-college Teacher Development in Science, and Community Education.

In FY 1980 Congress appropriated $732 million for the individual programs consolidated under Chapter 2. The funding level for Chapter 2 was $589 million in FY 1982, the first year of the education block grant—a difference of $143 million. In FY 1982 the U.S. Department of Education distributed only $437 million of its authorization under the education block grant. State education agencies (SEAs) administer Chapter 2 and are permitted to retain up to 20 percent of their allotment.

At least 80 percent of this allotment must be distributed to local education agencies (LEAs) based on relative enrollments in public and nonpublic schools, adjusted to provide higher per-pupil allocation to LEAs having the greatest number and percentage of children whose education costs are higher than average. The state also is responsible for defining "high-cost" students, which may include those from low-income families, economically depressed areas, or sparsely populated areas. But LEAs are under no obligation to use their funding for these high-cost students; local boards determine their own priorities and how to spend their allocations. The FY 1986 budget funded $529 million for Chapter 2, but $1.2 billion is needed to cope with the effects of inflation since FY 1980.

Teacher centers were included in the education block grant. Preliminary data of the U.S. Department of Education in fall 1982/winter 1983 revealed that only nine states had planned to expend funds for the purpose of teacher training and in-service staff development (Colorado, Delaware, Illinois, Indiana, Massachusetts, New York, Texas, Utah, and West Virginia). A National Education Association (NEA) survey also showed that most teacher centers were experiencing a reduction of programs and services as a result of the new funding pattern of Chapter 2. Many were forced to close down because state and local governments were unable to maintain the necessary funding requirements.[9] Yet teacher centers have proved effective for in-service education. Consistent with the intent of Congress (Higher Education Act of 1965), teacher centers provide in-service and curriculum development opportunities. Their programs and activities are largely designed and carried out by teachers themselves and directed toward the needs that they have identified.

The Emergency School Aid Act (ESSA)—Title IV, Elementary and Secondary Education Act of 1965—which assisted school districts in dealing with the difficult problems of desegregation, also was included in the education block grant. Many school districts have not been able to maintain desegregation programs because of the block grant and reduced funding. Those cities that received considerable desegregation assistance in the past seem to be suffering disproportionately. St. Louis, for example, has dropped from $7.8 million in aid to $750,000. Buffalo went from $6.7 million to $957,000.[10]

Along with decreased funding, administrative and application requirements have been substantially lessened. Although ESAA is still intended to meet the particular needs of low-income and disadvantaged children, the elimination of audit procedures and monitoring have led to a loss of accountability, and they may lead to lower quality services for our most needy youth. Further, findings show that the education block grant has resulted in a massive redistribution of federal funds from poorer school districts to wealthier ones and from public to private schools, since targeting features have been removed.[11]

Chapter 2 gives state and local school systems the advantage of flexibility in designing and implementing education programs. However, recent budget cuts have resulted in the elimination of effective programs in several critical areas formerly included under the individual grants. States and cities cannot pay the bill, so ultimately millions of children will lose the opportunity for quality education.

EDUCATION OF THE HANDICAPPED

The Education for All Handicapped Children Act (P.L. 94-142) was enacted to assist in expansion and improvement of programs and projects designed to provide a free appropriate public education to handicapped children at the preschool, elementary, and secondary levels.

According to a report from the U.S. Department of Education in FY 1982, a total of $1.1 billion benefited more than 4.2 million handicapped children through three formula grant programs (Handicapped State Grants, Preschool

Incentive Grants, and Title I State-Administered Programs).[12] However, a General Accounting Office (GAO) report concluded that only half or fewer of the eligible children have obtained the "free appropriate public education" called for in P.L. 94-142.[13] In 1982 the administration proposed substantial cost-saving changes in the regulations implementing P.L. 94-142, to restrict eligibility. Due to congressional and public pressure, however, it was forced to withdraw the regulations, pending further study.

The FY 1986 funding level was $1.4 billion for education of the handicapped. However, a doubling of funding would be needed to serve all those in need. Who will pick up the slack? Most states and cities certainly cannot afford to.

VOCATIONAL EDUCATION

The Vocational Education Act of 1963, as amended, provides assistance to states, LEAs, postsecondary institutions, public and private organizations, and individuals. This assistance is for: (1) improving vocational education programs; (2) developing personnel training programs and programs in new occupations; (3) providing part-time employment for vocational education students enrolled full time; and (4) supporting projects for research, curriculum development, demonstration, guidance and counseling services, personnel development, and sex equity.

These programs address a critical component of providing equal educational opportunity for youth and adults. Vocational education received $779 million in FY 1980 and has been steadily decreasing since then. The FY 1986 funding level was $839 million, though a funding level of at least $1 billion is needed to counter inflation, to provide the same level of 1980 services, and to enable states to reinstitute vocational training programs, for youth and unemployed adults, that have been closed down.

Vocational education has long been an institution managed at the local school level, but a strong federal role is required to coordinate national economic priorities and demographics. As the economy continues to shift to services and high tech industries, for example, national leadership is required to assess the trends, identify the job skills which will be needed, and cushion the transition in a fair and equitable manner (see Chapter 5). Leadership at the federal level also is required to direct the services and financial resources to those areas and individuals who could benefit most from vocational education.

Although it is not often readily admitted, we have an educational track system, by race and income class, that starts at an early age. For example, white children are nearly three times as likely as black children to be placed into gifted and talented special programs, while black children are more than three times as likely as white children to be placed into educable mentally retarded special programs.[14] By the time the children attend high school, 33 percent of black youth enter vocational tracks. By contrast, only 25 percent of white children are in vocational education, and instead are much more likely to move into academic tracks.[15]

Such track systems should be closely examined to eliminate racial and income class bias. However, while such reform is in progress, vocational education need not be a consolation prize for students who cannot perform at a higher level. If we commit our energies and resources to use vocational education to build job skills in high-demand, high-technology, and high-wage areas, and couple this commitment with a strong job placement emphasis, we can have a chance to achieve full employment in our nation. Such a commitment must involve the energies of the business, labor, government, and public school communities.

BILINGUAL EDUCATION

Under the Bilingual Education Act, enacted in 1968, programs are provided for the special educational needs of children of limited English proficiency to increase their educational capabilities.

A 1978 report by the U.S. Commission on Civil Rights found that 79 percent of elementary and secondary school students identified as speaking limited or no English were Hispanic, and 63 percent of these students were served by bilingual education programs.[16] Yet appropriations for bilingual education programs have steadily decreased from a peak of $192 million in FY 1980 to $173 million in FY 1986. Only 206,000 students are now receiving the benefits of the programs, which ought to serve an estimated non-English-speaking school population of 3.6 million. To maintain services at FY 1980 levels, $263 million is needed—a difference of over 50 percent from the FY 1986 appropriation.

Bilingual education programs are critical to achieve equal educational opportunity for children of limited English ability or those who are not fluent in English at all. Drastic budget cuts can only exacerbate the problem.

POSTSECONDARY EDUCATION

The U.S. Conference of Mayors believes that funding for federal programs supporting postsecondary education must be maintained; to do otherwise would be to devastate the quality of programs offered, severely reduce access to postsecondary education, damage equal educational opportunity, and limit the variety of programs currently available for choices by students of all ages. Mayors support funding of federal student financial assistance, both grants and low-interest loans, so that all students who so wish may have available the funds needed to pursue postsecondary education at either two- or four-year institutions.

The president's National Commission on Student Financial Assistance concluded that although the student aid delivery system is complex it functions quite effectively. Federal student aid programs have been remarkably successful in expanding educational opportunities for low-income, minority, and female students. Though the value of higher education assistance is widely recognized, the FY 1986 federal budget proposed major policy shifts which included $2.5 billion in cuts in student financial aid and other higher education programs. The impact of the administration's proposals would be severe for both poor and middle class students. It would deny access to a postsecondary education for millions of students who will simply be unable to afford it. New program requirements that increase the contributions from students would have the effect of advancing the economic segregation of the higher education system; that is, the poorer students would be limited in their choices to community colleges and trade and technical schools while students from economically well off families would attend more expensive and prestigious public and private universities. Expressed in terms of student impact, 1.7 million financial aid awards would be eliminated under the president's plan in academic year 1986-87, affecting 1 million students. Recognizing this impact, Congress retained 94 percent of Pell Grants and Guaranteed Student Loans funding for 1986.

A reduction in funding for student financial assistance would widen the already growing disparities. As seen in Figure 8-1, as recently as 1977 blacks and whites enrolled about equally in college. However, by 1982, 52 percent of white high school graduates enrolled in college, compared to just 36 percent of black high school graduates. Reductions in student financial assistance would adversely affect all low-income Americans, regardless of race, and of course especially affect minorities' chances to obtain higher education because of the lower income levels found among those population groups.

Knowledge is increasingly this nation's most important resource, and fortunately it is not only renewable but in infinite supply if properly cultivated. Moreover, a college education and employment are closely linked. As of March 1985 the unemployment rate among college graduates was 2.4 percent, compared to 6.9 percent for high school graduates and 11.4 percent for workers with an eighth-grade education or less.[17] Job stability, pay, and labor force participation rates are, of course, also much higher for college graduates. College is clearly a way for some to break out of the poverty cycle.

EQUAL ACCESS TO EDUCATIONAL OPPORTUNITIES

The Department of Education's Office for Civil Rights (OCR) is responsible for enforcing statutes that prohibit discrimination by recipients of federal education funds. When taken in conjunction with the administration's plans for other equal educational opportunity programs, it is clear that civil rights enforcement at the

Figure 8-1. Percent of High School Graduates Enrolled in College, 1977–1982.

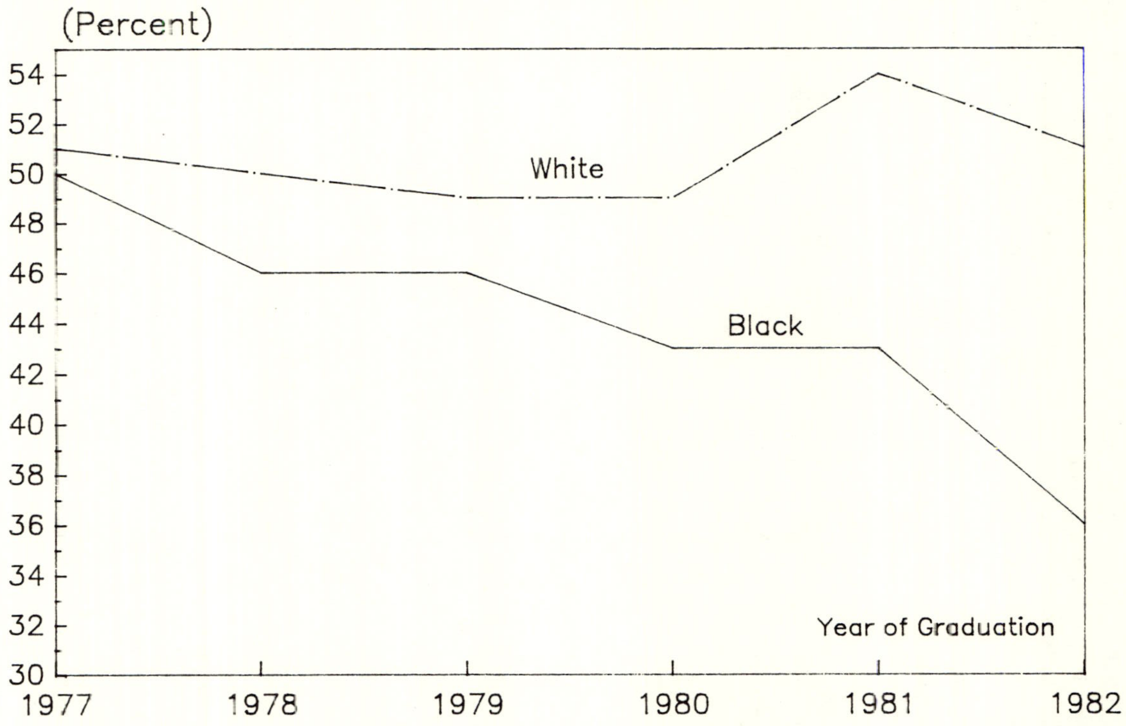

Source: U.S. Department of Labor, Bureau of Labor Statistics (BLS), *Monthly Labor Review* 106, no. 8 (Washington, D.C.: BLS, August 1983), Table 5.

Department of Education is steadily and dangerously declining. The Emergency School Aid Act, which authorizes grants to local districts for desegregation efforts, is now available only in block grants to states. Moreover, the Women's Educational Equity Act (WEEA), which funds projects for the promotion of equity in education programs and educational activities, has been substantially reduced. In FY 1980, $10 million went to WEEA. The FY 1986 appropriation was $6 million, unchanged since FY 1982. Nevertheless, the WEEA program has been very successful in improving the educational experience of women and girls.[18]

In addition to the disabling cuts in civil rights and equal educational opportunity programs, the Justice Department's Division of Civil Rights has not actively worked to ensure the civil rights of schoolchildren through school desegregation. Several civil rights laws apply directly to discrimination in education. They include Title VI of the Civil Rights Act of 1964, which prohibits discrimination by recipients of federal assistance on the basis of race, color, or national origin; Title IX of the Education Amendments of 1972, which prohibits sex discrimination by recipients of federal assistance; and Section 504 of the Rehabilitation Act of 1973, which prohibits discrimination of the handicapped by recipients of federal assistance.

Substantial changes in enforcement of these laws have been proposed over the last four years. Since compliance with the laws is critical to the achievement of equal education opportunity, any attempts to weaken enforcement efforts would threaten the attainment of this goal. Further, these laws apply to all federal education programs; therefore, lack of enforcement would defeat the specific objectives of these programs in serving the educational needs of children and adults.

A 1983 report of the U.S. Civil Rights Commission—*A Growing Crisis—Disadvantaged Women and Their Children*—cited a number of examples of the complexity of the problem.[19]

- The lower the level of educational attainment of the head of household, the higher the poverty rate. Female household heads run a higher risk of living in poverty than men at all levels of educational attainment. In 1981 the poverty rate for female heads with less than eight years of education was 49 percent, 28 percent for high school graduates, and 17 percent for those with one or more years of college.
- Inequitable access to vocational schools is a major barrier for minority women. Proportionately more minorities live in urban areas, but vocational facilities are located predominately in small cities and suburbs. Enforcement in vocational education of sex equity and civil rights provisions has been minimal, and equal opportunity for disadvantaged women in vocational education remains a goal yet to be achieved.

- Sex-segregated enrollment is found within various kinds of vocational education programs. Women tend to be in sales, office work, and health support programs; men are concentrated in agricultural, industrial, technical, and trade programs.
- Among three and four-year olds from poor families, about 13 percent of white and 22 percent of black children are enrolled in preschool programs. In wealthier families 24 percent of white and 30 percent of black children are in preschool programs.
- Elementary and high school students from poor families are more likely to be enrolled below their modal (the level normally attained by a child of a given age) grade than are nonpoor children.
- Federal programs such as Head Start, Follow Through, Title I compensatory education, and bilingual education have significantly improved the school performance of disadvantaged children.

FUTURE MATH AND SCIENCE NEEDS: IMPLICATIONS FOR TRAINING

As the wave of technological change has been cresting, we have been preoccupied with many other crises and priorities. At a time when the marketplace shows strong growth in job areas such as engineering, computer work, or electronics, all of which require math and science skills, the number and kinds of these courses in which U.S. students enroll have declined sharply. There has been an exodus of math and science teachers, driven from the classroom by low pay and readiness for the rewards of private sector employment. The national commitment to these priority areas has drastically decreased from what it was in the Sputnik era. Declining excellence has been the natural by-product of this process.

It is clear that only limited relief can be expected for these educational problems from state and local governments. Teacher layoffs, decreases in course offerings, school closings, and cutbacks for supplies are commonplace throughout the country. In most cases the economic recovery has not enabled jurisdictions to meet past levels of resource commitment, much less provide an infusion of resources for math, science, and other needs. Meeting the educational challenges of the future will be next to impossible if our schools are forced to choose between teachers and books, pencils, and paper.

Our present and future job skill requirements are not sufficiently linked with our public school systems. A lack of close coordination has its advantages, since we eschew the planned society. Nonetheless, the free market forces are now determining for us the crucial need for a math and science emphasis. Careful planning and an infusion of resources in our public schools would be a sound investment in retraining and extending our economic leadership in the world community. Within our nearly trillion-dollar federal budget, we already have the capacity in our Departments of Commerce, Labor, and Education, the Council of Economic Advisors, and elsewhere to examine job skill trends and insist upon certain curricula standards for math and science in our public schools.

A 1980 sampling of high school graduates in the United States revealed that (1) only one-third of those surveyed had taken three or more years of math; (2) though more than half of students in academic programs had taken at least three years of math, only a fifth of the general and vocational student graduates had three years of math; and (3) only 41 percent of academic students, 13 percent of general students, and 9 percent of vocational students completed three or more years of science courses.[20] The National Education Association (NEA) put the higher education math and science problem succinctly: "Science education at the postsecondary level is in trouble for a simple economic reason: trained people can earn much more in industry than they can teaching. Many teachers are leaving campus for other jobs and not enough young graduates are coming forward to replace them."[21]

While the needs are real, some of the high tech rhetoric has been overstated. The economy is shifting toward information services and high technology, but we are not becoming a nation of engineers. What our economy will demand is a well-educated workforce able to adapt quickly to the changing job descriptions created by our technology. Math and science education will be crucial but so too will be reading, logic, and computer literacy. The high tech revolution, more than anything else, will require a major reinvestment in public education and the "back to basics" movement. It will need to give particular emphasis to educational equity and access. As the computer age expands, the gap between educational "haves" and "have nots" will become increasingly meaningful. The stability of our existing social, political, and economic institutions will surely be threatened if the economic and social disparities are not closed. To assure continued progress of our institutions, students in poor urban school districts must have the same opportunity for access to high tech education as those in more affluent suburban school districts.

Recent congressional proposals for treatment of various aspects of the problem include: (1) promoting an assessment and plan for math and science needs; (2) focusing on providing low-cost loans to college students seeking math and science degrees who will enter teaching; (3) providing a tax credit for those who employ math and science teachers during the summer months; (4) establishing a block grant program to improve math and science teaching in elementary and secondary schools; (5) authorizing financial aid for continuing education for math and science teachers at the secondary level; and (6) establishing a teacher awards program for excellence in teaching. Dealing successfully with the demands of math, science, and technology will require a complete package with sufficient funding to get the job done. Planning, targeting, and directly funding local school districts are essential components of any effective national math and science policy.

To be most effective, local education agencies should play a major role in the planning and implementation of programs. Consequently, a funding mechanism that allows dollars to flow directly to local school districts would provide assurance of maximum achievement of program objectives. At the same time, these funds would assist certain local jurisdictions in absorbing any costs for programs and services that they cannot afford because of their long-standing diverse fiscal conditions vis-à-vis more affluent jurisdictions.

OTHER PROPOSED EDUCATIONAL CONCEPTS

Private schools are desirable to many parents who seek an opportunity for their children that they consider better than can be received in public schools. These parents have a right to exercise free choice, but the American taxpayer should not be expected to subsidize that choice. A federal or state subsidy encourages school systems that are segregated by income class, race, and perhaps by religion and sex. It leaves behind in public schools children from the lowest income class, whose parents cannot afford the difference between the subsidy and the private-school tuition. The goal of these subsidies is to widen educational disparities rather than to build a strong, unified nation.

Two such proposals, for educational vouchers and tuition tax credits, are discussed below. The concept of community education, which brings public schools and neighborhoods closer together, is also presented.

Educational Vouchers

Early in 1983 the Reagan administration proposed that states be given the option of using funds under Chapter 1 of the Educational Consolidation and Improvement Act of 1981 for vouchers. Funds would have continued to be allocated, under current law, to educationally disadvantaged children. The amount of the vouchers would have depended on the amount of Chapter 1 funds that each state or school district planned to spend on compensatory programs and on the number of students chosen to participate in those programs.

The proposal was based on the assumption that giving children from the nation's poorest families a voucher for approximately $500 would enable them to gain admission to a private school which would do a better job of meeting their educational needs than the schools they currently attend. There is little evidence to suggest that the lowest cost private schools would agree to accept the most economically disadvantaged children. Should annual tuition exceed $500, which is well below the average cost of most private schools, the very poorest families in the nation will be unable to finance the additional cost of tuition from their own resources. According to a U.S. Department of Education statement:

> This proposal is a simple measure intended to introduce more flexibility into the elementary and secondary education system of this country, and the approval of school officials, to give the parents of educationally disadvantaged children the same choices that other parents have in selecting a different and more educationally advantageous school program for their children. This Administration believes that parents of disadvantaged children should be able to exercise effective choice—through vouchers.[22]

Under the proposals, parents could use the vouchers to: (1) pay the cost of enrolling their children at private schools, (2) pay the cost of enrolling children at public schools outside their school district, or (3) enroll their children in compensatory education services made available by the home districts.

We should not assume, however, that an increase in parental choice will lead to an increase in student achievement. The choices parents make, according to Linda Darling-Hammond of Rand Corporation, are not solely based upon curriculum. The single most important factor in parents' decisionmaking is the school's proximity to the home. Under a voucher system, parents would probably choose schools by their ethnic and socioeconomic composition and, under a $500 voucher, by the lowest tuition cost. Consequently, vouchers would foster a system that would begin to resegregate schools by race and income level. Public schools would be at a loss, as public funds would be redirected to prefab, instant, bargain basement schools which would emerge across the land seeking voucher money.

Even if the parents of educationally disadvantaged children are aware of their choices, a voucher for approximately $500 would be insufficient to allow admission to any school based on parental choice, the national public school average per pupil expenditure being $2,917. Most critical is the fact that few private schools have programs designed to benefit students with special needs. The poor will be unable to meet the cost difference, and many private schools may not be able to give any financial assistance. Moreover, according to an official of the National PTA, "given the facts that disadvantaged students have been ill-served by many private schools, and few private schools have located in low-income areas to serve disadvantaged students, it is difficult to swallow the assumption that now low-income students will be better served by choice."[23]

Furthermore, no evidence is available to suggest that voucher programs would be successful in improving or providing educational opportunities and services in a more cost-efficient manner.

Finally, two other concerns have been raised concerning the voucher plan:

- Voucher payments on behalf of children attending private schools could raise questions about the constitutional principle of the separation of church and state.

- The voucher plan would result in an increase rather than a decrease in federal regulation because of the need to provide accountability, efficiency, and equity.

Tuition Tax Credits

Tuition tax credits are another means of financing private schools, with parents permitted an income tax credit to reimburse them for part of tuition paid. The administration proposed a tuition tax credit bill in the Ninety-seventh and the Ninety-eighth Congress which raised serious concerns, namely, that tax credits:

1. would be a drain on the federal treasury and would represent a lopsided federal commitment to private education over public;
2. would accelerate the "white flight" from public schools and legitimize openly racist institutions;
3. would foster poor public education by offering an alternative to those few lucky enough to get out of deficient schools; and
4. could breach the constitutional guarantees separating church and state.

Early supporters of tuition tax credits pointed out, with some validity, that many private schools were in financial trouble and that their very existence was threatened. This wavering status did indeed characterize many private schools ten to fifteen years ago, but recent statistics indicate a more positive outlook. Since the early 1970s private school enrollments have increased, as has the number of private schools. In 1971 there were 17,569 private schools. Today there are over 21,000. As these findings report, private schools are holding their own. The quality education they provide is not undermined by public schools, and certainly no bailout is required. On the other side of the ledger, however, public education continues to undergo an increasingly severe retrenchment, as indicated in previous sections of this chapter.

"The Effect of Tuition Tax Credits on Urban Schools" (August 1982), a study published by the Council of the Great City Schools and the American Association of School Administrators, included an examination of findings in sixty-five cities. Based on proposed administration education policies at the time, the study found that federal aid to public schools would be reduced, on the average, from $206 to only $105 per pupil within three years. Over that same period federal aid, through tuition tax credits to private school students in the same sixty-five cities studied, would soar from an average of $43 to $329 per pupil—an increase of 665 percent.

The NEA, which strongly opposed the administration's tuition tax credit proposal, examined tuition tax credits on the basis of public opinion, economic policy, education policy, and legal precedent.

> It is important to note that the general public does not favor tuition tax credits. In a Roper poll cited by Senator Ernest F. Hollings (D–SC), 64 percent of

Table 8-1. Votes for and against State Aid to Private Schools in Referenda, 1962-1982.

State	*Year*	*Vote against Aid*	*Vote for Aid*
New York	1967	72.5%	27.5%
Michigan	1970	57.0	43.0
Nebraska	1970	57.0	43.0
Maryland	1972	55.0	45.0
Oregon	1972	61.0	39.0
Idaho	1972	57.0	43.0
Maryland	1974	56.5	43.5
Washington	1975	60.5	39.5
Missouri	1976	60.0	40.0
Alaska	1976	54.0	46.0
Washington, D.C.	1981	88.0	12.0
Massachusetts	1982	62.0	38.0
California	1982	61.0	39.0

Source: National Education Association (NEA), *Tuition Tax Credits* (Washington, D.C.: NEA, June 1983), p. 3.

the public opposed tuition tax credits for non-public elementary and secondary education. And when state aid for non-public schools has been put before the voters in statewide referenda since 1967, they were overwhelmingly rejected.[24] (See Table 8-1.)

In early 1983 the National Coalition for Public Education produced more than 500,000 signatures opposing tuition tax credits as part of a nationwide petition drive. This effort was hailed by leaders in Congress as an important show of support of the public's "growing opposition to this ill-timed effort."[25]

If billions of dollars are allowed to be channeled to private education, the interest in public education will decline further. For those who remain trapped in an unsupported system, the future will be very bleak indeed. Because those left behind will not be a minority but a majority of inner city students, the future of our country could prove equally as bleak.

THE NEED FOR REVITALIZATION OF COMMUNITY EDUCATION

The U.S. Conference of Mayors has called consistently for the availability of more federal dollars to cities for community education programs. These dollars can be used to revitalize underutilized school facilities when appropriate for community purposes such as youth and senior citizens' recreation programs.

As tax dollars become scarce, mayors must find ways to save dollars and still maintain services. The community education process can be an effective vehicle for providing efficient services while conserving local resources. The process also provides a means for mayors to work with citizens, school officials, and local agencies to coordinate existing resources and merge expertise, thus avoiding costly duplication of effort and giving citizens an opportunity to contribute to the overall quality of community life.

According to the National Community Education Association, about 72 percent of all current taxpayers do not have children in school, and school enrollments are projected to increase only slightly this decade. By 1990 more than one-fourth of our population will be fifty or older.

Community education offers a process by which each community can identify its own problems and solutions, using its own unique resources. Community schools have these concepts in common:

- Local citizens are involved in planning and decisionmaking through community advisory councils.
- The schools are open to everyone in the community, for extended hours, and emphasize lifelong learning.
- The K-12 curriculum is enriched through use of community resources in and out of the classroom.
- Educational enrichment and recreation opportunities are offered to youngsters before and after school.
- Adults are offered numerous opportunities for social, cultural, recreational, and educational programs.
- Delivery of services from community agencies is coordinated to eliminate waste and duplication.

As indicated in the previous section on the education block grant, community education was consolidated under Chapter 2 of the Education and Consolidation Improvement Act of 1981. It has not been a priority item for states and local school districts which have tried to pick up the slack because of the reduction in federal funding. However, community education represents a vital link between the community and the success of public education. Clearly, there is an urgent need to renew the public interest in this essential component of society.

John J. Gunther, executive director of the U.S. Conference of Mayors, states:

> Our survival as a nation rests upon the viability of our cities, and the future of our cities and the public school system are inextricably bound together. Most community educators are well aware of this bond, and we are impressed by the support that local and state community educators have given to our efforts to improve urban education through city/school cooperation. . . .
>
> In any cooperative endeavor between cities and schools, there must be recognition that both are governmental entities accountable to the public and, as as result, both are influenced by politics. Let's remember that the schools

> belong to the people, not to the mayor, the superintendent, the board, the principals, or the teachers. The role of public officials, whatever their jurisdiction, is to serve the citizenry.[26]

Gunther's words are just as relevant and critical today as they were in 1979. Community education must take a leading role in the challenge for excellence in education if we intend to maintain the public system.

CONCLUSIONS

The facts presented here clearly demonstrate that education is on a destructive course in this country. Education is the cornerstone of our democracy and the foundation for our future. Nothing less than the highest priority should be given to this essential ingredient of our society.

Over the last five years, the federal government has reversed many of its efforts to maintain effectively the major programs and services needed to provide quality education and equal educational opportunity for all of the nation's children. The impact of these policy shifts is, in fact, a reflection of the "mediocrity" to which the report *A Nation At Risk* referred. *A Nation At Risk* was prepared through the U.S. Department of Education. Dwindling priority to education comes at a time when the demands of the future are rapidly increasing due to technological advances. It also comes at a time when cities are in the midst of long-standing economic difficulties that cannot be cured solely by economic recovery.

Some argue that the problems in education cannot be solved just by money. The mayors agree. But, it would be hypocritical to think that a reduced role for the federal government, particularly in the maintenance of federal education programs, would increase quality and equality in the nation's public schools. States and cities have sliced the financial pie down to the pan. A report of the U.S. Conference of Mayors states:

> Altogether, real federal grants to state and local governments, after accounting for inflation, would be reduced by 50 percent in budget authority over the five year period FY81 through FY86. In dollar terms, the decrease is over 24 percent. . . . The cuts in urban and low income programs stand in stark contrast to the treatment of defense spending, foreign military aid, interest on the public debt and other spending components of the budget. . . . State and local grants would decline from 11.7 percent in FY78 to 4.5 percent in FY88, while defense would escalate from 22.8 percent to 32.7 percent over the same period.[27]

To achieve quality education, all sectors must participate as partners, contributing the necessary resources to keep this vital element afloat. The mayors intend to participate actively in an all-out effort to protect the future of this country. We urge all partners in this endeavor to commit themselves to doing so also.

NOTES TO CHAPTER 8

1. Some examples are: National Commission on Excellence in Education (NCEE), *A Nation at Risk: The Imperative for Educational Reform* (Washington, D.C.: NCEE, 1983); Task Force on Education for Economic Growth, *Action for Excellence: A Comprehensive Plan to Improve Our Nation's Schools* (Washington, D.C.: Task Force on Education for Economic Growth, 1983); Twentieth Century Fund, *Making the Grade: Report of the Twentieth Century Fund Task Force on Federal Elementary and Secondary Education Policy* (New York: Twentieth Century Fund, 1983); John I. Goodlad, *A Place Called School: Prospects for the Future* (New York: McGraw-Hill, 1983); and Ernest L. Boyer, *High School: A Report on Secondary Education in America* (New York: Harper & Row, 1983).
2. Council of Great City Schools, "Federal Education Budget Policy, 1980–84: Effects on the Great City Schools" (Washington, D.C.: Council of Great City Schools, October 1984), p. 2.
3. National Education Association, statement on the Education Budget for FY 1984 before the Committee on the Budget, U.S. House of Representatives, February 24, 1983, p. 8, and statement on the FY 1986 budget, March 12, 1985.
4. National Education Association, statement on the Education Budget for FY 1984, p. 8.
5. Ibid.
6. Ibid.
7. Children's Defense Fund (CDF), *Black and White Children in America: Key Facts* (Washington, D.C.: CDF, 1985), p. 99, calculated from Bureau of Census, *Current Population Reports*, Series P–60, No. 144, 1984, Table 13.
8. Ibid., p. 100, calculated from *Current Population Reports*, Table 8.
9. National Education Association, Testimony on the Education Consolidation and Improvement Act of 1981, before the Subcommittee on Intergovernmental Relations and Human Resources, Committee on Government Operations, U.S. House of Representatives, September 20, 1983, p. 6.
10. The Council of the Great City Schools, Testimony on the Department of Education's Implementation of the Chapter 2 Block Grants, before the Subcommittee on Intergovernmental Relations and Human Resources, Committee on Government Operations, U.S. House of Representatives, September 20, 1983, p. 5.
11. Ibid., p. 13.
12. U.S. Department of Education (DOE), *Annual Report to Congress* (Washington, D.C.: DOE, 1983), pp. 1–3.

13. General Accounting Office (GAO), *Disparities Still Exist in Who Gets Special Education* (Washington, D.C.: GAO, 1984), p. 1.
14. Children's Defense Fund, p. 93.
15. Ibid., p. 94.
16. U.S. Commission on Civil Rights, *A Growing Crisis: Disadvantaged Women and Their Children*, Clearinghouse Publication 78 (Washington, D.C.: U.S. Commission on Civil Rights, May 1983), pp. 45–46.
17. U.S. Department of Labor, Bureau of Labor Statistics (BLS), News Release 85–355 (Washington, D.C.: BLS, September 2, 1985), Table 3.
18. Coalition on Women and the Budget, "Inequality of Sacrifice: The Impact of the Reagan Budget on Women" (Washington, D.C.: Coalition on Women and the Budget, March 1983), pp. 29–31.
19. U.S. Commission on Civil Rights, p. 64.
20. National Education Association, *American Defense Education Act* (Washington, D.C.: National Education Association, February 1983), p. 10.
21. Ibid., p. 11.
22. U.S. Department of Education, Press Release, May 17, 1983, p. 1.
23. National Coalition for Public Education, Testimony on Education Vouchers and ECIA, Chapter 1, before the House Subcommittee on Elementary, Secondary and Vocational Education, April 6, 1983, p. 7.
24. National Education Association, *Tuition Tax Credits* (Washington, D.C.: National Education Association, June 1983), p. 3.
25. Readers interested in pursuing this subject further should contact the National Community Education Association, Alexandria, Virg. (703 683–6232.
26. John J. Gunther, "Why Community Education Appeals to Mayors," *Community Education Journal*, Vol. 6, no. 5 (June 1979): p. 6.
27. U.S. Conference of Mayors (USCM), *The Federal Budget and the Cities* (Washington, D.C.: USCM, February 1985), p. iii.

9 HUMAN SERVICES AS A BASIS FOR SELF-SUFFICIENCY

Mayors fully agree with many national policymakers that the costs of federal government social service programs can and should be reduced over time as economic opportunities are built. With job training, affirmative action, and economic development, the vitality of urban centers can be restored so that the need for social services can be minimized among those who are physically and emotionally able to join the economic mainstream.

Nonetheless, it should be recognized that to remove social services in the absence of fruitful alternatives does nothing but abandon those in dire need. Moreover, many social services are required today to prepare citizens for a life of economic independence, reducing future government costs.

There are two major flaws in this nation's human services system: It is not funded at a level anywhere near sufficient to meet the need, and it is so complex and fragmented that it is not possible to make the best use of those resources that are available. A fifty-five-city survey conducted by the Conference of Mayors in October 1982 showed that in not one of the human service areas examined was over 50 percent of the eligible population served in FY 1981 or FY 1982. Social service programs reached only 7 percent of the eligible population in FY 1982; child day care served 16 percent; senior services were delivered to 15 percent.

Human service programs are supported by a wide variety of federal, state, and local public and private funding sources. They are provided by a similarly wide range of agencies. Often there is little coordination between the planning for and funding of services that benefit the residents of a given community. For example, a city may use a portion of its Community Development Block Grant allocation to support child day care in a particular neighborhood. The state may use a portion of its Social Services Block Grant to support day care in the same neighborhood. Due to the efforts of city human services officials and others, it is possible that those two funding services and programs are coordinated, but more often than not they are not coordinated. Providing social service funds directly to local governments at an adequate funding level could go a long way toward resolving these difficulties.

TYPES OF SERVICES

"Human services" or "social services" can involve a wide variety of assistance to those in need, including the disoriented older widow, the pregnant teenager, the severely handicapped adult, the abused child, the battered spouse.

It was once routinely assumed that poverty and all of its consequences would consistently dwindle over the years, capturing fewer and fewer families, and at some point society would gain control over poverty. However, the 1984 poverty rate of 14.4 percent is considerably higher than the rate of a decade previously, when the rate was 11.2 percent in 1974 (see Chapters 2, 6, and 11). One in every five urban residents lives in poverty. More than 67 percent of all minority children in female-headed households live in poverty—and the number of those households has increased by 50 percent in the last ten years. Moreover, the nation's economic recovery often does not reach those most in need; our population living in poverty is far greater in numbers today than before the last recession began.

In contrast to such payments and benefits as Aid to Families with Dependent Children (AFDC), Medicaid, Supplementary Security Income (SSI), and food stamps, social services are often intended to reduce dependency on public assistance programs; prevent the continuation of family problems; defer or prevent costly institutionalization; and generally help individuals, families, and communities cope with the varied effects of poverty. Thus, homecare, transportation, homemaker, meals-on-wheels, and other services can keep people in their homes and communities rather than in publicly subsidized institutions at a far greater cost. Adolescent pregnancy prevention and family planning can lead to reduction in welfare and health service expenditures.[1] Similarly, day care for children can free a parent to obtain work or job training. Foster care enables placement of a child in a home setting. Adoption services provide the maximum feasible stability for a child, preventing a host of social problems later. Counseling and protection in child abuse cases can stop abusive treatment and help prevent in the child the development of a variety of social maladies resulting from mistreatment. Other social services include assistance to drug and alcohol abusers, boarding home services, emergency services, various health- and housing-related services, independent living for the handicapped, multiservice programs for the aged, social services in corrections institutions, community planning, and many others.

RECENT DEVELOPMENTS IN SOCIAL SERVICES

The modern era of social services likely can be marked by passage of the Public Welfare Amendments of 1962, which provided for federal cost sharing, at a rate of 75 percent, for social services that reduced or prevented dependency on welfare. Following the urban rebellions, which awoke many to the need to break the poverty cycle, states began to draw heavily on federal social services assistance. Between 1967 and 1971 federal social services expenditures grew from \$242 to \$776 million.[2]

By 1972 Congress and the executive branch decided to place limits on the growth of social services spending, establishing a national ceiling of \$2.5 billion. In 1975 a social services block grant program was created, under Title XX of the Social Security Act, giving wide latitude to states in designing social services programs. Funding under Title XX reached its peak at \$3.1 billion in fiscal 1979.

The Omnibus Budget Reconciliation Act of 1981 renamed Title XX the Social Services Block Grant (SSBG) and made several key changes. These included elimination of state matching requirements and modifications in reporting requirements, enabling states to target services not just to AFDC and SSI recipients and to liberalize income eligibility for services if they like. Still greater flexibility was granted in the uses of funds, and, most importantly, federal funding was reduced by nearly \$600 million or 20 percent.

The FY 1986 funding level of \$2.7 billion falls far short of pre-SSBG levels, especially when inflation is taken into account. Considering that the fiscal 1979 social services (Title XX) funding level was \$3.1 billion, in today's dollars that funding level would actually be \$4.8 billion, more than \$2 billion a year greater than present social services funding.

IMPACT OF SOCIAL SERVICES REDUCTIONS

It likely is impossible to measure the full impact of these significant federal funding reductions. As proponents of the reductions like to say, the evidence of the impact is mostly "anecdotal." In millions of individual cases, the fortunate have turned to families and friends for help, others to churches and charities, and others have lived in states and cities that compensated for federal funding declines. Of course, in many other cases, people have had nowhere to turn, leading to countless individual tragedies, broken families, institutionalization when community services fall apart, welfare dependency, in some cases criminal activity, and growing incidences of poverty.

Recent studies indicate that many states are making up for much of the recent loss in federal funds. In fact, in an Urban Institute study of eighteen states, eleven were able to maintain social services funding in 1983 at 1981 (Title XX) levels and even "overreplace" lost dollars in most cases.[3] In nine of the eighteen states increased state spending for social services was the primary strategy to cope with the federal deemphasis; four states primarily relied on the strategy of shifting funds into social services from other federal sources (chiefly from the Low Income Home Energy Assistance Grant), and three states (Michigan, Minnesota, and New York) primarily required greater local contributions. It is encouraging that states and localities value social services to those in need so highly that they are making the financial sacrifices to maintain services. Several concerns should be considered, however.

First, as the National Association of State Budget Officers points out, states are increasing taxes with far greater frequency than in previous years, at least in part to compensate for federal funding losses. In 1983, nineteen states enacted permanent tax increases, mostly in the major tax categories. In 1984, twenty-four states enacted permanent tax increases, twenty-one states projecting permanent increases for 1985.[4] Many of the states with continuing economic difficulty and heavy social service burdens already have higher than average tax rates, which hinder their ability to compete for economic development.

The purpose of federal social service funding is to equalize the poverty burdens among all the state and local governments, the relatively affluent and the economically distressed alike. By reverting to more of a state-funded approach, jurisdictions with relatively few impoverished citizens are extending their competitive advantages; other states and localities are becoming increasingly unable to cope with their disproportionately high levels of poverty and all of the side effects.

Second, while some states are able to cope for the time being with reduced federal social services spending, other states clearly are not. In the aforementioned Urban Institute study, seven of the eighteen states surveyed were not able to keep pace. On a fifty-state basis, by extrapolation, perhaps nineteen states have suffered social services cutbacks for their citizenry. Several more would be added if one considered the effects of inflation from FY 1981 to FY 1983 in the Urban Institute study, in which case ten of the eighteen surveyed lost funds in inflation-adjusted dollars. In fact, considering the federal social services cutbacks stretching back to 1978, *all* states have lost considerable support for their social services networks.

The Urban Institute survey demonstrates that some states are reducing social services more than others. One might be tempted to applaud this variation as a result of democratic choice among the states, but it should be acknowledged that low-income citizens, as an historically powerless minority, are not as able to participate in the shaping of state decisions as is, for example, the large voting block of affluent suburbanites.

The low-income citizen of Boston likely had as little to do with Massachusetts' decision to increase state social services spending as that of St. Louis had with Missouri's decision not to replace lost federal dollars. Equity criteria, which can only be accommodated on a national scale, dictate that the St. Louis citizen should have as much chance as the Boston citizen to receive an essential social service.

A recent National Governors' Association (NGA) survey confirms the findings of the Urban Institute. Although most states are able to maintain social services, several of the thirty-eight states responding to the survey reported declines in major service areas: day care for children (eleven states), services to alcoholic/drug dependent persons (six states), adults in day care (ten states), recipients of meals-on-wheels (eight states), and so forth.

Third, the mix of services is changing as federal dollars diminish. The trend is toward continuing social services funding that responds to life-threatening situations. High priority is assigned to protective services (e.g., for abused children and battered spouses) and for adoption/foster services. Lower priority is assigned to day care, for example, since it is not considered by many states an immediate "crisis" to ensure that a parent can work or obtain job training.[6] Although it may be too early to discern a lasting trend, it appears that longer term needs and benefits are being sacrificed to ensure that emergency needs are provided for. This trend may adversely affect longer term social services system costs.

Fourth, temporary fiscal phenomena have enabled some states to maintain social services. As the NGA points out, many states received a one-time-only "additional" social service payment when Title XX was transferred to the Social Services Block Grant; Title XX reserves were carried forward at the same time the annual lump-sum SSBG payment was received. The NGA also noted that funds were shifted out of the low-income energy assistance block grant and into the SSBG in those states that had unusually warm winters.[7]

In summary, many states are preserving the social services network as best as they can, although other states are not, and the future is uncertain. Only the federal government can ensure full and equitable delivery of social services.

CHILD CARE

The supply of child care lags so far behind the demand that more than one in six U.S. children thirteen years older and under, including many preschoolers, may be going without care. The need for infant care is steadily climbing, as is the demand for afterschool programs so that young children are not left waiting up to four hours a day in empty homes, in school yards, or on neighborhood streets while parents work. The labor force participation of mothers with children has increased dramatically in the last forty years. Only 19 percent of women with children under age eighteen were in the labor force in 1947; in contrast, 60 percent of such women were employed in 1982—a threefold increase in about thirty-five years. As more and more parents of young children work, child care needs will become an even greater problem.[8]

- Almost 46 percent of mothers with children under age three are in the labor force.
- Almost 57 percent of mothers with children ages three to five are in the labor force.
- By 1990 at least half of all preschool children—11.5 million—will have mothers in the labor force, as will about 60 percent—17.2 million—of all school-age children.

Many mothers work because of economic necessity. Two-thirds of women in the workforce are either sole providers for their children or have husbands who earn less than $15,000 a year. Over one-third of single-parent working families, most of them headed by women, live below the poverty level.

Today one in five children is living in a one-parent family—a figure that is expected to grow to one in four by 1990. Moreover, 44 percent of all black children live with their mothers only. It is startling to realize that 75 percent of all impoverished black children in 1984 lived in female-headed households.[9]

Lack of affordable child care is a major factor in keeping women and children in poverty. The U.S. Commission on Civil Rights notes that the inability to locate affordable child care restricts not only women's employment and training opportunities but also their ability to participate in federally supported education programs. A recent Census Bureau survey found that 45 percent of single mothers who are not in the labor force would work if child care were available at a reasonable cost. The same is true for 36 percent of all mothers (whether in a single- or two-parent household) with family incomes under $15,000.

The United States for years has had a patchwork child care system to help meet the needs of lower income families. Since 1981 it has been rapidly unraveling. In FY 1982 the Title XX Social Services Block Grant, the largest source of direct support for child care, had its funding reduced from $3 billion to $2.4 billion, a 20 percent cut. The Child Care Food Program was cut by 30 percent. The amount of child care costs for which families can be compensated under the AFDC program was limited further.

Twenty-five states spent less for child care in 1984 than they did in 1981, despite increased need and inflation. Twenty-seven states served fewer children than they did in 1981. Therefore, at least half the states are not compensating for the loss of federal funds with sufficient resources of their own to maintain service levels. A Children's Defense Fund report provides a state-by-state analysis of the deficiencies in child care services. For example, in California there are an estimated 620,000 to 815,000 latchkey children—young children who unlock their homes' doors and care for themselves after school. New Mexico estimates they are meeting just 7 percent of the child care needs. More than half the counties in Georgia have no Title XX funds. In Massachusetts only about a third of families are able to find satisfactory, affordable child care. Cuyahoga County, Ohio is able to meet 53 percent of the need. These examples are echoed around the nation.[10]

The results of the cutbacks in child care are painful for women who are struggling to improve their family's situation through employment or training. Children are being left alone or have been switched to less familiar and often less supportive child care arrangements. Older children stay home from school to care for younger siblings.

ANTIPOVERTY PROGRAMS

At the same time that the national poverty rate today is as high as it was in the late 1960s, and unemployment continues at double-digit levels in many communities (because of structural, not cyclical problems), it is ironic that efforts continue to end the community action program by eliminating the Community Services Block Grant (CSBG). Mayors have supported economic opportunity programs for at least twenty years and have consistently supported an all-out attack on the multiple causes of poverty in the United States by all levels of government and with a national commitment commensurate with the problem. Low-income urban residents need community service programs now—certainly as much as they did before.

The CSBG was established in fiscal 1982, providing for funding and control of community action (antipoverty) agencies through state governments and providing states with administrative funds to distribute funds to and monitor the community action agencies (CAAs).

Funding for antipoverty agencies has diminished significantly in recent times. For example, in FY 1980 funding was at $561 million, whereas in FY 1986 it was just $370 million. This is a reduction of $191 million or, in terms of inflation-adjusted dollars, a reduction of 50 percent in six years. The president proposed termination of CSBG in 1986; however, Congress retained the program with full funding.

Unlike the case with the Social Services Block Grant, states are replacing almost none of the reduced federal antipoverty program dollars. Prior to the establishment of the CSBG, states had virtually no programmatic or financial relationship with these antipoverty programs; they did not invest dollars or staff into them. This historical independence from state government, the lack of a long-standing partnership, has hindered CAA funding since the CAAs were brought under state control.[11]

Another recent trend has been to direct funds away from large-city CAAs and more toward rural CAAs. The large-city CAAs had received a disproportionately heavy share of the antipoverty funding, in part because the higher funding levels were needed to reach concentrations of heavy poverty. Now funding is more spread out in the states and is being extended to areas that heretofore had received no antipoverty program funds.[12] This dilution of funds, from a large-city mayor's perspective, hinders antipoverty service delivery in precisely those areas that have the greatest need.

The services provided by CAAs in low-income communities are often among the most critical. A local CAA may serve as the umbrella agency for a Head Start agency, a weatherization program, and an emergency fuel program. It can serve as an Area Agency on Aging (AAA) or be designated by the AAA to provide services to the elderly. The CAAs provide emergency supplies and services, such as energy, food, clothing and shelter assistance, disaster relief and crisis loans, food pantries, home-delivered meals, food vouchers, and nutrition assistance to mothers and children.[13] The CAAs serve as advocates for low-income people to improve employment, housing, community development, and sanitary conditifons. They link citizens served by CAAs to existing service programs or fill in the service gaps themselves when those programs do not reach these often forgotten, lowest of income areas. For example, they can provide services such as dental care when no such program exists elsewhere. These services should not be considered expendable.

HEAD START

Project Head Start was launched in 1965 to help economically disadvantaged three to five year olds achieve their potential. Head Start offers a unique approach, emphasizing strong parental involvement, comprehensive service delivery, and strong community support.

Ninety percent of Head Start families live below the poverty level. In Newark, for example, the average income of Head Start families is $5,724. Two-thirds of participants are minorities; 12.5 percent are handicapped.[14]

Head Start is widely recognized as one of the federal government's most effective programs. A twenty-year study of preschool program participants and graduates found that two years of preschool programs provide economic benefits that outweigh costs by seven to one. Preschool graudates are less likely to be classified as retarded or otherwise in need of special education. The children do better on school achievement tests; they are more likely to graduate from high school and more likely to receive additional vocational or academic training after high school. As adults, they are more likely to be employed and satisfied with their jobs. The jobs are higher paying than jobs obtained by non-program attendees. Moreover, the attendees are more likely to be self-supporting in adulthood—that is, less likely to be public assistance, Medicaid, and food stamp recipients. They are also less likely to become teen parents or involved in criminal activity.[15]

Despite its remarkable achievements, Head Start is funded at a level to reach only 18 percent of those who are eligible—about 442,000 children out of nearly 2 million eligible. Each year that the program funds are frozen at the previous year's level risks dropping about 19,000 children from Head Start.

HUMAN SERVICES RECOMMENDATIONS

Mayors offer several recommendations to provide for adequate social services funding, greater child care services, a thriving head start program, increased participation by local government in social services delivery, and full funding for community action programs.

Social Services Funding Should Be Restored

To combat the federal deficit, mayors proposed a budget freeze for at least a year in all non-means-tested programs. Funding levels for the post-budget-freeze period should be examined to ensure that growing demand for services can be met as best as possible. Funds for the block grants were cut 20 percent in FY 1982. Although there have been modest increases since then, funding has not reached pre-SSBG levels. Restoration of funds to the level of several years ago would make positive contributions to urban programs.

Most Americans have a complex network of support services at their disposal: day care for their children, a variety of good preschool learning environments, a nursing home for a family member, a therapist or counselor in event of family emergency, Blue Cross/Blue Shield, and so forth. Some minimal approximation of this network for the lower income is necessary. This need has been particularly felt in recent years when disposable incomes of the low income are declining significantly while affluent families are benefiting to such a great extent from federal tax and expenditure policies (see Chapter 2).

The Role of Local Government Should Be Increased

Funds provided to the states through the Social Services Block Grant should be passed through to local governments that wish to receive them, if the locality is of sufficient size and has a demonstrated service delivery capacity. Local government officials should be involved in the state planning and resource allocation process so that locally identified needs can be taken into account. Preferably, federal social services dollars should be provided directly to local governments so that they can be better targeted to areas of special need and more simply administered. Cities have proved themselves over time to be the most equitable of jurisdictions in reaching people who have the greatest need.

Child Care Funding Should Be Adequate

To respond to the growing demand for child care as increasing numbers of parents of young children work, quality child care should be available on a fee-for-service basis for those able to pay, and sliding fee subsidies should be awarded when the costs of care preclude employment or result in arrangements that have a deleterious effect upon the welfare of children. This should be accomplished through adequate funding of both institutional and family day care systems and of components that support such systems, such as child care information and federal training for child care workers. Attention should be given to adequate health and safety standards for child care centers.

The Children's Defense Fund supports a $500 million earmark for child care, to be added to the Social Services Block Grant. In view of the magnitude of need to involve more women in the workforce to break the cycle of poverty and dependency for them, their families, and future generations, this is a reasonable proposal.

An additional $500 million would increase child care funding by about 80 percent from the current level of $623 million. There are about 2 million children under six years old with working mothers in families where the income is $12,000 or less. There are 1.1 to 1.2 million children under six with working mothers in families having incomes below the poverty level. The $500 million earmark would lift the total number of children served to a minimum of 850,000, so that a sizable portion of the need would be met. Moreover, this single action would dramatically increase equal employment opportunities for women, reduce welfare dependency, and stimulate the national economy. These net benefits would considerably outweigh the costs.

Community Action Programs Should Be Maintained

To maintain the mayors' commitment to eliminating poverty in this nation, community action programs should be supported at an adequate funding level, funds being provided directly by the federal government to local agencies. Substantial cuts have been made in these programs over the last several years, and the system has been changed to one of block grants to the states. These decisions should be reversed. If there are federal concerns with the structure, activities, and effectiveness of these antipoverty programs, then the program should be thoroughly analyzed and improved rather than abandoned.

Head Start Programs Should Reach More Children

Currently, Head Start programs reach only 18 percent of eligible children. To reach 30 percent by 1990, a $200-million-per-year increase in Head Start funding over a five-year period would be needed, thereby increasing Head Start funding from $1.1 billion to $2.1 billion a year.

NOTES TO CHAPTER 9

1. Michael F. Gutowski and Jeffery J. Koshel, "Social Services," *The Reagan Experiment* (Washington, D.C.: Urban Institute Press, 1982), p. 313.
2. Ibid., p. 309.
3. Eugene C. Durman et al., "Block Grants and the New Federalism: The Second Year Experience," draft report of February 6, 1984 (Washington, D.C.: The Urban Institute), p. 6.
4. Phone conversation with National Association of State Budget Officers, Dr. J. Miller, May 17, 1984; data from unpublished report.
5. National Governors' Association, "Block Grant Implementation," working draft, May 1984, Table 5.
6. Durman; and National Governors' Association. The studies show similar trends in the mix of social services.
7. National Governors' Association, pp. 12–14.
8. These data and child care data that follow in this chapter are derived from an unpublished paper on this subject prepared for the Mayors' Committee for a National Urban Policy by the Children's Defense Fund, and from Children's Defense Fund (CDF), *A Children's Defense Budget* (Washington, D.C.: CDF, 1985), pp. 203–14.
9. Computed from U.S. Census Bureau, *Money Income and Poverty Status of Families and Persons in the United States: 1984*, Current Population Reports, Series P–60, No. 149 (Washington, D.C.: U.S. Government Printing Office, 1985), pp. 20–21.
10. Helen Blank, Children's Defense Fund, *Child Care: The States' Response* (Washington, D.C.: CDF, 1984), pp. 4, 10–11; and updated in Children's Defense Fund, *A Children's Defense Budget*, p. 207.
11. Durman, pp. 35, 38.
12. Ibid., pp. 40, 45.
13. National Governors' Association, pp. 30–35.
14. Children's Defense Fund, p. 215.
15. Ibid., p. 216.

10 FOOD AND NUTRITION
The Most Elemental of Government Gestures

The nation's mayors see clear, unmistakable evidence of hunger in their cities every day. Tens of thousands of people do not line up for cheese in the cold of winter or the heat of summer unless they have no alternative, unless they need food and do not have the money to buy it. Growing numbers of people, including many families with children, do not come to soup kitchens unless they must. Up to 20 million Americans go hungry a minimum of two days a month, millions going hungry several days each month.[1]

Mayors recommend that the primary federal food assistance programs—food stamps, child nutrition, and WIC (supplemental food program for Women, Infants and Children)—should be supported as entitlement programs. The nation should ensure that all citizens eligible for and in need of food assitance provided by these programs can receive it. Mayors also offer revisions to food stamp programs, support for child nutrition programs, and support for emergency food programs. These recommendations will be detailed below.

HUNGER AND MALNUTRITION IN AMERICA'S CITIES

The Conference of Mayors has worked diligently in recent years to document the problems faced by people in cities and to develop solutions to those problems. In October 1982 the Conference conducted a survey on the combined impact of federal budget cuts, economic conditions, and high unemployment on urban residents. It found that in none of the human service areas examined was even 50 percent of the eligible population being served for the fifty-five cities surveyed. City officials estimated that only 43 percent of the emergency service needs of citizens were being met for such basics as shelter, food, and emergency medical help.[2]

In June 1983 the Conference developed case studies on hunger in eight cities across the nation. Despite differing local economic conditions and rates of unemployment, all of the cities examined had experienced a recent dramatic increase in the demand for emergency food assistance, and only three of the eight cities were able to serve all of those in need of food assistance. Two of those cities were just barely able to meet needs.

In August 1983 the Conference of Mayors convened a meeting of mayors; other key city officials; representatives of private corporations involved in food processing, packaging, and distribution; and representatives of nonprofit organizations, both national groups and those involved directly in service delivery in cities. The U.S. Department of Agriculture (USDA) was represented, as was the Congress. The purpose of the meeting was to identify the actions that can be taken by all of us working together to respond to the increasing demand for emergency food assistance in cities.

A number of efforts that are currently underway in cities or could be developed to respond to the problems were discussed. But it was clear that the magnitude of the problem was so great that there was no way people in cities, even with the public and private sectors working together, could respond to the problems using the resources available to them. Only the federal government has the resources to do that.

To encourage further local programs, in October 1983 the Conference published "Responses to Urban Hunger," which contains information on public-private efforts to provide emergency food assistance in our cities.[3] It includes descriptions of emergency food hotlines, food banks, local coalitions, municipal food policies, surplus food commodities distribution, urban gardening, and other local efforts.

That report shows, however, that although pleased with the results of their efforts, the city officials and others involved in food distribution programs have a number of serious concerns that are shared by other officials in cities across the country. They point out, for example, that although local efforts have provided temporary relief to numerous city residents, they often do not serve a sufficiently high proportion of people in need in a systematic way. In addition, by investing such a significant portion of their resources in emergency feeding programs, many local agencies have had to cut back on other essential services. The problem of hunger is indeed continuing to grow in cities, despite a general national economic recovery. And the gap between the demand for assistance and local public and private resources available to meet the demand continues to widen.

It is important to note that there is a connection between hunger and poverty, and the poverty rate as of 1984 was 14.4 percent, compared to 11.2 percent ten years earlier. Over the course of those ten years, the number of persons living in poverty increased by 10.3 million, a 44 percent increase—quadruple the rate of the general population increase in the United States during the same years. Only people with inadequate incomes are likely to find themselves unable to purchase enough food to prevent hunger. The antipoverty programs that are presently in place do not reach all people in need and do not provide benefit levels high enough to allow those they do reach to escape poverty.

In no state does the combination of Aid to Families with Dependent Children (AFDC) and food stamp benefits come up to the federal poverty line. In half of the states two-parent households are ineligible for AFDC regardless of employment status or income level. In no state is a single person who is not elderly or disabled eligible for cash federal welfare payments. There is, in fact, not a "safety net" to keep all of our citizens from experiencing poverty and lack of basic necessities.

Critics of the welfare system contend that the poverty count is overstated by failure to include in-kind benefits such as food stamps, housing assistance, and medical assistance. Inclusion of such payments and subsequent lowering of the poverty count would only provide a false sense of accomplishment as to how well we as a country are meeting the needs of our citizens.

Such playing with statistics would in no way change the plight of the poor; it would only deny their existence. To count housing and medical assistance would be particularly misleading. Without medical assistance most low-income people would be forced to go without needed medical treatment. Even today there are numerous cases in which pregnant women arrive in the hospital for delivery having received no prenatal care. Government programs that allow people to take care of their health are not comparable to disposable income.

Without housing assistance poor families would not have the resources to provide minimal housing for themselves. Rather, they would be compelled to live in substandard conditions, seeking abandoned, unheated buildings or crowding several families into small quarters. To count the value of decent, subsidized housing as disposable income would imply that poor families have more available resources to meet other basic necessities than is actually the case.

Despite the above-mentioned deficiencies in antipoverty programs, there are positive factors in food assistance programs. The federal food assistance programs were designed for the expressed purpose of combating hunger and poor nutrition among the residents of our country. Until the past three years these programs had been fairly successful in accomplishing their mission. Unfortunately, that is no longer the case. Excessive budget cuts in federal food programs were enacted, purportedly, to target services to the "truly needy" and to eliminate waste, fraud, and abuse. In fact, they have made the programs so restrictive that large numbers of poor people are no longer able to participate. Benefit levels are so inadequate that many poor families are forced to choose between eating and heating their homes or eating and seeking medical care, or the adults must go without food so that children may eat.

The hardships caused by deep cuts in federal food programs were exacerbated by simultaneous cuts in other federal assistance programs designed to help low-income persons: AFDC, low-income energy assistance, and subsidized housing programs, to name a few. At the same time, the nation suffered through a harsh recession. Many families facing unemployment, often for the first time, found that, although they could not provide for their families' needs once their unemployment benefits were depleted, they were not eligible for government assistance.

Additionally, the deinstitutionalization of the mentally ill—that is, their discharge from hospitals and placement in the community—along with insufficient services for them in the community, have exacerbated the problems of homelessness and hunger.

Many in the private sector have undertaken a Herculean effort in trying to answer the nutritional needs of families and individuals who are unable to provide for themselves. A tremendous number of new soup kitchens and food pantries have opened their doors in the past three years. The lines at these emergency centers have multiplied and, in most cases, the doors have had to close because food supplies had been depleted.

The private sector simply does not have the resources or the orientation to replace the billions of dollars that have been cut from federal assistance programs. Only the public sector can ensure that the basic needs of its citizenry are met.

Despite the economic recovery, which seems targeted particularly to suburbs and other areas that never experienced severe depressionlike conditions, food assistance problems continue to increase. Ninety-five percent of cities surveyed in 1984 by the U.S. Conference of Mayors' Task Force on Joblessness and Hunger reported that the demand for food assistance increased during 1983 over 1982 levels. The average increase was 71 percent, ranging from 20 percent in Denver to 250 percent in Seattle. In fact, Seattle reports a sixfold increase in demand for emergency food since 1980. San Antonio distributed 1 million pounds of food in 1982 and over twice that amount, 2.3 million pounds, in 1983. Holy Apostle's Church in New York City served 25 people a day in 1982 but over 400 a day by the end of 1983. Cuts in federal nutrition and other programs were cited by 75 percent of cities studied as a cause of the growing need for food assistance; continued unemployment and the high cost of necessities were also chief causes.[4]

Fully half of the cities studied—Detroit, Chicago, Seattle, New Orleans, and many others—were unable to meet the demand for emergency food assistance. Even in the 50 percent of cities that are able to meet the demand for emergency food, city officials acknowledge that they only serve those who seek assistance; many who do not ask go hungry.[5]

A November 1984 survey by the Food Research and Action Center demonstrates that the trend continues. Nearly two-thirds (65 percent) of emergency food facilities reported an increase in the numbers of those seeking food in 1984 over 1983. There was an average increase of 20 percent in the numbers of persons served over the previous year. Over 70 percent of the soup kitchens and food pantries reported that private charity cannot meet the need for food assistance. Moreover, 60 percent of respondents indicated that families with children constituted the majority of persons served.[6] Through actual and frequent home visits by a team of physicians and nutritionists (to satisfy even the most callous among us), it was found that those receiving food from food banks and soup kitchens were invariably in deep need, with virtually nothing in refrigerators and cupboards and no food stamps remaining.[7] A Conference of Mayors' survey indicated that the majority of mayors expected hunger to increase in 1985; only 4 percent anticipated a decrease.

The economic recovery has not solved or even reduced the hunger epidemic in the United States. As stated by the Physician Task Force on Hunger in America, "It appears that most Americans who are 'recovering' economically were never hungry, and those who are hungry are not recovering."[8]

Some may contend that the United States is no longer the land of plenty. However, no one should argue that the nation lacks sufficient resources to meet the nourishment needs of the children, the elderly, and others who are, for now, dependent upon the most token and elemental of all government gestures.

POLICY RECOMMENDATIONS

The policy recommendations offered below are designed to change the notion that food assistance should be available only to those who can find their way fast enough through the bureaucratic maze. Rather, food assistance is a matter of right, a necessary first step before all the other steps to individual and societal progress can be taken.

Support for Federal Food Assistance

The fundamental federal food assistance programs—food stamps, child nutrition, and WIC (Special Supplemental Food Program for Women, Infants, and Children)—enable many Americans to acquire and maintain a minimally adequate diet and, until recently, together have made significant progress in reducing hunger and malnutrition in this nation. The primary federal nutrition assistance programs should be supported as entitlement programs to ensure that all who are eligible for and in need of the assistance provided by these programs can receive it.

In recent years the food stamp program was proposed by the executive branch to be cut 52 percent from the pre-1980s policy baseline levels; child nutrition was proposed to be reduced 46 percent; and the WIC food supplement program for low-income women and children, 64 percent. Many of these proposed reductions were restored by Congress. Food stamp funding was still reduced 14 percent and child nutrition 28 percent, but the WIC program received some increase.[9] Nonetheless, in the four years between 1982 and 1985 about $12.2 billion was cut from food stamps and food nutrition, including school breakfast and lunch programs.[10] The essential food and nutrition programs should not be subject to the vicissitudes of executive or legislative branch attitudes as to how "tough" on low-income citizens they feel they must be in any given year. Even if one accepts the extremist viewpoint that low-income people are somehow deserving of their condition, one should at least exempt the children from that contention. Early indications are that Congress may be inclined to retain and in some cases strengthen food assistance programs in the fiscal year 1986 through 1988 period.

Food Stamps

The food stamp program has proven to be a highly effective means of assuring that 20.8 million persons and 7.2 million U.S. households have a nutritionally adequate diet. The 1986 program cost was $11.8 billion. The program in 1984 reached about 62 percent of all persons living in poverty. This is an excellent outreach record in comparison to many other governmental efforts. Nonetheless, food and nutrition assistance is so integral to family and child well-being that broader coverage should be sought.

Food stamp eligibility rules and regulations are often confusing and seemingly punitive, designed to keep those in need of assistance from receiving food. One study recorded ninety USDA regulations changes over a thirty-month period.[11] The emphasis should be on ensuring that the hungry obtain food rather than creating so much turmoil that millions of the eligible are shut out. Eligibility could be made less restrictive by raising the assets limit and the limit on the value of vehicles, both of which are out of date.

The gross income test, which was implemented in 1981 to remove about one million of the working poor from the food stamp rolls, should be reconsidered. This test removes those with incomes a little above 130 percent of the poverty line, but with very high expenses. Benefits should once again be targeted only to persons who have accessible income below poverty level.

Further, consideration should be given to ensuring that groups of persons living under the same roof but maintaining separate household accounts are each treated as a separate household unit when computing income and assets limits. When people are experiencing economic hardship they often "double up" with parents and other relatives, and they should not be penalized for doing so by losing food stamp eligibility.

The above are a few options that could be offered to assure that those eligible for food stamps are able to receive them. No specific option or combination is advocated; however, policymakers should strive for universal coverage. Moreover, the level of monthly food stamp allotments should be examined. A 1985 Congressional Budget Office study points out that the Thrifty Food Plan (TFP), the USDA nutritionally adequate diet upon which food stamp benefits are based, may not be sufficient to meet minimum needs. Because of a three- to fifteen-month lag in indexing the TFP for inflation and because food prices may be higher in low-income neighborhoods, some adjustments may be necessary.[12] The USDA's National Household Food Consumption Survey revealed that over 80 percent of all households whose expenditures equal the thrifty food plan level fail to obtain the recommended dietary allowances for nutrients.[13] The Congressional Budget Office suggests the option of raising allotments by 15 percent to overcome deficiencies in the TFP formula. Average benefits under that option would increase by about $25 per month, to about $198, at an additional cost of $1.2 billion.[14] Even with this increase, the average food stamp benefit would only be lifted from forty-nine to sixty-one cents per meal. An increase in limits in the food stamp benefits formula on deductions for shelter and child care costs could also be considered, since more than one-fourth of food stamp households with children are affected by the limits.

Moreover, the Food Stamp Act could be amended to allow states to provide cash benefits in lieu of food stamps to low-income elderly. Only about half the eligible elderly take part in the food stamp program, in large measure due to what is often perceived as the very visible "welfare stigma" attached to this program.[15] Additionally, workfare—a work requirement as a condition to receiving food stamps and AFDC in some states—should be reformed to turn it into a meaningful job training program for those whose health and family circumstances permit work. Finally, outreach programs should be funded and expanded to ensure that eligible low-income people participate.

Child Nutrition Programs

The sharp reduction in recent years in child nutrition programs has reduced the number of children receiving school lunches each day by 3 million. Half a million fewer children participate in the school breakfast program, and a half million fewer also receive summer lunches. These reductions have come at a time when there is clear evidence of child health problems due to inadequate nutrition. In autumn of 1983 Massachusetts' Department of Public Health found that between 10,000 and 17,500 low-income children in that state are stunted, largely due to chronic malnutrition. In Chicago, Cook County Hospital reported a 24 percent increase from 1981 to 1983 in the number of children admitted for failure to thrive, acute diarrhea, or dehydration, conditions often linked to poor nutrition.[16] Nationally, malnutrition occurs in about one-half million U.S. children, with high infant mortality rates, low birth weights, growth failure, and a variety of chronic diseases associated with undernutrition found in clearly excessive and well-documented frequencies among low-income children.

Mayors recommend lowering the price and increasing eligibility for the reduced-price breakfast and lunch programs. The National School Lunch Program (NSLP) serves about 23 million students a day (1983 data) at an annual program cost of $3.2 billion. About 92 percent of elementary and secondary school students are in schools that participate in NSLP. In contrast, the School Breakfast Program (SBP) serves 3.4 million children a day at a cost of $350 million (also 1983 data). Greater participation rates in the latter program could be achieved by increasing reimbursement rates to schools. The nutritional quality of the SBP should also be improved. Efforts to restrict income eligibility guidelines should be resisted, and in fact options presented in 1985 by the Congressional Budget Office (CBO) to expand eligibility seem reasonable.[17] The CBO also points out that it is within federal authority to require schools to participate in one or both of these programs on the grounds that all states receive funds for public education.[18] Additionally, nonprofit organizations should again be allowed to sponsor summer food programs.

The Special Milk Program has received a 50 percent funding reduction in recent years and should be restored at least to previous funding levels. Kindergarten children should be allowed to receive milk regardless of whether or not the school participates in other nutrition programs. At present, the milk program is only allowed to operate in schools that do not operate a breakfast or lunch program, and kindergarten children generally do not participate in these programs.

As indicated above, the WIC program should be made an entitlement program to remove the cap on participation levels. This program, established in 1972, provides food, nutrition screening, and counseling to 3.1 million low-income pregnant and postpartum women as well as to their infants and children up to age five. The 1986 cost of the program was $1.6 billion.

WIC is a grant program and therefore is not available to all those eligible. WIC serves about 30 percent of eligible women, 45 percent of eligible infants, and 20 percent of eligible children. All of the 7 million eligible persons could be served by converting WIC to an entitlement program, at a 1985 cost of about $3.8 billion.[19] Such a policy, coupled with intensified outreach to the eligible population, would reduce infant mortality rates and improve child health considerably (see Chapter 12).

Numerous studies have demonstrated WIC's effectiveness in increasing birthweights and reducing neonatal mortality.[20] Moreover, WIC saves up to $3 in short-term hospital costs in treating low-birthweight disabilities for each WIC dollar spent. A Missouri study found that WIC participation saved $100 in Medicaid costs per newborn, on the average.[21]

Emergency Food Assistance

Support for emergency food assistance, through funding for food supplies, distribution of surplus commodities, and reimbursement for the distribution of those commodities, should be continued as long as the current problems continue. These programs are not the solution; they are merely an immediate, temporary response. But they compensate in part for the inability of the fundamental food assistance programs to meet the needs of many Americans. Surplus commodities cannot provide a nutritionally balanced diet, but they help. Soup kitchens cannot provide three meals a day to a hungry family, but they help.

Involving the Private Sector

Although many private food manufacturing and packaging companies have donated food they are unable to sell, many more have not. Awareness of the need must be developed among these companies to bring them on board. Additional creative incentives should be enacted to encourage corporations to provide more assistance than they are now giving. Finally, the successful private sector experiences in handling and processing food should be shared by the federal government with corporations throughout the United States.

Data Collection

The U.S. Conference of Mayors and other organizations have documented clear evidence of increasing hunger in the United States. Nonetheless, if more detailed data, collected by the federal government, are needed to fund emergency food and nutrition programs, then, by all means, mayors recommend that such data be collected, analyzed, and acted upon. If Congress or the executive branch believes the data on hunger are insufficient, it does not follow that hunger is not present. It only means we are turning away from the problem.

Finally, we must state the obvious: Ensuring full employment in our nation is the best of all possible ways to increase nutritional levels.

NOTES TO CHAPTER 10

1. Physician Task Force on Hunger in America, *Hunger in America: The Growing Epidemic* (Boston: Harvard University School of Public Health, 1985), p. 4.
2. U.S. Conference of Mayors (USCM), "Human Services in FY 82" (Washington, D.C.: USCM, 1982).

3. U.S. Conference of Mayors (USCM), "Responses to Urban Hunger: Public-Private Efforts to Provide Emergency Food Assistance in America's Cities," (Washington, D.C.: USCM, October 1983).
4. U.S. Conference of Mayors (USCM), Task Force on Joblessness and Hunger, "Status Report: Emergency Food, Shelter, and Energy Programs in Twenty Cities" (Washington, D.C.: USCM, January 1984), pp. 1, 2.
5. Ibid., p. 5.
6. Physician Task Force, p. 11, citing Federal Food Research and Action Council survey.
7. Ibid., pp. 11, 22.
8. Ibid., p. 5.
9. John L. Palmer and Isabel V. Sawhill, eds., *The Reagan Record; An Assessment of America's Changing Domestic Priorities* (Cambridge, Mass.: Ballinger Publishing Company, 1984), p. 185.
10. Physician Task Force, p. 97.
11. Ibid., p. 109.
12. Congressional Budget Office (CBO), *Reducing Poverty Among Children* (Washington, D.C.: CBO, 1985), pp. 72–73.
13. Physician Task Force, p. 89.
14. Congressional Budget Office, p. 73.
15. From a paper prepared for the U.S. Conference of Mayors' urban policy report by the Food Research and Action Center, "Federal Food Assistance" (Washington, D.C.: Food Research Action Center, December 1983), p. 6
16. American Federation of State, County, and Municipal Employees (AFSCME), "The States, the People, and the Reagan Years" (Washington, D.C.: AFSCME, April 1984), p. 3.
17. Congressional Budget Office, pp. 74–81.
18. Ibid., p. 78.
19. Ibid., pp. 94, 96.
20. Select Committee on Children, Youth and Families, Staff Report, "Opportunities for Success: Cost-Effective Programs for Children" (Washington, D.C.: U.S. Government Printing Office, August 1985), pp. 6–9.
21. Ibid., p. 6.

11 PUBLIC ASSISTANCE REFORM
A New Agenda for Alleviating Poverty

Curbing poverty requires a new agenda to (1) provide for those who cannot work; (2) assist the working poor with proper incentives and some income supplementation; and (3) provide job training and job creation for the unemployed. Combining current programs into this three-level approach will help reduce inequities and lack of coverage.

The poverty rate in the United States declined by nearly one percentage point in 1984, and some economists predict a continuing moderating trend in this figure. Nonetheless, the poverty rate at 14.4 percent in 1984 is considerably higher than the 11.2 rate of a decade earlier. In the years between 1974 and 1984, the numbers of Americans living in poverty increased by 10.3 million, a 44 percent increase at a time when the general population of the nation increased by 10 percent. For some groups the situation is much worse. For example, the poverty rate for central city blacks in 1983 (latest year of available data) was 44.6 percent; for central city Hispanics it was 41 percent.[1]

A large proportion of poverty is concentrated in our cities, and urban governments bear a considerable part of the burden of fighting poverty. During the last several years we have witnessed a dramatic and progressive deterioration in the nation's responsibility for meeting the needs of its poor and dependent citizens. Federal budget cuts have included a series of attempts to reduce deficits at the expense of the poor, the disabled, and the disadvantaged—the very people who most need the assistance of a responsible and caring government (see Chapter 2).

Most Americans, irrespective of ideological and political affiliation, recognize the responsibility of society to help provide for its less fortunate members. It is inevitable in a competitive economic system such as ours that some individuals, often through no fault of their own, require assistance in order to live and participate in society. Aid to dependent and vulnerable populations has traditionally been met through private charity, religious commitments, and government support. Government programs have increased substantially in the last half century with the establishment of the federal programs of Social Security retirement, survivors and disability insurance, Aid to Families with Dependent Children (AFDC), food stamps, Medicaid and Medicare, Supplemental Security Income (SSI), public housing, state and local general assistance, and other programs. Taken together, this series of domestic programs has helped to reduce the extent of poverty in this country. The poverty rate fell from 22.4 percent in 1959 to below 12 percent for most of the 1970s. Now poverty rates are back to levels found in the 1960s.

Unfortunately, growing federal budget deficits have diverted attention from difficult and growing problems of poverty and dependency and have forced the advocates for the poor into the uncomfortable position of defending the status quo against changes that are neither conceptually nor practically sound. It is essential, however, that we turn again to the task of restructuring a social agenda for the 1980s that positively addresses the problems in our current policies and programs.

Creative new domestic policy proposals must be advanced now both to alleviate the immediate suffering of many and to lay a foundation for social productivity, health, and security during this century and into the next. At a minimum, action must be taken in the following three areas:

- Restoration of a true national safety net for those in our society who are unable to work;
- Creation of positive work incentives for those who are able to hold jobs, including the working poor and the marginally employed; and
- A greatly expanded and revitalized focus on employment, including job training and job creation in both the public and private sectors.

Before discussing each of these recommendations, some general comments about the nature of poverty and the problems with current policies and programs are provided.

POVERTY IN THE UNITED STATES

Current economic conditions have shown us all too painfully that poverty in the United States is a multifaceted condition and is not restricted to the mythology of the lazy welfare recipient living on the public largesse. People are poor for many reasons, not the least of which is the lack of jobs. The welfare population includes the young and the old; fathers both incapacitated and unemployed;

mothers who have lost husbands and mothers who never had husbands; the able bodied and the disabled; people who work; people who do not work; and people who, according to various interpretations, should work. People end up in poverty and often on welfare because of poor education, poor helath, inability to find work, inability to support a family, injury, unwanted pregnancy, divorce, desertion, or physical or mental handicaps.

Despite the diversity of reasons for poverty, three population groups are greatly overrepresented among the poor: women, children, and minorities. In 1984 the poverty rate for all children was 21 percent. For children in female-headed families it was 54 percent, and for black children in such families, 66 percent.[2]

In addition, the high incidence of poverty in the nation's cities makes this a particularly important issue for the Conference of Mayors. In 1983 the poverty rate for U.S. central cities was 19.8 percent, well above the overall rate of 15.2 percent. For central city residents in female-headed families, the poverty rate is even higher: Although later data are not yet available, 1981 Census data show 45.5 percent overall and 57 percent for blacks. Most damaging and frightening of all is the incidence of poverty among urban children. For all central city children under age eighteen, the 1981 poverty rate was 27.8 percent. For female-headed central city families, the rate was 60.6 percent for children under age eighteen and a shocking 70.2 percent for central city children under age six.[3]

The alarmingly high rates of poverty among children and particularly children in female-headed families lead us to focus on AFDC as a principal target of reform. AFDC was established by the Social Security Act of 1935 and provides cash assistance primarily to low-income mothers and children. States set need standards, benefit levels, and a number of other parts of this program. Children under age eighteen (and under nineteen in some states) are eligible. There are about 10.8 million AFDC recipients, nearly 7.4 million of whom are children. In September 1984 the national average monthly payment per recipient was \$111.68 or \$3.67 per day.[4] The median monthly payment for a family of three is \$329. Twenty-four states plus the District of Columbia have in their AFDC programs the additional feature of coverage for children in impoverished two-parent families where one parent is unemployed (AFDC/UP).

Reform of AFDC is made difficult by societal misperceptions about the extent of public assistance and the characteristics of those receiving assistance. AFDC recipients do not live luxuriously. As of January 1985 the maximum AFDC level for a family of three was less than 75 percent of the federal poverty level in every state but Alaska. In fact, the median state payment for a family of four was Virginia's AFDC system, where the payment equaled just 42.7 percent of poverty.[5]

Certainly there are numerous long-term AFDC recipients but perhaps fewer than generally imagined. Each year about a third of AFDC families leave the program and are replaced by others. Half of the recipients stay in the program under two years, although half will stay in the program for at least eight years. Only 4 percent receive as much as half of their income from AFDC during the period in which they raise children.[6]

Most welfare recipients—nearly two-thirds—are children. It should be kept in mind that AFDC is primarily intended to help impoverished children have some semblance of a fair start in life.

Often people will claim that welfare is getting out of hand, as "more and more people climb on the rolls." In contrast to this belief, over the past decade, as an additional 3.9 million children fell into poverty (a 41 percent increase), 800,000 fewer children (a 10 percent decline) received AFDC benefits in an average month. Unfortunately, only 53 percent of the nation's poor children receive AFDC.

It is said that AFDC recipients are content to sit back and collect welfare. However, about 45 percent of families who received AFDC in 1980 also earned income that year, averaging 32.1 weeks of work. Increases in earnings is a major cause (nearly 40 percent) of AFDC case closings.[7] The Massachusetts and Utah voluntary work programs demonstrate that "welfare mothers" want to work and will work in jobs of a reasonably meaningful nature, especially when training opportunities are provided and child care can be arranged.

AFDC is replete with problems and over the years has been the subject of innumerable attempts at reform. First, large interstate variations in both eligibility and benefit levels constitute an obvious inequity. For example, a maximum monthly payment for a three-person family in Tennessee is $138; it is $524 in Minnesota. In 1985, maximum benefits for a family of three ranged from 13 percent of poverty income in one state to 79 percent in another. The inadequacy of benefit provided by many states is another problem. Despite myths to the contrary, AFDC benefits have lagged far behind the rate of inflation. Between 1970 and 1985 the real value of the average maximum AFDC benefit for a family of four declined 33 percent. Third, there are substantial gaps in eligibility, particularly for intact families and single persons. Welfare policies often encourage family separation and serve as a work disincentive. Twenty-six states will not provide AFDC payments to two-parent households, assuming neither parent is incapacitated, no matter how low the income, thereby encouraging family breakups to help children survive. Moreover, even a small amount of income can remove an AFDC recipient from the program. For example, a mother with two children in Kentucky is disqualified if she works more than twenty-five hours a week at minimum wage.[8]

Although benefits are low, rising welfare costs have become a growing problem for state and local governments. In fiscal year 1985 federally funded AFDC benefits totaled 8.5 billion, with states nearly matching that amount. Some states require their cities and towns to share in AFDC costs. These states include California, Colorado, Maryland, Minnesota, Montana, New Jersey, New York,

North Carolina, North Dakota, Ohio, and Wyoming.[9] This obviously results in an added fiscal burden for cities in those states.

In addition to AFDC, most states and localities finance and operate General Assistance (GA) programs which are designed to help low-income persons who are ineligible for federal categorical income supports. Recent cutbacks in AFDC have forced state and local GA programs to assume ever greater burdens, adding to the fiscal pressures on many states and cities. In the state of New York, for example, the number of persons transferring from AFDC to GA rose by 65 percent between November 1981 and April 1982.

Recognition of problems in our existing income support programs is not new. Over the past twenty years, numerous proposals for comprehensive overhaul of the welfare system have been developed and debated. The most prominent include the work of the Heineman Commission on Income Maintenance Policy, the Nixon administration's Family Assistance Plan, and the Carter administration's Program for Better Jobs and Income. These and other proposals for comprehensive reform have sought to replace categorical programs with new, single, and simplified systems, such as guaranteed income through the mechanism of a negative income tax. But despite considerable time and effort, no comprehensive reforms have been adopted. We now find ourselves desperately trying to keep things from getting worse and paying little or no attention to long-range systematic improvements.

AN AGENDA FOR CHANGE

The time has come to move away from the negative approach to public assistance and to put forth a responsible agenda for social reform that attempts to sort out the problems of poverty and devise potential solutions in a new way. Although the political climate is hardly considered ready for reform, the extent of the problem is so great that a full analysis of the agenda's potential is a minimal request at present. We turn now to a discussion of a promising agenda for change that can be pursued simultaneously on several fronts: restoration of a true national safety net for those who cannot work; creation of positive work incentives for those who can work; and the development of expanded and revitalized job programs to lift families from dependency to self-sufficiency.

Restoration of a National Safety Net

We must recognize that even under vastly improved economic conditions there will always be some in our society who cannot be expected to work outside their own homes. These include the disabled, those with young children, and those with major health or emotional problems. We must ensure that these families and individuals are provided a basic minimum standard of living regardless of where they live and irrespective of state and local budgetary pressures.

We recommend establishment of a single noncategorical income maintenance program with a national minimum benefit level designed to provide a decent standard of living for families and individuals who cannot reasonably be expected to work. This minimum benefit level would vary from state to state or region to region only by differences in the costs of living. The benefit level would be established at a certain percentage of the official federal poverty level (e.g., 70 percent), and the minimum benefit level would therefore automatically increase with inflation. The current federal, state, and local patchwork of AFDC, AFDC/UP, and GA programs should be consolidated and replaced with a simplified federal benefit program for those unable to work. Shifting full responsibility to the federal level would create a more efficient and equitable system. Poverty is a national problem and must be recognized as a national responsibility rather than left to the discretion of already fiscally strapped states and localities. One should not be able to escape paying for the costs of poverty by moving across a city line or to a more affluent state; rather, all should share in combating poverty, thereby building the capacity to do so.

We emphasize that the vast majority of the recipients are children. The goal of such a program is to provide basic necessities for the development of our most valuable national resource: our children. Therefore, closely aligned with basic income support would be a nationally defined education and service strategy to strengthen family life, with primary emphasis on children and on long-range help in moving people from dependence to self-support.

In 1985 AFDC federal, state, and local payments totaled \$16 billion, of which 8.5 billion were federal funds. The cost of a new program would depend on the level set for the national minimum benefit. For example, a national minimum benefit set a 80 percent poverty level and financed entirely by the federal government would have a total federal cost of about \$20 billion today.[10]

Options to Federal Assumption of AFDC Costs

Mayors have long recognized that the causes of poverty are national in scope and that the most equitable way to find AFDC is through federal assumption of public assistance. However, there are a number of reforms of a lesser magnitude than full federal assumption of AFDC, but which considerably improve the present system. Many of these options, listed below, are drawn from a 1985 analysis by the Congressional Budget Office.[11]

National Minimum Benefit Level. To reduce interstate disparities in benefit levels and ensure that AFDC benefits keep pace with inflation, a federally mandated minimum level, based on a percent of the poverty level, could be set. Under this option, states would continue to pay their full share of AFDC costs. States currently having low benefit levels would have to raise benefits to the federal minimum, causing the federal share to increase as well. States of course could supplement the benefit levels, as desired. A national benefit level set at 70 percent of poverty would cause benefits to be increased in forty-three states. The added cost to the federal government would be $3.1 billion, while states would contribute an added $2 billion, assuming a 70 percent national minimum.[12]

Mandatory AFDC Unemployed Parents Program. Under this option the incentive would be removed for one parent to leave home so that the family can become eligible for AFDC. The twenty-six states that do not now have the AFDC-UP program would be required to participate. Under this program, the primary earner can be employed up to ninety-nine hours per month without losing AFDC eligibility for his or her family. The cost increase to the federal government would be about $500 million per year.

AFDC Coverage for All Low-Income Families. A more comprehensive reform would require states to provide AFDC payments to families that meet income and assets requirements, regardless of employment status or presence of both parents in the household. As is the case with the current AFDC law and all of the options discussed here, AFDC benefits diminish and are eventually eliminated as family income rises. However, incentives to break up the family or to work under ninety-nine hours a month would be eliminated. The added federal cost of this option is about $1.1 billion.

Evaluation of Asset Limits. Currently asset limits are low for AFDC eligibility ($1000 per family not counting house, furniture, clothing, and $1,500 for a car). If asset limits are revised periodically to more realistic levels, families would not be encouraged to spend down their assets to qualify for AFDC.

Creation of Positive Work Incentives

There are a variety of ways to assure that AFDC parents who can work do not threaten their family security by taking a job. As the Congressional Budget Office (CBO) states:

> Increasing the amount of earnings that is not counted in calculating benefits could give AFDC families a greater incentive to work, since they would be allowed to retain a larger fraction of earnings as a net income gain. To the extent that AFDC families would work and earn more as a result, this would lead to lower program costs as earnings would replace some benefits.[13]

The Omnibus Budget Reconciliation Act of 1981 changed AFDC in ways that made welfare more profitable than work for many recipients. Because of increased benefit penalties for earned income, many employed AFDC mothers could secure more cash for their families by quitting work and going on public assistance full time, receiving the added advantage of Medicaid in the process. Studies have shown that the vast majority of working low-income mothers chose to remain in their jobs even though it was more economical for them to quit their job and go on AFDC.[14] Legislative changes by Congress partially restored AFDC work disregards (i.e., disregarding a part of income earned by very low income families in computing AFDC eligibility). However, work incentives are less today than they were in 1981, and incentives to obtain additional income remain inadequate. The entire subject of the payment formula, added income, and eligibility criteria is in need of full analysis and reform. The CBO estimates that greater work incentives can be built into the AFDC system at a rather modest cost of $455 million, with $260 million of these costs paid by the states.[15]

We further recommend restoring and expanding work incentives through the tax system—through expansion and reform of the existing Earned Income and Child Care Tax Credits. The objective here is to provide income supplementation for the working poor through the tax system, both to enhance work incentives and to ensure that working persons who require additional income are not forced to quit their jobs and enter the welfare system in order to receive help.

The Earned Income Tax Credit (EITC) is a refundable tax credit for all families with children earning less than $11,000 per year. It is available to any qualifying family that submits a claim to the Internal Revenue Service (IRS). Only families who work receive the credit, which is 11 percent of the first $5,000 in income, with declining rates to $11,000. For example, families can receive a maximum of $550 if their annual income is $5,000. Because the credit is refundable, families do not have to pay taxes to claim it; the IRS will send them a check for the amount they are due even if they do not owe taxes.

The EITC was introduced into the tax system by conservative Democratic senators in 1975. It was viewed as a way to reward people for taking, and keeping, low-paying jobs. That principle could now be expanded by widening the level of income eligibility and raising the amount of the credit.[16] The 1981 federal income tax reduction did not reduce taxes for the working poor, and Social Security tax increases affected the working poor disproportionately (see Chapter 2). An expanded EITC would have the effect of providing partial Social Security tax refunds to the working poor and would help ensure that all income levels of Americans share in the 1981 federal income tax reductions.

The EITC has lost considerable ground to inflation in recent years. Many working families who are living in poverty can no longer qualify for EITC, even though they could years earlier at the same constant dollar level of earnings. The working poor who still qualify receive a credit whose real dollar value is declining yearly. The CBO suggests that the EITC could be restored to its 1979 real dollar value and indexed for inflation at an added 1986 cost of $2.6 billion.

Such an indexing feature would make the EITC consistent with other features of the individual income tax system that are now indexed (the personal exemption, the zero bracket amount, and the width of the tax brackets).[17]

The Dependent Care Tax Credit is also an existing universal mechanism that provides a tax credit to families for child care costs up to $2,400 for one child or $4,800 for two or more children. The credit amount is 30 percent of child care expenses for incomes of $10,000 a year or less—proposed by the executive branch to be increased to 40 percent in the 1986 budget—with a gradual phase-out of the credit as incomes move up to $60,000. The credit is often out of reach of many low-income earners because it is not refundable and therefore unavailable to many low-income families who do not earn enough to file taxes. Expanding this credit and making it refundable would help to provide assistance to many low-wage earners, thereby offering another positive incentive to work.

In considering these tax reforms, it must be kept in mind that middle and especially upper income taxpayers have received huge tax reductions in recent years, while lower income workers did not. These two proposed tax revisions could remedy that inequity by assisting the working poor.

Development of Expanded and Revitalized Jobs Programs

The third part of our recommended agenda focuses on job creation and job training. This is a critical need and is perhaps the most important part of a program for increasing the productive capacity of our society. We must address the difficult task of (1) creating jobs, both in the private and public sectors, that can be performed by current AFDC recipients and other low-income citizens; (2) training presently unemployed and unskilled workers for those jobs; and (3) revitalizing the institutions that help people find employment (see Chapters 3 through 6 for detailed policy).

One part of this program should be the establishment of a unified and restructured unemployment compensation/manpower system that is responsible for providing assistance to all persons who can be expected to work outside their homes and maintain jobs. Temporary stipends could be provided through the unemployment insurance system for unemployed persons in training and until such time that they become employed. Those persons in training programs, therefore, would receive higher amounts of unemployment insurance benefits than those who do not enroll. A new comprehensive employment plan, proposed in Chapter 5, can be built primarily upon existing legislation and programs, fundamentally restructuring them to provide an integrated system of training, job placement services, and public service employment opportunities to assist those who are able to work and whose life circumstances permit work.

The vast majority of AFDC households are headed by single women; 60 percent of the women are high school dropouts, and many have little or no work experience. More than half of the children are of preschool age, requiring special day care arrangements. Until our society acknowledges this set of circumstances and actively plans employment programs around them, we collectively are at least as responsible for "perpetuating welfare" as the recipients themselves.

The Community Work Experience Program, Workfare, which requires AFDC recipients to earn their benefits through wages on a job, is a flawed concept in the sense that the training infrastructure is not now in place. Our employment and training programs reach less than 5 percent of the eligible population; without training, the odds are slim that the AFDC recipient can achieve an independent life apart from AFDC. Employment and training funds have been reduced by half in recent years, and for the past five budget years the Work Incentive Program (WIN) has been proposed for elimination by the executive branch. WIN's purpose is to train and place AFDC recipients into jobs. WIN's efficiency can and should be improved in preference to eliminating the program—a step that guarantees insufficient results. With an adequate training and placement strategy, the conditions that led to the implementation of AFDC one-half century ago can be attacked systematically, and AFDC can then be reduced steadily year by year.

CONCLUSION

The agenda suggested above represents an attempt to refocus the nation's energies on meeting the needs of its children, its poor, and its dependent populations. We can begin work on this urgently needed agenda by building on policies and programs that already exist while restructuring them in ways that reflect both the causes and conditions of poverty. Perhaps the most crucial feature of this proposal is an attempt to redefine welfare in ways that are emanable to change. This is obviously a long-term agenda, but work on each of the major components can proceed independently.

Taken together, the agenda represents a commitment grounded in three fundamental beliefs: first, that children are a resource to be nurtured and protected; second, that work is valuable, necessary, and fulfilling and should be encouraged; and third, that those in our society who cannot work or who cannot be financially independent are entitled to our compassion and assistance. Liberals and conservatives, Democrats and Republicans, share these beliefs. It is time to translate them into effective policies and programs.

NOTES TO CHAPTER 11

1. U.S. Bureau of the Census, *Money Income and Poverty Status of Families and Persons in the United States: 1984*, Series P-60, No. 149 (Washington, D.C.: U.S. Government Printing Office, 1985), Table 15; and *Money Income: 1983*, Series P-60, No. 145, 1984, Table 15.

2. *Money Income: 1983*, Table 15.
3. U.S. Bureau of the Census, *Characteristics of the Population Below the Poverty Level: 1981*, CPR P-60, No. 138 (Washington, D.C.: U.S. Government Printing Office, 1983), various tables.
4. Children's Defense Fund (CDF), *A Children's Defense Budget* (Washington, D.C.: CDF, 1985), p. 100.
5. Ibid., pp. 100, 269 (as corrected).
6. Ibid., p. 101.
7. Ibid., p. 100.
8. Ibid., p. 103.
9. U.S. House of Representatives, Committee on Ways and Means, *Background Material and Data on Major Programs Within the Jurisdiction of the Commitee on Ways and Means*, February 8, 1983.
10. For detailed cost projections, see Center for the Study of Social Policy, *Cost Analysis of Selected Welfare Policy Proposals Put Forth by Former Secretaries of Health, Education and Welfare* (Washington, D.C.: Center for the Study of Social Policy, October 22, 1982).
11. Congressional Budget Office (CBO), *Reducing Poverty Among Children* (Washington, D.C.: CBO, 1985), pp. 33-70.
12. Ibid., pp. 35-38.
13. Ibid., p. 46.
14. John L. Palmer and Isabel V. Sawhill, eds., *The Reagan Record: An Assessment of America's Changing Domestic Priorities* (Cambridge, Mass.: Ballinger Publishing Company, 1984), p. 364.
15. Congressional Budget Office, p. 49.
16. For more detailed information, see Center for the Study of Social Policy, "Expanding the Earned Income Tax Credit: Needed Help for the Working Poor" (Washington, D.C.: Center for the Study of Social Policy, October 1982).
17. Congressional Budget Office, p. 61.

12 QUALITY HEALTH CARE FOR ALL AMERICANS

Mayors struggle throughout the year with their cities' budgets, balancing them in the face of seemingly insurmountable odds. Therefore, mayors comprehend fully the budgetary difficulties at the national level and, in particular, the extraordinary burdens placed on federal budgets by health costs which increase at triple the inflation rate. Undeniably, a thorough reexamination of our entire health care delivery system is in order, with cost containment as a top priority in this review.

Mayors have as an equally high priority the need to bring greater equity into our nation's health system. The low income, the elderly, young mothers and their infants, and minorities are usually the ones asked to bear the burden of current health system cost containment measures. However, simply reducing services to these groups can only meet narrow year-to-year budgetary objectives. These measures are inadequate substitutes for comprehensive, systemic reforms. Moreover, the lowest paid, nonsupervisory hospital workers are usually the first to fall victims to hospital cost containment measures, when little effort is made to economize elsewhere in the health system. Mayors accept fully the federal goal of health cost containment as long as those policies are equitable, and mayors ask federal policymakers to join them in improving the availability of health care for all Americans.

FEDERAL RESPONSIBILITIES FOR INEQUITIES IN OUR HEALTH SYSTEM

Although the U.S. Constitution does not mention health, it permits growth of activities pertaining to improving the nation's health by granting certain powers to the federal government. Regulation of interstate commerce and the authority to tax and spend funds for the general welfare have allowed federal leadership on many national health fronts. The history of federal assumption of health responsibilities is evident in the current range of legislation extending from entitlement and categorical programs to the health block grant programs.

Lacking any deliberate plan, in a process largely the result of temporary power shifts, interests, and, to some extent, needs, the federal government over the years assumed increasingly greater funding responsibilities for health care for vulnerable and special population groups, many of whom reside in large urban areas. This culminated, some suggest, in the advent of Medicare and Medicaid and was accompanied by real funding growth for public health programs in the years up to 1982.

In recent years we have seen an erosion in the nation's commitment to public health. With the arrival of block grant legislation in 1982, funding for national health programs in twenty-one former categorical grant areas was slashed by 25 percent, and funding levels still have not been restored. Funding of health block grant programs is about $327 million less today than in 1981 in real (inflation-adjusted) dollars. Local participation in funding decisions has been reduced or eliminated.

Moreover, in recent years the federal government has reduced its share of funding of Medicaid and Medicare by $19.5 billion.[1] Federal Medicaid matching funds were cut 3 percent in 1982, 4 percent in 1983, and 4.5 percent in 1984, with a permanent 3 percent reduction proposed for future years.

The nation had been progressing steadily toward some form of universal health coverage, as the federal government accepted ever-growing responsibility of health care for the indigent. The dream that everyone could have access to affordable health care once seemed achievable. However, the current outlook is not so optimistic.

Today, more than 12 percent of U.S. citizens—21 million adults and 7 million children—are considered medically disadvantaged. These people have the following characteristics:

- They lack health insurance;
- They do not have a regular source of medical care because of financial problems or bcause they do not know where to seek care; and
- They needed health care in the previous twelve months but were unable to obtain it.[2]

Medicaid is usually thought of as the health safety net for the low income. To the contrary, over half of the nation's population living in poverty are ineligible for Medicaid. Because Medicaid is tied to receipt of Aid to Families with Dependent Children (AFDC) or Supplemental Security Income, a variety of low-income individuals, children in two-parent families below poverty level, first-time pregnant low-income women, the working poor, and millions of people with incomes just above the poverty level are often shut out from any form of public or private health insurance.

Eighty percent of those without a job for a year are without health insurance. Equally significant, about half of all those uninsured (12 to 15.5 million U.S. citizens) are employed. Many of the 15 million part-time employees are uninsured as well.[3] Most tragic in its discriminatory implications for the U.S. health system, 59 percent of the poor and near-poor blacks and 62 percent of the poor and near-poor Hispanics were uninsured all or part of the year.[4]

Exacerbating the problem of lack of health coverage have been the recent cutbacks in AFDC. Since 1981 AFDC has been cut by 10 percent, resulting in 365,000 families and 700,000 people losing their AFDC payments and, consequently, their Medicaid eligibility.

Nor does Medicare mean that the health problems of the elderly are provided for. In fact, the elderly pay 29.9 percent of their total health costs directly out of pocket, not even counting the Medicare premiums they pay. Again, it is the poor who are disadvantaged by the health system. The elderly with annual incomes of $5,000 or less pay an average of 21.5 percent of their incomes on medical care, compared to 3.1 percent paid by the elderly with incomes over $20,000.[5]

Private hospitals across the nation take a disproportionately small share of the medically indigent, transferring them when possible to public hospitals. Indeed, in a 1983 survey of public hospitals in seven large U.S. cities, 76 percent of the patients treated were unemployed, and half of the uninsured patients seeking care were using public hospitals for the first time.[6] However, public hospitals and community health centers cannot cope with the financial burdens. A 1982 U.S. Conference of Mayors survey of fifty-five cities demonstrated that, after federal reductions accompanying block grant implementation, there had been a 42 percent cut in local health programs serving the cities' indigents.[7] During 1982, 239 community health centers were closed.[8] Moreover, in recent years nearly 50 public hospitals have been sold to for-profit hospital chains, which serve significantly fewer low-income uninsured, Medicaid and Medicare patients, and minorities and which are likely to increase significantly the price of their services from fees charged by public hospitals.[9]

Therefore, we still live in a time when the capability of remaining in good health is strongly correlated to one's financial means. Despite the evolution of such a "survival of the financially fittest" national health policy, the U.S. public generally does not approve of such inequitable health programs. A Harris survey indicated that, by a margin of 62 percent to 34 percent, Americans preferred to cut military spending before health programs. By three to one they would cut national defense before cutting Medicaid. Harris concluded from the poll findings that "there is something sacred about federal health programs to the American people," and the public gets "fighting mad" when they think "that America could well be systematically stripped of all its compassion for decency and humanity."[10]

Mayors urge that the nation restore reductions in health programs and move back on track toward universal health coverage of all in need. Specifically, mayors have consistently advocated policy revisions in the following areas:

- full federal responsibility for medical care for the medically indigent;
- revisions in the block grant concept such that they provide direct funding to cities;
- adequate assistance to low-income mothers and children to reduce infant mortality and to improve the health of low-income children to the levels enjoyed by other children;
- adjustments in federal reimbursement policies regarding public and community hospitals; and
- reestablishment of a national data collection system.

FEDERAL HEALTH CARE RESPONSIBILITY FOR THE MEDICALLY INDIGENT

It has been the long-standing policy of the U.S. Conference of Mayors to advocate federal responsibility for the full health care costs of the medically indigent. The history of the nation makes it clear that states and cities, acting independently, cannot create a health system that enables all citizens to receive adequate health care. In fact, many states fail to provide the full range of Medicaid services for which the federal government will cover a share of the costs. For example, Medicaid programs in Texas and Mississippi cover only 25 percent of persons living below the poverty line.

The three principal goals of a nation's health programs should be quality, cost containment, and equity. However, the United States will fail in its equity goals if it depends on fiscally impoverished jurisdictions to somehow locate the funds to provide for the heavy concentrations of low-income people who are dependent upon public sources for their health and survival.

The costs to extend coverage to all are, of course, staggering. More than twenty-five national health insurance bills have been offered in Congress in the last decade, their costs ranging from $33 to $71 billion.[11] Other, less comprehensive, approaches may offer intermediate remedies.

Coverage for the Working Poor

Some 12 million people are among the working poor. The nation could require expansion of private health insurance to the workplace for all, with federal subsidies when necessary. The $10 to $14 billion annual cost of this proposal would be borne in large part by employers, although varying levels of employee payment or federal subsidy or both could share the burden. This extension would add about 3.5 percent to today's total national health expenditures.[12]

Coverage for the Unemployed

Over 5 million unemployed people have no health insurance, public or private. Numerous proposals have been offered to bring health coverage to the unemployed. One approach would require employers to retain health coverage for longer periods of time after a worker is laid off. Another approach is to establish national and state private insurance pools, with pay-ins from employers, current employees, and public funds. Under this plan the unemployed could purchase health insurance at low rates (or receive insurance at no cost once assets dwindle to a certain low level). Another approach would extend to Medicaid the low-income, long-term unemployed, at a cost of $5 to $6 billion annually.[13]

Coverage to Families Without a Household Head in the Labor Force

Many of the above groups (i.e., recently laid-off workers and the working poor) could be helped to some degree by the private sector health insurance market, given some level of public stimulus and support; however, in families where there is no one in the labor force, direct public support is essential. Extending Medicaid to the 3.5 to 4 million people in this category who do not now have health insurance would cost about $3 billion annually, adding 1 percent to total national health expenditures.[14]

Cost Implications

The total cost to extend health coverage to the 12 percent of U.S. citizens who are not now insured would cost somewhere between $18 billion to $24 billion—an addition of about 7 percent to national health expenditures.[15] Not all of these expenditures need be federal. For example, employers could pay an insurance premium tax to help insure those not now covered; moreover, those currently employed could contribute in a similar way, assuming they are earning sufficiently high wages to afford such a contribution.

It is difficult to devise cost estimates for national health insurance because of the necessity of comprehensive health care reform, involving such issues as hospital cost containment; responsible and equitable pay for physicians; the interrelationship of private and public hospitals, interconnected with the community health center and clinic network; the types of coverage to be extended to various target groups (the elderly, the unemployed, the poor and near-poor, etc.), and coordination among all the health and insurance programs. Explicit decisions should be made as to who should be included and excluded rather than allowing a patchwork system to continue to evolve that leaves millions without medical care.

As the national health system is developed and refined, mayors advocate health coverage for all U.S. citizens, including the currently uninsured, the unemployed, and the other medically indigent, with public financing responsibility for these groups borne by the federal government. Poverty, unemployment, and their many effects can only be treated at a national level, using the resources of all the people. Unlike the federal government, the cities, counties, and states cannot rely on massive deficit spending to meet priority needs.

In summary, the elements of the national health care system should be:

- federal financing to cover the minimum health needs of the medically indigent, including the unemployed who need assistance, with particular attention to mothers, children, and the elderly;
- the promotion of illness prevention and the early detection of disease;
- the assurance of quality care and equal distribution of resources; and
- coverage for long-term care and for high-risk populations.

PUBLIC AND OTHER HOSPITALS THAT TREAT THE UNINSURED

With such a high pricetag for national health insurance, coupled with $175 billion annual deficits and health costs which still are increasing at or near double-digit levels (despite the general moderation of inflation), national policymakers are not actively seeking more universal forms of health coverage.

At a much lower cost than national health insurance, the nation could implement improved federal support for public hospitals and other hospitals that treat the uninsured. Such support can take the form of periodic federal grants to hospitals, based upon the proportion of uninsured and underinsured patients accepted, or per-patient payments to hospitals for documented charity care.

Public hospitals are particularly capable of achieving federal health equity goals. In contrast, private hospitals often adopt the philosophy, as expressed by one of their spokespersons, that "we support indigent care through the payment of our taxes."[16] Many private hospitals take only a small fraction of their proportional share of Medicaid patients, the uninsured, and minorities.

As a result of current national health policies, the uninsured have 48 percent fewer hospital days, on average, than the insured.[17] At a cost of $6 to $7 billion, public hospitals can be reimbursed to a full extent for services rendered to the uninsured, and private hospitals can be given the needed economic incentive to accept patients of all income levels.[18]

Reimbursement programs should have the following features:

Adjustments for Free Care: As providers of last resort, public and community hospitals offer disproportionately high levels of care to uninsured or underinsured people. This care, or portions of this care, is nonreimbursable and therefore free to the recipient of the care. Financial assistance should be provided by the federal government to ensure that public and community hospitals are not penalized for providing needed health and medical care for a population that can obtain care nowhere else.

Safeguards Against "Dumping": "Dumping" refers to the refusal by private caregivers to provide health care to low-income and other patients for whom reimbursement presently is not possible. Such patients are often sent to or dumped on public and community hospitals.

Dumping is reportedly on the increase in many communities. For example, Chicago's Cook County reported a 500 percent increase in patient transfers from private hospitals to their public hospitals in 1983 over 1982.[19] Federal guidelines and enforcement of levels of permissible patient transfers should be adopted to avoid excessive financial burdens on public and community hospitals.

Enforcement of Hill-Burton Regulations: The Hill-Burton program provides federal construction money and loans to health facilities. The program's regulations require provision of set amounts of free care for the poor in exchange for Hill-Burton assistance received by the health facility. The U.S. Department of Health and Human Services' Office for Civil Rights now reviews Hill-Burton hospitals for compliance only once every three years, and even then enforcement is weak. Enforcement should be stepped up to ensure that private hospitals meet their part of the agreement in receiving public construction funds.

Review of Hospital Cost-saving Incentives: Given the large overhead and other costs associated with hospital-based care, services provided in hospitals are almost always of higher cost than those provided in an ambulatory (walk-in) setting. In large part due to reimbursement policies of many public and private insurers, however, services are frequently provided in hospitals rather than in an outpatient setting. Overall costs to the health system could effectively be reduced if appropriate services were reimbursed based on the service provided, not the place of provision.

Table 12-1. Infant Mortality Rates, Selected Cities, 1982 (*deaths per 1,000 live births*).

City	*Black*	*White*	*Black-to-White Ratio*
Pittsburgh	30.0	13.4	2.2
Newark	29.9	15.2	2.0
Hartsford	26.6	21.6	1.2
St. Louis	26.1	13.0	2.0
Chicago	25.9	14.3	1.8
Washington, D.C.	25.2	5.5	4.6
Phoenix	24.9	15.1	1.7
Kansas City	24.3	14.5	1.7
Baltimore	23.7	20.8	1.1
New Orleans	23.5	13.4	1.8

MOTHERS AND CHILDREN

Our nation's inequitable health policies are epitomized by the excessive and disproportionate rate of infant mortality among minorities and the low income in general.

National infant mortality rates in recent decades have declined steadily and significantly, from 33 infant deaths per 1,000 live births in 1950, to 25 in 1965, to 10.6 in 1984.

However, infant mortality rates remain at substantially higher than average levels in cities, among minorities in cities, and among poor urban minorities in particular. In some parts of Detroit the infant death rate is 33 per 1,000 live births—the same rate as that of Honduras, the poorest country in Central America.[20] In central Harlem the infant mortality rate increased from 21.5 in 1977 to 27.6 in 1982.[21] Chicago, Baltimore, and several other cities reported recent increases as well.

Nationally, black babies die at *double* the rate of white babies. In some cities this black-to-white ratio is even higher, getting as alarmingly high as six to one, as is the case in Wilmington, Delaware. Table 12-1 demonstrates the inequities in our health care, nutrition, and social systems.[22]

Moreover, the maternal death rate is three times as high among minorities as among whites, a condition that can only be attributed to inequities in health care and living environments. Neonatal deaths (of infants who live beyond birth but less than twenty-eight days) are also twice as high for blacks as for whites. What is most troublesome is the insufficiency of national concern over these inequities; this issue is rarely discussed, even in this era of "pro-life" debates.

Federal budget cuts in a variety of social services areas, the loss of health insurance due to unemployment rates that remain in or close to double digits in many cities, Medicaid cuts, maternal and child health grant reductions, and the unwillingness of many private hospitals to accept Medicaid patients have all combined to decimate local health care delivery systems. Transfers themselves from private to public hospitals (as patient dumping occurs) also endanger infant lives.

State and local health departments report large budget reductions made in response to external factors beyond their control. In fact, forty-four states reported reductions in prenatal and delivery systems following implementation of the maternal and child health block grant and concurrent funding reductions in 1982. Moreover, twenty-eight states do not provide Medicaid coverage to pregnant women and children in poor two-parent families; ten states do not cover first-time pregnant women. Half of all women of child-bearing age have no health insurance of any kind. In 1981 in central Harlem 33.8 percent of pregnant women received late or no prenatal care, an increase from 24.8 percent in 1976.[23] In an Oregon study of low-income women 10 percent reported that they were receiving no prenatal care, 13 percent had made no plans for delivery, 9 percent planned simply to show up at a hospital in labor, and 5 percent indicated that they would have home births for financial reasons.[24]

The unavailability of health care and insurance leads directly and conclusively to infant deaths. A study in South Carolina, which has the second-highest infant mortality rate in the nation, demonstrated that mothers who had five or more prenatal visits had an infant death rate of 12 per 1,000; in contrast, mothers who had less than five visits had a truly alarming rate of 68.[25]

Additionally, a landmark study of all births in New York City in 1968 showed that

> death rates of infants born to mothers in each of four categories of risk were lowest among infants whose mothers had adequate care, slightly higher if their mothers had intermediate care, and the highest if the mothers had inadequate care. Mothers who began prenatal care in the first eleven weeks of pregnancy and had at least nine visits had an infant mortality rate of 6.0 per 1,000, compared to a rate more than three times as high (19.0 per 1,000) for women who delayed their first visit until the twenty-eighth week or later and had fewer than five visits. The researchers concluded that, "Generally, adequacy of care . . . is strongly and consistently associated with infant birth weight and survival, an association that is pronounced throughout the entire first year of life."[26]

Federally financed maternal and child health programs have proved cost effective. In Alabama, for instance, health officials estimate that for every $1.00 spent on maternal and child health services, the state saves from $5.00 to $10.00 in costs that would otherwise have occurred from mothers' and children's lack of access to prenatal and primary health care.[27] Michigan analysis indicates that for every $1 spent through prenatal care programs, $6.12 could be saved in newborn intensive care costs. Colorado research demonstrated a $9 to $1 cost savings ratio. Nationwide, the Institute of Medicine calculated that for

Table 12-2. Percentage of One- to Four-Year-Olds Immunized against Childhood Diseases, by Race, 1982.

Disease	*Minority*	*White*
Diptheria-Tetanus	48.4%	70.6%
Measles	53.1	66.7
Mumps	47.8	61.5
Polio	39.1	62.6
Rubella	50.2	65.9

Source: Children's Defense Fund, *Black and White Children in America* (Washington, D.C.: Children's Defense Fund, 1985), p. 82.

every $1 spent in prenatal care, $3.38 would be saved in the costs of care for low-birthweight infants.[28]

Resources available through the Medicaid program and the Maternal and Child Health block grant must be maximized to ensure adequate prenatal and postnatal care. Major federal social welfare initiatives of the 1960s, particularly the Medicaid, Title V Maternal and Child Health, and Neighborhood Health Centers programs, have had a major impact on infant mortality and poor children's health status. In great part because of these programs, poor children average 65 percent more physicians' visits in a recent year than they did in 1964.[29] Infant mortality rates dropped by 40 percent between 1965 and 1979.[30] However, as the above discussion demonstrates, there is still a long way to go.

Our nation must reach out to the total population to a much greater extent than it does today. For example, Table 12-2 demonstrates the disparities in disease prevention by race between white and minority children. About two-thirds of young white children are immunized against these preventable diseases, while often less than half of minority children are immunized. Greater outreach would be most cost-effective; studies indicate that for every $1 spent on the Childhood Immunization Program, the federal government saves $10 in medical costs.[31]

Mayors urge national policymakers to end their complacency toward these most crucial issues. They advocate:

- greatly increased Medicaid services for low-income and near-poor women;
- substantial maternal and child health care funding, with assurances that cities and counties receive funding for the full costs of care provided; and
- restoration of child nutrition programs, which were reduced 25 percent in the early 1980s, cutting 500,000 participants from the WIC (Special Supplemental Food Program for Women, Infants and Children).

MEDICAL CARE FOR THE ELDERLY

Medicare, enacted twenty years ago, serves 31 million elderly and disabled people through two subprograms, financed through two separate trust funds. To bring costs under control and ensure solvency of the fund numerous proposals are being offered designed to produce $18.7 billion savings over the 1986-1988 period in this $81.7 billion (1986 estimate) program.

Most of the proposals involve shifting the burdens of payment for care to the elderly or local public facilities that serve the elderly. These increases in cost sharing are manifested in greater co-payments (a fixed charge that the elderly pay for each service received), increased deductibles (the amounts that must be paid by the elderly before insurance coverage begins), increased co-insurance (a fixed percentage charge on hospitalization and physician charges) and higher monthly premiums to purchase Medicare.

It should be recognized that cost sharing is already at high levels. Currently, the Part B (the voluntary Supplemental Medical Insurance Program) premium is $15.50 monthly; the Part B annual deductible is $75; there is a 25 percent co-insurance payment for most Part B services; the elderly must pay the difference between what the provider charges and what Medicare pays for any given kind of medical care; they pay a first-day hospitalization deductible ($356); they pay daily co-insurance on hospitalization in excess of sixty days ($89), which rises after ninety days ($178); they pay daily nursing home co-insurance (after the twentieth day). And all of these forms of cost sharing, except the Part B deductible, rise annually with inflation. Additionally, the deductible is proposed in the 1986 budget also to be indexed for inflation. The average older American spends $1,500 of his or her money each year on health care, not counting Medicare and other insurance premiums.

For the low-income elderly medical expenses reach 20 percent, and often much higher, of their income. In fact, the low-income elderly can easily spend nearly every cent of their income just on health costs and rent, making a decent meal a "luxury." To make ends meet, the elderly poor average 35 percent fewer physician visits and 27 percent fewer prescription drugs than the elderly with incomes greater than the poverty level and having supplementary forms of insurance.[32]

In Chapter 13 mayors advocate a comprehensive examination and reform of the Medicare program. The reforms must go far beyond the current simplistic responses of raising co-payments, co-insurance, deductible levels, and premiums. Shifting of cost burdens to the elderly should be resisted to the extent possible. In particular, mayors advocate greater levels of assistance to the low-income elderly; for example, through sliding scale premiums based on income and assets. Certain age gaps currently in Medicare coverage—namely, for eyeglasses, hearing aids, drugs, and most of the long-term care costs—should be considered for inclusion in the comprehensive reform package for those who need this help most.

Finally, mayors strongly resist any and all attempts to cut Medicare costs by increasing the age of eligibility above sixty-five years of age. Such proposals are highly discriminatory against blacks and other minorities. Because of poorer health care, difficult living conditions, nutritional problems, and the like, the life expectancy of minorities is much lower than that of whites; for example, minority males have a life expectancy of just 67.1 years, compared to 71.6 years for white males.[33] For black males, life expectancy is even lower at 65.5 years.

PREVENTION AND CLINIC PROGRAMS

Mayors urge the federal government to ensure sufficient federal funding for all public disease prevention and clinical programs, especially those that impact most directly on urban areas; for example, drug abuse, alcoholism, rodent control, lead-based-paint-poisoning prevention, AIDS treatment, VD control and treatment, and tuberculosis programs. Many urban areas can afford little more than methadon maintenance programs for drug addicts, even though a comprehensive, live-in environment with counseling, supervision, and peer group reinforcement is the only known effective treatment. Rodent control is uneven from city to city and within city borders. Tuberculosis rates for minority children are more than four times the rates for white children. VD epidemics are common. Alcoholism programs reach only a fraction of these who need them. Proliferation of AIDS is frightening and tragic. Generally speaking, these clinical programs are grossly underfunded, and fiscally strapped cities with disproportionately large numbers of those who need clinical services cannot meet the need.

With respect to AIDS, early indications are that Congress is responding with major research funding increases. Funds are also needed at the community level for the treatment and prevention of AIDS. In-home care programs, blood testing, subsidized rent programs, group homes, and public education (including information on safe sex practices) are examples of ways a community may help.

HEALTH BLOCK GRANTS

The Omnibus Reconciliation Act of 1981 resulted in major changes in the structure and funding of public health programs. Through this legislation the Congress created four block grants to states from twenty-one former categorical health programs and retained six programs in categorical form. Funding was reduced 25 percent the first year, and today funding is still considerably less than before the funds were blocked. The four block grants—maternal and child health; preventive health (including emergency medical services); primary care (community health services); and alcohol, drug abuse, and mental health—failed to include such features advocated by local governments as:

- Direct funding for local governments or pass-throughs. A pass-through occurs when the federal government has a prearranged agreement with the state to pass through a certain proportion of funds to local governments, after the states take their level of funding and administrative funds. When states control expenditures of health funds, these funds are not necessarily distributed on the basis of greatest need to urban areas having large concentrations of those in poverty and near poverty, and certain programs needed by urban areas may be eliminated altogether.
- Mandated local participation in the planning process. When cities lose the opportunity to control or influence decisions over the expenditures of health funds, often this omission is accompanied by the redirection of funds away from those in greatest need.
- National health standards and uniform data collection. By adopting a block grant approach to health expenditures, national standards for services delivered are no longer in effect in many cases. The result is that those in greatest need may not obtain the level of assistance or the quality of care required. Moreover, with the states controlling the expenditure of block grant funds, it is no longer possible to obtain consistent and comparable data across states.

Lack of adequate funding for health block grants is responsible for many of the health problems discussed throughout this section. Mayors advocate sufficiency of funding, with requirements for direct funding, or pass-throughs, to local governments based on need; mandated local participation in the state health system and fund distribution; and the reestablishment and strengthening of national health standards and uniform data collection.

Relative to the latter point, much of our current data collection system was lost upon initiation of health block grants, when states imposed their own health standards and data submission requirements. With the loss of comparable data state to state and city to city, serious health problems and inequities can now go unmeasured and consequently are more likely to go unnoticed. This deficiency, in turn, leads to funding declines to hard-pressed urban areas and to the neglected urban poor. A national health data collection system must be designed.

NOTES TO CHAPTER 12

1. National Health Law Program, "In Poor Health: The Administration's 1985 Health Budget" (Los Angeles: The Program, March 1984), p. 1.
2. The Robert Wood Johnson Foundation, "Updated Report on Access to Health Care for the American People" (Princeton, N.J.: the Foundation, 1983), pp. 8–9.
3. Robert J. Blendon et al., "Health Insurance for the Unemployed and Uninsured," *National Journal*, May 28, 1983, p. 1148.
4. National Health Law Program, p. 17.

5. Ibid.
6. Ibid., p. 18.
7. U.S. Conference of Mayors (USCM), "Human Services in FY '82: A Survey of Human Services Officials in the Nation's Cities" (Washington, D.C.: USCM, October 1982), pp. 1, 3-4.
8. Geraldine Dallek, "Reagan Health Policy: Two Year Assessment," an unpublished paper from the National Health Law Program.
9. Geraldine Dallek, "For-Profit Hospitals and the Law," *Clearinghouse Review* (December 1983): 860.
10. Dallek, "Reagan Health Policy," p. 5, citing American Public Health Association, *Nation's Health*, July 1982.
11. Blendon et al., p. 1148.
12. Ibid., p. 1149.
13. Ibid.
14. Ibid.
15. Ibid.
16. Dallek, "For-Profit Hospitals," p. 862.
17. Ibid., pp. 860-63.
18. Blendon et al., p. 1147.
19. National Health Law Program, p. 18.
20. The National Urban Coalition, "The Situation in Urban America: A 1983 Report on America's Cities" (Washington, D.C.: The National Urban Coalition, 1983), p. 17.
21. Ibid.
22. Ibid., p. 121, citing U.S. Bureau of the Census data.
23. National Health Law Program, pp. 11-12.
24. Dallek, "Reagan Health Policy," p. 17, citing a survey by the Oregon Health Sciences University, School of Nursing.
25. National Health Law Program, p. 12.
26. Statement by Antoinette Parisi Eaton, M.D., before the Joint Economic Committee, November 2, 1983,
27. Testimony of Dr. Robert Goldenberg before U.S. Senate Finance Committee, April 1, 1981.
28. U.S. House of Representatives, Select Committee on Children, Youth and Families, Staff Report, "Opportunities for Success: Cost-Effective Programs for Children" (Washington, D.C.: U.S. Government Printing Office, August 1985), pp. 10-12.
29. E. Richard Brown, "Medicare and Medicaid: The Process, Value, and Limits of Health Care Reforms," *Journal of Public Health Policy* (September 1983): p. 335.
30. Congressional Research Service, "Infant Mortality," Committee Print, 98-J, June 1983, p. 9.
31. House Select Committee, pp. 16-19.
32. U.S. Department of Health and Human Services, *Health, United States, 1984* (Washington, D.C.: U.S. Government Printing Office, December 1984), p. 53.
33. U.S. Bureau of the Census, *Statistical Abstract of the United States, 1985* (Washington, D.C.: U.S. Government Printing Office, 1984), p. 69.

13 THE URBAN ELDERLY

National trends toward an older populace will have a profound effect on U.S. cities. Each day over 5,000 U.S. citizens celebrate their sixty-fifth birthday, increasing the total number of older citizens in this country by 600,000 per year.[1] In 1980 those aged sixty-five and over accounted for 11.3 percent of the total population. By the year 2035 the number of elderly persons will have more than doubled, and the number of people over age eighty-five, the most frail and dependent upon support services in our society, is projected to triple.[2] Moreover, of the nearly 27 million persons currently sixty-five years of age and older, nearly two-thirds live in urban areas, with half of these, including disproportionate numbers of minority and low-income elderly, located in central cities. On a national level, one of every nine citizens is currently over sixty-five. In many cities, however, this ratio is already as high or higher than one in five.

This "graying of America" has already had an impact on the policies governing such diverse areas as demands for goods and services, public revenues, cultural and educational programs, voting patterns, business and consumer goods, housing and transportation patterns, the delivery of health and social services, and leisure time activities. In response to an aging citizenry, city governments are establishing and revising local policies to redirect zoning, regulatory, and taxation powers and to initiate local programs to benefit the elderly.

National policies and programs that complement and assist local communities in effectively addressing the needs of the elderly are crucial if the United States is to respond intelligently to what former Health and Human Services Secretary Richard Schweiker termed "the most profound sociological trend of the coming years."[3]

At present cities are assuming more and more of the financial burden of providing programs for the elderly. Cities administer federal programs such as the Community Development Block Grant Act and the Older Americans Act, pay increased shares of social services costs, and serve the low-income elderly through local relief programs when federal benefits terminate. Unfortunately, the transferring of responsibility from the federal to the local level is not readily accomplished due to funding constraints.

Local governments' abilities to fund aging programs are generally constrained by such factors as reductions in federal and state support; limits placed on their taxing authority, particularly with property taxes; competing demands for public services; increased costs of personnel and materials needed for service delivery; and loss of local revenues due to local economic difficulties. In hearings conducted in 1982 by the House Select Committee on Aging on the impact of federal budget cuts, mayors repeatedly testified that services for the elderly in their cities had been significantly reduced as a result of dramatic shifts in the federal budget. Further, although recent federal policies emphasize deinstitutionalization, House Select Committee surveys reveal that programs most severely affected were those designed to assist the elderly in living independently. Most cities are simply not in a position to make up losses of federal dollars from local revenues, and the urban elderly suffer.[4]

What is needed is an effective partnership among all levels of government and with the private sector. The federal government should ensure that basic services such as health care and income support are provided equitably throughout the nation. While mayors and local officials are in a better position to understand the particular needs of a community's older citizens, they require significant financial assistance which is readily available only through federal resources. Federal involvement is also needed to disseminate information about the successes and failures of local projects across the nation. When a local program greatly benefits older residents, the federal government should assist in replicating it in other regions. Programs must be developed that provide quality care to the frail elderly and that promote independent living for those who are able, thereby helping the elderly to help themselves.

Mayor Richard Fulton of Nashville, the 1983 president of the U.S. Conference of Mayors, called upon policymakers to respond to these goals.

> As a nation we seek often incompatible goals: reduction of entitlement expectations, and care for our older citizens. . . . We at all levels of government must face such problems forthrightly and search vigorously for ways of providing assistance without building dependency. . . . We must look . . . [to] preventive health care alternatives . . . [and] to part-time and flex-time employment. We must seek to provide in our national programs the flexibility, that will allow our states and our cities—our service providers—to care for those with the greatest need.[5]

As identified by mayors and other local officials, the priority needs and major concerns facing the urban elderly are those of economic security, health care, adequate housing and the improvement of administrative systems. The following sections present priority needs of the urban elderly and recommend a number of changes in national policies and programs to meet these needs.

ENSURING GREATER ECONOMIC SECURITY

Perhaps the single most important determinant in an older person's attitude toward retirement is economic security. Most other necessities of life—adequate housing, access to transportation, nutritious meals, and the quality of health care—are dependent to some degree on ability to pay. In 1984 over 12 percent of the elderly population lived in poverty. Over 21 percent of the Hispanic elderly were poor, as were nearly 32 percent of the black elderly.[6] In addition to the number of people living at the poverty level, many elderly may be classified as marginally poor—that is, living just above poverty level—and, therefore, usually ineligible to participate in many means-tested programs.

Intermediate income families also face severe financial difficulties. The typical urban retired couple with an intermediate income in 1979 ($8,562) spent 29 percent of their income on food ($47.75 per week), 33 percent on housing ($325 per month), 10 percent each for transportation and health, and 7 percent on clothing and personal care, leaving only 11 percent for all other needs.[7] In a Harris poll 17 percent of the elderly population, representing 4.3 million persons, responded that not having enough money to live on was a serious problem for them.[8] This figure is likely understated, since many elderly do not admit to neediness.

The overall poverty rate for the elderly has declined in recent years and is below the general population's poverty rate. As the House Budget Committee points out, "the poverty line alone, however, should not be the sole factor used to assess the economic standing of the elderly. As a group, the aged are very dependent upon Federal assistance."[9] In fact, in a 1984 study released by the Senate Aging Committee, it was found that three-fourths of the elderly had incomes below $10,000 per year, and only 7 percent had incomes over $20,000 per year (1981 data). For the low-income elderly, 93 percent of their income is derived from Social Security, Supplemental Security Income (SSI), Public Assistance, and other federal programs.[10]

The lowered poverty rate for the elderly is used as a rationale to reduce federal assistance to the elderly; however, any such reductions would undoubtedly increase the poverty rate among the many elderly who presently are just above the poverty line. Recent proposals of the executive branch to reduce Medicare/Medicaid, transportation subsidies, the community development block grant, the community services block grant, Social Security, nutritional programs, the Older Americans Act funding, and the moratorium on elderly housing under the 202 program collectively could reverse the recent progress in the overall poverty rate for the elderly.

Social Security is the sole source of income for some 28 percent of retired persons[11] and a major source for 38 percent.[12] Yet this source remains inadequate and annually faces considerable danger of major cuts. The amount of Social Security benefits one receives depends on how long he or she has worked for an employer who paid into the Social Security fund and how much the employee earned during this time period. Social Security incomes are likely, therefore, to be especially low in cities with large numbers of unskilled workers.

In contrast to earnings-based programs, eligibility for Supplemental Security Income is based on need. However, federal benefit levels are less than the poverty line and do not take into account regional variations in the cost of living. States may supplement SSI benefits out of their own funds, but supplementation has usually been based on what the state can afford rather than any need standards.[13]

In order to prevent the 10 percent of elderly citizens whose incomes are just above poverty thresholds from dropping into poverty, it is essential that adequate cost-of-living increases be granted to Social Security and SSI recipients. These should be based on the prices of goods, including medicines and special foods, that elderly people must buy.

The cost of purchasing food, housing, and medicine is higher in cities than in the surrounding areas. Among the only federal benefits that take these costs into account are food stamps, which adjust for excessive shelter and medical costs, and Medicaid, which, at state option, can insure people with high medical costs compared to their incomes. Cuts in the food stamp inflationary adjustment have therefore severely affected the urban elderly. Excessive verification requirements and a lack of outreach prevent many eligible people from receiving food stamps. All levels of government should act to correct these problems. Recent proposals to count in-kind benefits (such as food stamps, Medicaid, and housing assistance) as income should be firmly rejected. Such proposals would both prevent elderly people from receiving needed benefits and act as a disincentive to local governments in establishing programs to serve the elderly.

High cancer rates and the incidence of other disabling diseases can lead urban populations to "age" rapidly. During the past few years terminations of disability benefits have forced many people who could not work onto state welfare roles.[14] There have been delays in processing Social Security disability appeals. Consequently, cities have needed to provide shelter and emergency assistance to people wrongfully denied federal benefits. Legal services programs have valuably assisted clients in obtaining federal entitlements. Some states have been vigorous in challenging disability benefit terminations. Mayors support these challenges and work with states in such efforts. Under current Social Security disability law, in order to get benefits, a person must prove that he or she is unable to do any "substantial gainful" work due to a physical or mental impairment expected to last at least twelve months or to result in death. If Social Security finds that a person is able to perform some types of jobs, but those jobs are not available in the local community, the person will still be denied federal benefits. Locally funded welfare programs must therefore often pay for people who are disabled for many years. Mayors recommend that the Social Security disability program be strengthened to provide benefits for older workers who cannot perform jobs available in the local community.

Unfortunately, even older people who are physically able to work have difficulty securing employment. Age discrimination and disincentives to work prevent them from remaining in the labor force.

A 1981 survey has shown that 85 percent of employees aged fifty-five and over would like some form of paid employment after they retire.[15] Another survey indicated that as many as 70 percent favor an approach whereby older employees could reduce their work schedule by up to three months per year.[16] For the nearly four in ten who are forced to retire,[17] the cessation of work can usher in a difficult period, characterized by anxiety and depression for both physical and financial reasons.

The Age Discrimination Act can help to open employment to older Americans. However, since the act is new, the community must be educated about its value, and advocates must help elderly workers of all incomes to assert their employment rights. Regulations must be promulgated to enforce the act.

Job opportunities should also be expanded through programs such as the Federal Senior Community Service Employment Program (SCEP). This program, authorized through Title V of the Older Americans Act, currently funds 54,200 part-time public service positions nationally for low-income people aged fifty-five and older. There is a need to double these job and training slots and to adjust eligibility requirements to enable the marginally poor to participate. The Department of Labor administers SCEP through states (20%) and through eight national organizations (80%). Mayors and local governments should be involved in more effectively coordinating this program with other community services.

However popular, the SCEP should not be regarded as the sole answer to the employment and economic needs of the elderly. Job opportunities for older people can be expanded in both the public and private sectors. To be effective, these opportunities must relate to the special working conditions of the elderly, including part-time employment, flex-time, job sharing, and working at home. Older workers can be trained for careers in emerging occupations—particularly in the delivery of senior services. Tax incentives should be provided to employers in selected fields who will train and hire older workers.

Government should take the lead in expanding employment opportunities for older workers by first reexamining its own employment practices and abolishing mandatory retirement. In local government, to save money, workers are often hired on a contractual or self-employed basis. The workers then do not receive pensions or other fringe benefits. Government should think carefully about these practices, for they perpetuate poverty; the same workers who contract with the government to provide in-home care for the elderly may retire without pensions and need subsidized care for themselves. On a national level, Congress should exercise oversight regarding age discrimination in federal agencies. Personnel policies should be adjusted to enable job sharing. Government should act to remove disincentives to work often found in pension and fringe benefit programs.

Many mayors believe that increased employment opportunities for older citizens can assist in reducing the escalating cost of health and social services. Older people can contribute as producers, taxpayers, and consumers, and programs that allow them to do so also allow them to remain independent and self-reliant. Mayors also recognize the need to assist retired citizens. Whether through skilled or unskilled labor, through paid employment or homemaking, older citizens have already contributed much to society. They should be provided with adequate incomes.

PROVIDING A CONTINUUM OF HEALTH CARE

The overall goal of a national health policy should be to give the older person the level of health and social care required for remaining independent in the community for the longest possible time. When a person is no longer able to function in the community, high-quality, affordable institutional care should be provided.

A recent survey of noninstitutional elderly shows 65 percent reporting their health as good or excellent.[18] For these senior citizens a preventive and maintenance social/health care program is beneficial. However, because the medical needs of older persons progress as they age, it is important that health care systems form a continuum of care. Long-term care is required by 50 percent of the population age eighty-five and older.[19]

Many communities are initiating efforts to promote preventive health care and alternatives to institutionalization for the elderly. Among these local programs are health screening, exercise and physical fitness, nutrition, alternative living arrangements, and counseling. Cities have led the development and operation of multiservice senior centers as catalysts for the planning, coordination, and delivery of support services.

To further improve preventive care, mayors recommend the strengthening of public and private health insurance. The cost of medical treatment is rapidly escalating, making it nearly impossible for many uninsured consumers to pay for their own care. In 1981 U.S. citizens spent $255.8 billion for health care, nearly 10 percent of the gross national product. Although older citizens represent only 11 percent of the population, they accounted for nearly 30 percent of medical costs. An average of $2,259 per person was spent on elderly health care in 1981, nearly three times that spent by those under sixty-five.[20] With an increase of 17 percent annually, institutional health care costs are rising much faster than the national cost of living. Hospitalization care accounts for 43 percent of health expenditures by the elderly today, an additional 26 percent being expended on nursing home care.[21]

Often, retired or unemployed people below the age of sixty-five are unable to obtain health insurance. They are not yet eligible for Medicare, nor are they covered by their former employers. Some states have contemplated passing laws that would mandate employers to continue health insurance benefits for laid-off workers. However, the Employee Retirement Income Security Act (ERISA) prevents states from regulating self-insurance plans. States have been afraid that if they regulate group insurance to mandate continued benefits, employers will simply switch to unregulated self-insurance plans. ERISA should be amended to correct this problem. The Hill-Burton Act assists low-income people in obtaining free hospital care, but Hill-Burton obligations are now expiring for many hospitals, and there is no comparable obligation for doctors or pharmacies to provide uncompensated preventive care.

Of the total payments for health care for the elderly, 63 percent come from publicly funded programs, 91 percent of which are from Medicare and Medicaid.[22] In fiscal year 1980 Medicare paid approximately 44 percent of the medical bills of the elderly, amounting to $35 billion. This figure is projected to reach $103 billion by 1990.[23] Moreover, $12.8 billion was spent in 1984 by Medicaid to provide health care for the low-income elderly, amounting to 38 percent of Medicaid expenditures. In an effort to reduce public costs, federal officials in recent years have repeatedly sought to cut Medicare/Medicaid expenditures and to raise the beneficiaries' shared costs. Older citizens pay anywhere from 29 to 47 percent of health costs as out-of-pocket expenses—amounts greater now than before the enactment of Medicare and Medicaid.[24] Yet the existing health care system may actually encourage spiraling costs by emphasizing institutionalized, acute, and long-term care over preventive or in-home care.

Public health insurance is now structured to cover acute care, even though preventive care, which is not covered, would be less costly. For example, Medicare does not cover dentistry or prescription drugs. Seniors who cannot afford dentures quickly develop nutritional problems. Seniors who cannot obtain drugs to control high blood pressure or diabetes may require hospitalization, at great public expense.

One alternative to institutionalization involves home health care. In the past policymakers have erred by classifying some services needed by the homebound as "social" and others as "medical." Health insurance paid only for services classified as medical and rehabilitative.

Health care should be viewed in context with essential social and economic support services. A person may require assistance with bathing, shopping, and cleaning to remain in the community. Some cities and states have therefore picked up the costs of chronic care in their Medicaid personal care programs and the costs of other supportive services under social services block grants. Effective programs amalgamate public and private funds; coordinate existing community-based support services; and promote the informal support of family, friends, and neighbors to enable a person to remain at home.

As part of the Omnibus Reconciliation Act, states were permitted to seek "community care waivers" from the federal government under the Medicare and Medicaid program. The waivers allow Medicaid and Medicare reimbursement for home-based care programs when homecare is shown to be cheaper than institutionalization. Mayors applaud this effort, but several barriers remain in the financing of home health. First, some states have failed to obtain waivers out of fear that the numbers of eligible people requesting homecare would grow, and Medicaid caseloads would therefore increase. People needing homecare do not always go to institutions when home-based services are unavailable; sometimes they scrape along without any care or die early, at no cost to the Medicaid program.

Second, the community care waiver can only allow service to those who would otherwise require institutionalization. Services to prevent people from reaching this point are often not available. At the same time the waiver provision was enacted, the federal government reduced funding under the social services block grant. Many states therefore cut back homemaker services. Due to shortfalls in federal Older Americans Act funds, many localities are unable to offer home-delivered meals during weekends. Neighbors often cannot fill such service gaps in cities because they too are disabled—urban elderly populations tend to live in isolated, gerontological enclaves.[25]

Third, due to inconsistencies in the structure of the Medicaid program, people may be forced into institutions before they become eligible for public health insurance. In a nursing home Medicaid recipients pay a portion of their monthly incomes toward the cost of care, and the government pays the remainder of the bill. In the community a person must incur medical expenses over a *six*-month budget period in many states to qualify for Medicaid. The person's monthly income is compared to a monthly income standard and multiplied by six. When the person incurs this dollar amount of medical bills, he or she is certified for Medicaid for the remainder of the six-month period. Patients with constant, predictable medical expenses cannot use anticipated bills to qualify for Medicaid. For several months they may therefore be without health insurance. Elderly people have difficulty meeting the costs of daily living and paying out-of-pocket expenses for homecare while awaiting Medicaid certification. This can force them to seek nursing home placement.

Federal policies should consistently encourage home-based care by: funding social as well as health services, ensuring weekend and evening service, and providing Medicaid coverage to people with high anticipated or monthly medical bills. States and localities should fully utilize community care options, even if it would result in granting more people service, for it would lower long-run costs in the process.

When nursing home care is required, it must be accessible to all. In part because intermediate-level nursing home costs are not covered by Medicare, nursing homes have become the haven of the rich, who can afford the high rates, and the poor, who are covered by Medicaid. Unfortunately for those elderly who do not qualify for Medicaid and who need long-term care, the logical conclusion of this policy is that they are forced to spend their entire savings on nursing home bills until their personal resources are exhausted and they then become eligible for Medicaid. This causes particular hardships to families who need resources for other purposes. If one spouse remains in the community while the former wage earner enters a nursing home, the community spouse may be left impoverished, without the income or resources necessary to maintain the family home. Congress should reform the maintenance allowance and resource criteria in the Medicaid program.

Because Medicaid reimbursement is frequently less than that provided by other insurers or self-pay patients, nursing homes have discriminated against Medicaid recipients. Beds for Medicaid recipients are limited, and care may be inferior. The states should exercise oversight to prevent discrimination. States can enact "all payers rate systems" which ensure that private pay charges are no more than Medicaid reimbursements and result in the equal treatment of patients. This has been done in Minnesota.

Mayors recognize the need to control spiraling health care costs, but controls cannot be at the expense of consumers. Low hospital reimbursement rates and the new Diagnostic Related Group (DRG) Medicare system have resulted in premature patient discharges. Urban public hospitals are not able to handle the patients with unprofitable treatment plans who are dumped at their doors. Some have been forced to close.

Instead of reducing health care services to the poor, mayors favor systems that reduce costs by emphasizing preventive care. Research must continue on the causes, costs, and cures of diseases such as Alzheimer's. Sliding fee scales should be established for public health services, and health maintenance organizations should be expanded. Private and public hospitals should be assessed for care to the medically indigent, or required to provide an amount of uncompensated services, so that financial burdens will not fall disproportionately on the public sector. Families and friends of the chronically ill can be encouraged to provide supportive services through federal tax incentives. Finally, improvements in community care systems can foster independent living, thereby preventing more costly nursing home care.

PROMOTING A CHOICE OF SUITABLE AND AFFORDABLE HOUSING

One of the stated goals of the Older Americans Act is the provision of decent and affordable housing for the elderly. Clearly, that goal is far from being met. Approximately one-half of all homeowners and one-fourth of all renters living at or below the poverty level are sixty-five years of age and older. Meeting rising costs of utilities, maintenance and repair, property taxes, insurance, and other living expenses can prove nearly impossible for many elderly on retirement income. Nearly a quarter of those aged sixty-five and over spend in excess of 35 percent of their income on housing.[26]

Seven out of ten elderly own their own homes, but the homes are often unsuitable for their needs. Older widows, for example, have difficulty maintaining the large, multiroom homes purchased when they were raising families. In addition to the loss of companionship and usually a sharp reduction in the household budget, the older widow, often without the handyman skills needed for routine maintenance, must either seek expensive labor or forgo needed repairs. This is a real problem for the older homeowner and may also adversely affect the community, since house deterioration devalues not only the single dwelling but surrounding homes as well.

Cities have responded by establishing home repair programs and by revising zoning laws to encourage alternative housing. Some innovative approaches to the problems of elderly homeowners are shared housing and accessory apartments (apartments for seniors built into single-family homes). Existing housing facilities should be renovated to better accommodate elderly persons. Mayors recommend the provision of tax incentives and federally financed loans for renovations including the installation of handrails, accessory apartments, and wheelchair ramps.

A number of creative funding mechanisms are emerging to enable the elderly to use the equity of their home or to share ownership/equity. In 1978 the Federal Home Loan Bank Board authorized federal savings and loans associations to offer a number of new mortgage instruments, including Reverse Annuity Mortgages (RAMs). This type of loan allows elderly homeowners to take advantage of the equity they have built up over the years to obtain the additional income necessary to meet living expenses while continuing to live in their homes. A RAM loan provides the homeowner a monthly cash payment over a set period of time, usually ten years, with the home as collateral. RAMs, shared equity, syndicated financing, use of pension systems, and revolving funds can help solve some of the financial problems of the urban elderly.

Housing problems are different for the one-third of those sixty-five and over who are renters. The availability of affordable rental units is a prime concern for the marginally poor who do not qualify for housing assistance. Gentrification and other development activities, which convert rental units to condominiums or cooperatives, also displace older residents, offering them the task of leaving their homes to find new shelter at affordable rates. Some cities have mandated lifetime tenancy for elderly residents when apartments are converted to condominiums. Still, rising rent costs exacerbate housing problems. Elderly residents are eligible for units in most public housing, and some projects are especially designed for their occupancy. As of 1980 there were approximately 1 million units of public housing, of which 44 percent were occupied by persons aged sixty-two and over. During 1980, 15,200 units of public housing were completed for occupancy and 5,200 were filled by elderly residents.[27] Waiting periods for federally subsidized units exceed two years in many cities due to the large number of qualified elderly seeking suitable housing at a price they can afford.

One of the federal housing programs especially designed to meet the needs of the elderly is outlined in Section 202 of the Housing Act. Operated in conjunction with federal rent subsidy programs, Section 202 provides direct, low-interest construction and permanent financing loans to nonprofit organizations that develop housing projects for the elderly and handicapped. The executive branch previously led an effort to reduce construction of new units from 17,000 a year in FY 1980 to 12,000 in FY 1985. Moreover, the FY 1986 executive budget proposed virtually to eliminate the Section 202 Loan Program, although Congress retained the program at the 12,000 unit level for 1986.

It has been estimated that 200,000 new units of elderly housing would have to be provided each year for the next ten years simply to meet the need as it existed in 1978.[28] Mayors recommend federal policy to encourage the construction and rehabilitation of these units. The federal government should also reevaluate the subsidy formula for public housing authorities. Public housing buildings in many urban areas are now old, and budgets have not been sufficient to maintain them properly or to provide the security guards and supportive services needed by older residents.

Supportive services are needed by elderly homeowners and renters alike. The federal government should revise policies that discourage friends from providing voluntary aid. SSI payments, for instance, should not be reduced by one-third when an elderly person lives in the household of another. Multipurpose senior centers should continue to be developed to coordinate services to the elderly, and operating subsidies should be restored to mass transit systems which help older citizens reach needed services.

Pilot demonstration programs were established in 1978 to study the benefits of congregate housing, a program that coordinates housing and support services. The program authorized the Department of Housing and Urban Development (HUD) to extend multiyear grants to eligible public housing authorities and nonprofit Section 202 borrowers to enable the functionally impaired or isolated elderly to remain, or to return, to a semi-independent lifestyle. In 1981 there were twenty-nine of these grants in operation serving approximately 1,300 residents.[29]

Congregate housing is a concept that mayors endorse. With proper supportive services, people who would otherwise need institutional care are able to remain in the community. Counseling, assistance with legal problems, recreation, help with shopping, and hot meals are among the services provided in some congregate settings. However, problems have developed for seniors who wish to participate in some of these services but not others. For example, many congregate housing projects require that residents purchase one meal per day as a condition of their tenancy. Because other housing is not available, people who cannot eat the meals for religious or dietary reasons may unwillingly consent to the program. As Representative Fernand J. St Germain (Rhode Island) said:

> Residents in federally subsidized housing frequently have trouble affording the special foods they must eat and the medicines they must take. Often they are elderly or disabled or both. They live on limited, fixed incomes in many cases. No argument of administrative convenience can support the requirement that these people pay up to $150 a month to buy meals that they do not want.[30]

Legal challenges to the mandatory meals plans have met with mixed success.[31] Providers have argued that congregate services are inadequately funded and that they cannot finance meal services without total participation. Congress should now legislate voluntary meals, and subsidize congregate meal plans to make them affordable.

Solving housing problems for the nation's elderly will require controlling costs of rental units, encouraging the development of alternative living arrangements, improving and expanding public housing, creating innovative funding mechanisms to aid older homeowners, and establishing supportive services. Mayors endorse this broad approach.

PROMOTING EFFECTIVE COORDINATION OF SUPPORT SERVICES

As public resources shrink, federal, local, and state authorities will need to create new partnerships that promote coordinated public-private and intergovernment efforts to achieve common goals. Although the present network of public and private agencies has been fairly successful in bringing national and local focus to many of the concerns of older Americans, much of its potential to respond to the needs of the urban elderly has been eroded by the complexity, fragmentation, and other constraints involved in coordinating programs at the local level. In 1980 the House Select Committee on Aging identified 45 major federal programs that directly benefited the elderly and an estimated 150 others that were of indirect benefit.[32] A recent study by the National Association of State Units on Aging stated that government programs are so complex that it is difficult to ascertain even the numbers of existing services having the potential to benefit older persons.[33] Some professionals describe the maze of bureaucracy as "too many bureaus with too many purposes and too little funding."[34] Each of these programs has its own objectives, funding regulations, administrative system, clients, and other factors contributing to fragmentation and difficulty in local coordination. What is needed and what is beginning to emerge is a growing recognition of the multifaceted needs of older people which will encourage agencies to take steps to simplify operations and work together toward common goals.

One issue that has demanded extensive coordination of public and private resources is that of elder abuse. States received federal funding to write protective services legislation in the 1980s. The various new laws give social workers access to investigate cases of adult abuse, provide for health care and social services to remove an adult from an abusive situation, establish public guardians, or alter the powers of conservators. To implement these statutes successfully the public must learn to recognize the signs of abuse. Legal and social workers must jointly intervene. Services must be financed to remedy abusive situations. Since conservators or guardians frequently make decisions for their wards that affect the state (e.g., whether to enter a nursing home, what treatment to obtain at public expense), it may best serve the elder's interest to have volunteers or nonprofit organizations appointed as conservators. Legal services programs could be funded to assist in creating appropriate protective arrangements. Cities can help to coordinate complex protective service networks through their area agencies on aging. However, since similar services may also be used by nonelderly disabled adults, it is important that social service departments cooperate to provide care.

To promote local coordination of services for the elderly, the federal government established, as part of the Older Americans Act, an "aging network" of public and private agencies for promoting coordination primarily through State and Area Agencies on Aging (AAAs). New language in the Older Americans Act requires that an adequate proportion of Title III funds be spent on legal services. This is important because legal services are essential for ensuring that older people obtain all the public benefits to which they are legally entitled. As required by the 1973 amendments to the Older Americans Act, the AAA is responsible for the development of a comprehensive and coordinated system within a state-determined Planning and Service Area (PSA), usually a multicounty geographical area. However, at the present time, only 18 of the nearly 700 AAAs are administered by city governments.

A key factor in local coordination of programs for the urban elderly is the successful relationship between the city government and the AAA. Most AAAs are administered by county governments, councils of government, or nonprofit organizations and generally lack the authority, resources, or clout necessary to counteract existing administrative and turf barriers. Effective working relationships between many cities and their AAAs have been developed through collaboration techniques such as contracts for services, memorandums of agreements, collocation of services, membership on AAA governing and advisory bodies, and information sharing. Yet there remains a need to bridge gaps between many city halls and AAAs and to strengthen and complement their mutual efforts to assist older Americans.

In addition to programs funded through the Older Americans Act, a number of other federal and state programs require multilevel coordination. Programs ranging from food stamps to crisis assistance appropriately serve many age groups, but special outreach is needed to facilitate the participation of the handicapped and elderly. Generally, these programs are administered directly by state governments through state-level agencies. They can be funded either by the federal government's passing funds through the state or by targeting funds directly to cities, counties, towns, special purpose governments, nonprofit corporations, and other types of health and social agencies. With the enactment in 1981 of nine new federal block grants, states were provided with increased discretion and flexibility to combine funding of services, target resources, and allocate funds to areas of state-determined needs. Local governments thus need to negotiate new relationships with state governments to ensure that local needs are met.

Ultimately, it is at the local service delivery level that the various programs must effectively come together if they are to be of benefit to the elderly, and city governments are in a pivotal position to develop and coordinate these efforts. Financing, however, is a key factor to programming and coordination, and recent years have witnessed reduced levels of funding for programs such as Medicare/Medicaid, Community Development Block Grants, Section 202, and jobs and training programs. As mayors repeatedly have testified, city governments cannot fill funding gaps.[35] How well a community succeeds in overcoming funding difficulties will depend upon unique local conditions, including the needs of older citizens, the city's role and involvement in aging programs, community resources, local experience, and leadership.

No two U.S. cities have the same programs, policies, or administrative systems for meeting the needs of older residents; therefore, each city should be encouraged to develop its own approach to its particular problems, based on local resources, experiences, and traditions, as well as on the powers granted to the municipality by its state government. Private contributions such as those garnered through the United Way, the business sector, churches, unions, and voluntary associations should be encouraged, and the informal support systems provided for the elderly by family and friends should be relied upon. Such an approach is in tune with current federal policies that reward local initiatives.

NOTES TO CHAPTER 13

1. U.S. Senate, Special Committee on Aging, *Developments in Aging, 1980, Part I* (Washington, D.C.: U.S. Government Printing Office, May 1981), p. xiv.
2. Richard Schweiker, *Final Report of the 1981 White House Conference on Aging, Volume 2* (Washington, D.C.: U.S. Government Printing Office, June 1982), p. 41.
3. Ibid.
4. U.S. House of Representatives, Select Committee on Aging, *Services to the Urban Elderly: Impact of Budget Cuts and Block Grants*, Hearings (Washington, D.C.: U.S. Government Printing Office, July 21, 1982), p. 2.
5. Ibid., p. 42.
6. U.S. Bureau of the Census, *Money Income and Poverty Status of Families and Persons in the United States: 1984* (Washington, D.C.: U.S. Government Printing Office, 1985), p. 21.
7. Data by phone from U.S. Bureau of Labor Statistics, May, 1985.
8. Louis Harris and Associates, Inc., National Council on the Aging, Inc., *Aging in the Eighties: America in Transition*, November 1981, p. 69.
9. U.S. House of Representatives, House Committee on Budget, *President's FY 1986 Budget* (Washington, D.C.: U.S. Government Printing Office, February 1985), p. 83.
10. Ibid.
11. *Congressional Record*, November 4, 1981, p. H8107.
12. Schweiker, p. 50.
13. For example, District of Columbia SSI payments in 1984 were $329 monthly for a single person, whereas the AFDC standard of need for one person was $612.
14. See, Avery v. Heckler, 584 F. Supp. 312, (D. Mass 1984).
15. Travelers Insurance Company, *The Travelers Pre-Retirement Opinion Survey*, January 1981.
16. Cyril F. Brickfield, "Income and Employment Patterns of Older Americans" (Paper presented at Japan-United States Symposium, Washington, D.C., September 26, 1983), p. 9.
17. Louis Harris and Associates, Inc., p. xiii.
18. National Center for Health Statistics, *National Health Interview Survey* (Hyattsville, Md.: U.S. Department of Health and Human Services, 1985), p. 107.
19. 1981 White House Conference on Aging, *Report of the Committee on Health Maintenance and Health Promotion* (Washington, D.C.: U.S. Government Printing Office, 1982), p. 2.
20. Pamela Fessler, "Soaring Health Care Costs for the Elderly: A Problem Growing Worse Every Year," *Congressional Quarterly*, November 28, 1981, p. 2337.
21. U.S. Senate, Special Committee on Aging, p. xxii.
22. Ibid., p. xxiii.

23. Fessler, p. 2337.
24. Ibid., p. 2339.
25. U.S. Bureau of the Census, Current Population Reports, Series P-23-138, *Demographic & Socioeconomic Aspects of Aging in the U.S.* (Washington, D.C.: U.S. Government Printing Office, 1984), p. 35.
26. Raymond J. Struyk, "The Housing and Neighborhood Environment of the Elderly: Challenges for the 1980s" (Paper presented at Japan-United States Symposium, Washington, D.C., September 26, 1983), p. 6.
27. U.S. Senate, Special Committee on Aging, pp. 153-54.
28. *Washington Post*, January 21, 1978, p. E-20.
29. U.S. Senate, Special Committee on Aging, *Developments in Aging: 1980, Part 2* (Washington, D.C.: U.S. Government Printing Office, 1981), pp. 279-80.
30. *Congressional Record*, October 28, 1983, p. H8845.
31. See Johnson v. Soundview Apts., 81 Civ. 4803 (JES) (S.D.N.Y., 1984); and Mayoral v. Jeffco, 726 F.2d 1361 (10th Cir. 1984).
32. U.S. House of Representatives, Select Committee on Aging, *Future Directions for Aging Policy: A Human Service Model, 1980* (Washington, D.C.: U.S. Government Printing Office, 1981), p. 28.
33. National Association of State Units on Aging, *State Units on Aging: Understanding Their Role and Responsibility* (Washington, D.C.: National Association of State Units on Aging, 1983).
34. William E. Oriol, "Modern Old Age and Public Policy," *Gerontologist* 21, no. 1 (February 1981): p. 71.
35. U.S. House of Representatives, Select Committee on Aging, *Services to the Urban Elderly*, pp. 4-151.

14 THE FEDERAL PARTNERSHIP IN CRIMINAL JUSTICE REFORM

Continuing high levels of crime, especially in urban areas, limit severely the potential of our cities and nation in achieving full vitality and prosperity.

Crime rates have declined by 15 percent from 1981 to 1984, leading some federal policymakers to deemphasize the federal role in crime control. Nonetheless, the U.S. crime rates are still double what they were in the mid-1960s. Crime in cities today is double the suburban crime rates and quadruple the rural crime rates. Comparisons of crime rates in the United States and other countries indicate that ours is among the most violent of all cultures.

The incidence of crime is recognized as a national problem. However, the response to crime occurs primarily at the local level. In the courtyard of the FBI Building in Washington in bronze lettering is a quotation from J. Edgar Hoover: "The most effective weapon against crime is cooperation—the efforts of all law enforcement agencies, with the support and understanding of the American people." If crime is to be controlled, a concerted effort at all government levels is needed. The U.S. Conference of Mayors calls for a national commitment to respond more adequately to crime in this country.

THE FEDERAL PARTNERSHIP IN CRIME CONTROL

For at least nineteen years the Conference of Mayors has supported federal assistance for local efforts to control crime. Recently, East Orange, New Jersey Mayor Thomas Cooke testified: "[The U.S. Conference of Mayors'] main concern is that funds get to jurisdictions that need them most and that those funds be flexible enough that they can be used to address locally identified priorities."[1] State and local governments are primarily responsible for crime control, but federal efforts are also needed to address special needs, to support the development of new techniques and approaches, and to provide the latest information and training concerning successful crime control technology and methods.

The federal partnership in funding crime control has traditionally not been large. Nonetheless, similar to education and public transportation funding, the federal role, though small, is critical; a diminishing commitment adversely affects all government levels' abilities to respond.

Federal appropriations for crime control have decreased dramatically since the 1970s. Annual federal appropriations in criminal justice for fiscal years 1973 to 1978 averaged over $800 million,[2] whereas fiscal 1985 justice assistance funding was just $227 million. Of that fiscal 1985 amount, the new Justice Assistance Act, the primary vehicle to provide criminal justice funding to state and local governments, made available $69 million.

In fiscal 1975, $895 million was authorized for the Law Enforcement Assistance Administration, to be used to improve crime control capability at all government levels. Of that amount, $480 million was allocated to state and local governments through formula grants. In fiscal 1975, 23 percent of the Department of Justice's budget was allocated to state and local governments' criminal justice systems; ten years later that proportion had fallen to a mere 2 percent.[3]

In contrast, state and local government spending for criminal justice has remained high. In 1979 state and local governments paid 87 percent of all government costs for criminal and civil justice, local governments absorbing 59 percent of all government costs in this area. Not even during the peak federal funding years under the auspices of the Law Enforcement Assistance Administration did direct federal assistance to state and local governments' criminal justice systems account for more than 5.3 percent of state and local spending.[4]

Today's system of funding crime control efforts requires the greatest financial commitment from those urban centers least able to pay the bill; namely, cities with the highest incidences of poverty and other conditions that contribute to criminal behavior. Crime and the conditions that breed crime are or should be a concern of the total U.S. society. Individuals should not be able to escape these costs by moving across an arbitrary boundary into a more affluent, relatively crime-free jurisdiction. A greater proportion of federal funding ensures that costs are shared more equitably among the nation's population.

TRENDS IN CRIME

To help ensure that the federal government once again assumes its full share of the partnership responsibilities in crime control funding, greater public awareness is needed about the high levels of crime in the United States, especially in

Figure 14-1. Crime in the United States, 1960-1984.

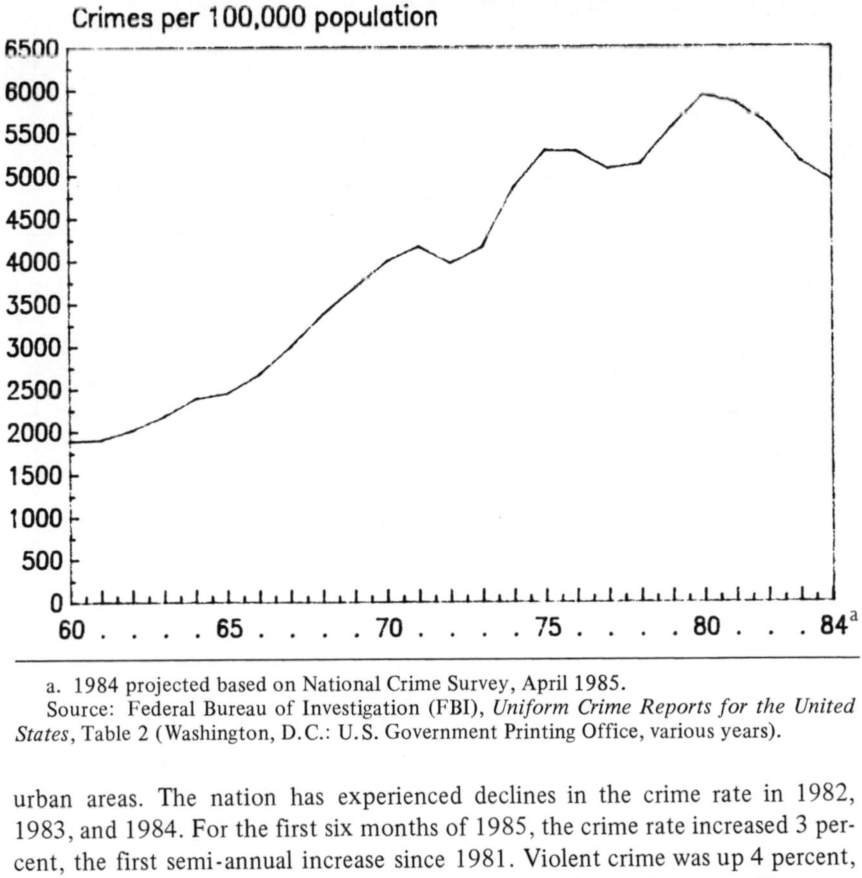

a. 1984 projected based on National Crime Survey, April 1985.
Source: Federal Bureau of Investigation (FBI), *Uniform Crime Reports for the United States*, Table 2 (Washington, D.C.: U.S. Government Printing Office, various years).

urban areas. The nation has experienced declines in the crime rate in 1982, 1983, and 1984. For the first six months of 1985, the crime rate increased 3 percent, the first semi-annual increase since 1981. Violent crime was up 4 percent, property crime 3 percent. Rapes and aggravated assault rose 7 percent. However, the long-term trend may be moderating somewhat.

Nonetheless, as seen in Figure 14-1, the crime rates of today are still very high by historical standards. Today's crime rates would be considered epidemic by the standards of just two decades ago, when the crime rates per 100,000 in population were less than one-half today's level.

Various causes are suggested for the recent downturn in crime rates. In Figure 14-2 it can be seen that the prison population is considerably larger than it was a few years ago. In fact, the rate of incarceration in federal and state prisons has doubled in the past twelve years as a result of new programs to prosecute career criminals, tougher sentencing laws, and mandatory prison terms for violent or repeat offenders. With such a growing share of the population incarcerated, there are fewer "crime-prone" individuals available to commit crimes.

Figure 14-2. Rate of Imprisonment in Federal and State Prisons.

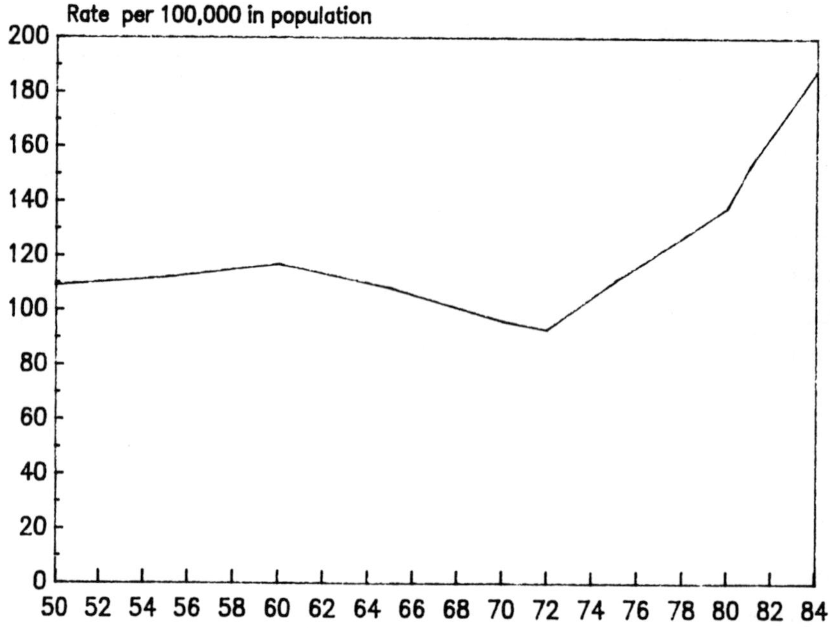

Source: Bureau of Justice Statistics (BJS), *Prisoners 1984* (Washington, D.C.: BJS, April, 1985).

At the same time, the nation has also experienced a decline in the proportion of the population in the most crime-prone years—from fourteen through twenty-four. The crime rate is falling faster than is the decline in the fourteen-to-twenty-four age group, and therefore, demographic changes do not constitute *the* reason for the declining rate. Nonetheless, coupled with the substantial increases in incarceration among this same age group, the decline in the population proportion of teenagers and young adults is a factor to be considered. Increased citizen involvement in crime prevention activities such as through Neighborhood Watch programs and improved police force efficiency have also deterred some criminal activity.

Regardless of the causes of the decline in crime, it must be acknowledged that crime levels remain excessive, with 11.9 million reported crime incidents in 1984 alone—and many additional crimes going unreported to local law enforcement agencies or unreported by the local agencies to the FBI. Violent crime in 1984 was 31 percent greater than it was ten years previously and 3.5 times greater than twenty years ago. Murder and manslaughter in 1984 were double the levels of twenty years previously. Incidences of rape have quadrupled from 1964

Figure 14-3. U.S. Crime Rate by Size of Jurisdiction, 1983.

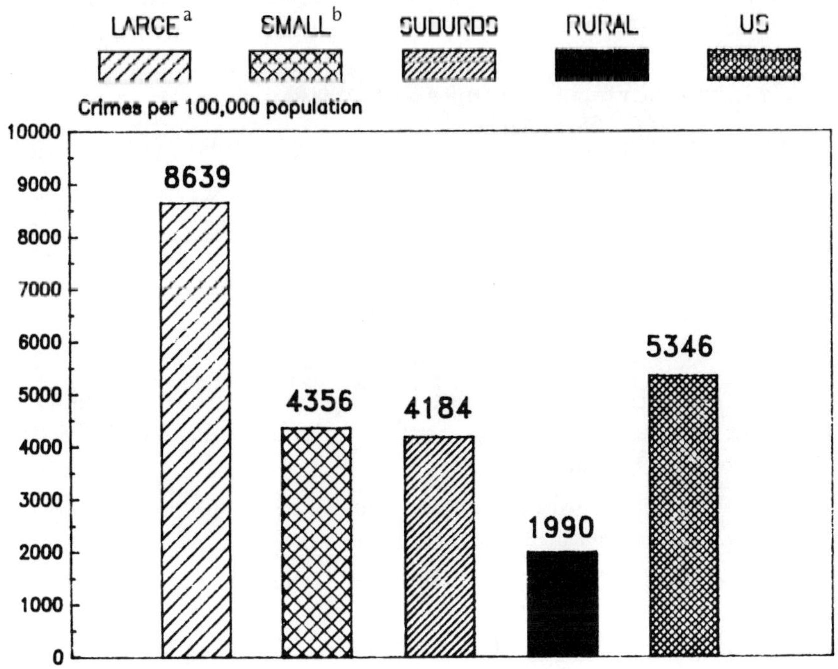

a. Largest cities: 250,000 and above.
b. Small Cities: Under 25,000.
Source: Federal Bureau of Investigation (FBI), *Uniform Crime Reports of the United States* (Washington, D.C.: U.S. Government Printing Office, 1984), pp. 152–53.

levels. Robberies in 1984 were 3.7 times 1964 levels. In 1984 one in every seven U.S. households, on the average, was victimized by violence or theft.

In Figure 14–3 we see that crime rates are especially high in the larger cities when compared to rates in the suburbs, smaller cities, rural areas, and the United States in general. Crime continues to devastate community and family life in urban areas—from the standpoint of the victims of crime and also from the standpoint of those drawn into a life of crime by substandard housing, inadequate education, and a lack of marketable skills and employment opportunities. Crime and criminals are a blight on our community, and criminal activity will continue to flourish if not dealt with effectively. If all citizens were to experience the same level of crime as experienced by urban citizens, there can be little doubt that substantial federal criminal justice assistance would become a national priority.

It appears that we are experiencing the start of some momentum to control crime. Now is the time to sustain the momentum through restoration of the full federal partnership.

NEW LEVELS OF FEDERAL CRIMINAL JUSTICE ASSISTANCE

Funds to state and local governments are largely provided through the Justice Assistance Act of 1984. Such funding, at $60 million for fiscal 1986, is but a small fraction of historical funding levels. A decade ago federal criminal justice assistance was thirteen times higher than today's level.

Restoration of the federal partnership, with funding closer to historical levels, would assist in:

- ensuring the sharing of costs and the coordinated transfer of successful technologies developed around the country to local jurisdictions experiencing crime-related problems;
- establishing comprehensive national criminal justice information, research, and statistical mechanisms;
- providing funding to state and local jurisdictions responding to emergency situations;
- developing mechanisms that respond to the needs of victims of and witnesses to crime in the operation and functions of the criminal justice system;
- reducing drug and alcohol abuse and the trafficking in illegal drugs;
- helping to improve the security of neighborhood businesses in high-crime areas;
- developing effective strategies to reduce the complex problem of family violence;
- addressing the problem of severely crowded local jails and state prisons and developing workable processes to alleviate the crowding;
- initiating constructive alternatives to incarceration for nonviolent crimes; and
- alleviating inmate idleness through the implementation of effective literacy and job-training programs.

A system is required to target such assistance to jurisdictions most in need. Funding levels should be prioritized by a jurisdiction's crime rate, which is a standardized measure of the amount of crime reported per 100,000 resident population.

The strategies, implemented through restoration of the full federal partnership, will be discussed below.

SHARING COSTS AND COORDINATING TRANSFER OF TECHNOLOGIES

The essence of a successful intergovernmental partnership in the fight against crime is a clear understanding of the vital role each partner plays in that working relationship. Mayors believe that the most effective relationship is one in which all levels of government are involved in the exchange of information, the sharing of costs, and the transfer of technology concerning effective crime control methods.

Technologies that have been shown to prevent, reduce, or control crime should be made known to all state and local jurisdictions. This is clearly a federal function and one that is best performed at the national level. Direct financial assistance should be provided to assist state and local units of government to ensure that programs and projects that have proved successful in addressing national crime priorities and the functioning of justice systems are correctly implemented.

The cost of these new technologies is often beyond the level the states and localities can afford. If the burden of funding is left solely to these units of government, new technologies will often not be implemented. Because of its resources, the federal government is in a unique position to provide funding for crime reduction strategies that would not otherwise be undertaken. With a renewed commitment at the federal level to join the intergovernmental partnerships to reduce crime, state and local governments will continue to extend themselves fully and join in the financing effort. Federally initiated programs and projects should be coordinated with local law enforcement efforts to maximize their effectiveness and promote a more workable transition of inmates back into society.

Crime control and the administration of justice remain primarily state and local responsibilities. The federal government can and should, however, play a role that combines: effective leadership, assistance based upon local initiatives and priorities, appropriations for successful technologies and programs, and capacity for transfer of credible information that jurisdictions, on their own, are unable to obtain.

RESEARCH AND STATISTICS

Research permits accurate assessment of current conditions, capabilities, strengths, and weaknesses of the criminal justice system and its agencies, and it permits the testing of new programs and policies for their efficiency and effectiveness. The obligation falls equally on all levels of government to support assessment and evaluation and to create a climate receptive to the role research can play in improving the administration of justice.

The federal government has a special responsibility and role to play in developing and testing methods to improve the criminal justice system. Because of its resources, its economies of scale, and its national perspective, the federal government is in a position to undertake the funding of research projects that test short-term research and development activities. Financial assistance should be provided to state and local criminal justice agencies and public and private nonprofit organizations to carry out research efforts initiated at the federal, state, and local levels. Special attention, however, should be given to those problems identified at the local level.

Without objective, reliable, and accurate statistics on crime and the activities of the criminal justice system, policies and procedures aimed at reducing the level of crime or improving the effectiveness of the criminal justice system are often ineffective and wasteful. Adequate attention must be focused at all levels of government on the accuracy of collected data, its storage and retrievability, its consistency in quality from jurisdiction to jurisdiction, and its ability to be aggregated for purposes of national-level analyses.

Mayors recommend that the Congress provide financial support to the Bureau of Justice Statistics at an adequate level to encourage state and local units of government in collecting, analyzing, and disseminating justice statistics and developing justice information systems that produce statistical and operational data.

EMERGENCY FEDERAL LAW ENFORCEMENT ASSISTANCE

Mayors strongly support federal assistance to state or local units of government in the event of emergency situations, such as the Atlanta child murders or an extraordinary influx of drugs. Such emergency funding, allocated at the discretion of the attorney general, would provide local jurisdictions with the ability to respond to the emergency circumstances that produce the extraordinary problem. Local and state governments are not equipped with either the needed resources or the expertise to respond completely to these tragedies.

It is more efficient to provide outside funding as extraordinary emergencies arise than to expect each local law enforcement agency to build its strength to a capacity large enough to meet every conceivable contingency. The executive branch included such an emergency fund in its fiscal 1986 budget for the Department of Justice.

VICTIMS AND WITNESSES OF CRIME

A workable program of assistance to victims and witnesses of crime is in the formative stages in the United States. Proposals are being developed at all levels of government to ensure that victims and witnesses are treated fairly and with understanding by the criminal justice system.

A victims' "bill of rights," embodying principles for the treatment of victims and witnesses by and within the criminal justice system, will likely evolve from these local-state-federal actions. This bill of rights would take steps to:

- protect victims, witnesses, and their families from intimidation from offenders;
- provide emergency medical and social services;
- advise victims of scheduling changes and continuances affecting their attendance at judicial proceedings;
- advise victims of the opportunity to address the court at the time of sentencing;
- avoid, to the extent possible, disclosing the addresses of victims and witnesses to the defense; and
- provide directions to probation officers to include a "victim impact statement" which reflects the effects of the crime upon the victim as well as the appropriateness and amount of restitution.[5]

Current federal plans call for funding of up to $100 million to assist the forty states that now have victim assistance programs. More states will surely add programs as a result of the availability of federal funds.

State programs are now struggling because of a shortage of funds, case backlogs, cumbersome administrative procedures, and a lack of publicity. The new federal funds should help cure administrative difficulties, and initial plans call for the federal treasury to provide 35 percent of whatever funds the state distributed to victims in the previous year.

With the new funds, states should feel able to publicize their crime victims assistance programs more than they are at present, without as much fear of encouraging more requests for assistance than can be budgeted and administered. However, it will likely take a few years for states to devise workable procedures, restrictions, budget levels, and so forth that will balance available funds against demand for help. Assistance in the transfer of knowledge and the development of programs and procedures designed to assist victims and witnesses should therefore be included as part of the overall federal assistance effort. Model victim/witness programs and other efforts to assist local jurisdictions in this area should be the focus of federal involvement.

DRUG AND ALCOHOL ABUSE CONTROL

Illegal trafficking in controlled substances has contributed markedly to the crime problem in this nation. The profit of those organizations involved in the distribution and sale of illegal drugs is estimated to be in the billions of dollars each year, and the sale of these substances in the streets creates an underground economy based in crime and violence. In fact, revenue from the sale of illegal drugs is greater than the combined annual budgets of several of our major cities.

The extent of the relation between crime and drugs is known to be awesome in proportions but never accurately measured. However, a study of 354 heroin addicts in Baltimore found that these "walking crime machines," as termed by Senator Paula Hawkins, committed 774,777 crimes over a nine-year period. The average addict committed crimes 255 days a year, burglary being the most frequently committed crime, for an average of 2,188 crimes per heroin addict during the study period.[6] One need only extrapolate these averages to the entire addict population of a city or nation to grasp the inextricable connection between drug abuse and today's excessive crime rates. One can speculate that drugs are the primary reason why today's crime rates are well over double the rates of two decades ago.

This nation must commit itself to reducing substantially the trafficking of illegal drugs. Mayors call upon the federal government to direct greater priority attention to the issue of illegal drug trafficking and, in so doing, to recognize and definitively act upon the need for coordination and cooperation among federal, state, and municipal enforcement agencies in the conduct of activities directed to halting the sale and distribution of illegal drugs. The twelve Organized Crime Drug Enforcement Task Forces, begun in 1983 to facilitate partnerships at all levels of government to reduce trafficking, are an impressive start in this direction.

Federal appropriations to state and local governments through the mayors' proposed grant program will assist them in curbing the sale and distribution of illegal drugs at the local level and at the same time coordinate these efforts with federal law enforcement authorities. In addition, federal funding would provide drug and alcohol counseling programs both within corrections facilities and in the local community. With the proper treatment and community support, many persons who experience the damaging effects of chemical dependency would be rehabilitated. The number of crimes directly related to drug and alcohol abuse could be lowered and recidivism rates significantly reduced. According to popular perception, such alcohol and drug rehabilitation programs are widely available; to the contrary, their numbers are woefully inadequate relative to the need.

SECURITY FOR NEIGHBORHOOD BUSINESSES IN HIGH-CRIME AREAS

City residents and businesses bear most of the costs of crime; suburbs can often escape these costs in their immediate environment by zoning out poverty and other conditions associated with high crime rates. This pattern gives suburban businesses a competitive edge. Urban neighborhood commercial establishments often struggle to stay in business, crime and high-cost (or unavailable) insurance being major causes of their instability.

Portions of the discretionary grant funds can help these marginal businesses survive, through assistance for security systems, where alarms are fed into local police rapid response teams. Other devices, such as sophisticated bolting systems and various forms of safety glass, would also help.

Finally, states should be encouraged, through incentives, or required to ensure that businesses in high-crime areas have access to affordable insurance throughout the state. Such an insurance program, if properly designed, could do as much for neighborhood commercial vitality as many other forms of economic development assistance.

DOMESTIC VIOLENCE

One of the most serious social problems facing the nation is the violent abuse of children and spouses in U.S. families.

There are few statistics on family violence, and it is probable that most incidents go unreported. The Department of Justice's National Crime Survey captures an average of 456,000 cases of family violence a year, but Justice officials freely acknowledge that such incidents are badly underestimated. One study estimates that between 1.8 and 5.7 million couples experience violence.[7] Reported cases of child victimization doubled between 1976 and 1981.

These cases, of course, are more than "family spats." A weapon is used in 31 percent of the cases, and injuries are caused in 49 percent of the cases. In cases involving spousal violence (in 93 percent of the cases, the victim is the wife or ex-wife), injuries result 58 percent of the time.[8] Mayors call for a thorough investigation into the causes and remedies of family violence. The creation of the Attorney General's Task Force on Domestic Violence was an initial step in addressing this problem. The federal government, however, could take a more active role in providing support to state and local units of government to undertake research and provide technical assistance in developing effective strategies to assist in relieving this national crisis.

JAIL OVERCROWDING

The problems facing the nation's local jails have reached enormous proportions.

- According to statistics released by the Bureau of Justice Statistics, the local jail population increased by 41 percent from 1978 to 1983.[9]
- At least 60 of the country's 100 largest jails are under court orders to reduce populations because of overcrowding.[10]

- Between 1978 and 1983 jailed persons as a ratio of the total U.S. population increased from 76 to 98 per 100,000—a 29 percent increase.[11]
- Of the 3,943 jails in the United States, 888 (25.4 percent) were built before 1925.[12]
- Occupancy among large jails, where the majority of inmates are held, increased from 77 percent of capacity in 1978 to 96 percent in 1983, many jails having higher levels than this average figure.[13]

Local jurisdictions are forced to release an increasing number of individuals to make room for new arrivals in jails. The reality of this situation must be faced while keeping in mind the public's concern over violent crime and other crime while persons are released on bail. It has been estimated that at any given time there are approximately 1.6 million people released pending adjudication of their charges, a figure approximately equal to the combined totals of those on probation and parole.[14] In Figure 14-2 it was shown that the state and federal prison population has grown rapidly as well. At present, state prisons are estimated to be at 110 percent of capacity.[15]

Mayors recommend that the federal government play a leadership role in assisting state and local units of government in developing strategies to review the use of incarceration as a means of punishment, deterrence, and rehabilitation of criminals. For example, effective mechanisms for pretrial release that ensure community safety and appearance in court exist in many jurisdictions. However, many local jurisdictions with crowded jails holding a large number of pretrial detainees are not aware of approaches that have proved successful in other jurisdictions. Access to documented and effective strategies is key to relieving the crisis faced by many local jails, avoiding costly litigation, and doing so in a way that is sensitive to concerns about crime in the community.

Mayors support the provision of federal assistance to local jurisdictions dealing with overpopulated jails. The federal assistance should provide local jurisdictions an opportunity to receive objective, unbiased information and help jurisdictions implement those options uniquely suited to their individual priorities, available resources, and community concerns.

Because strategies to reduce overcrowding must be national in scope, credible, and equally accessible to all jurisdictions, the most cost-efficient aid to local jurisdictions is the use of federal monies to: (1) systematically collect and review successful problemsolving approaches throughout the country, (2) objectively analyze and transfer such information to local and state governments, (3) ensure that states and local jurisdictions are given the freedom to use the information and appropriation in a manner consistent with local initiatives and priorities, and (4) provide some financial assistance in the implementation of capital expansion and alternatives programs.

ALTERNATIVES TO INCARCERATION

The severe overcrowding of jails requires innovative approaches. One strategy that is being increasingly employed is alternative sentencing. Any alternative to incarceration is at the discretion of the judge and court in each local jurisdiction and is usually tested with nonviolent first-time offenders.

Alternative sentencing essentially means that a person convicted of a crime is required to make restitution. This may be done through fines, compensatory service, personal development programs, or other means.

There are several advantages to alternative sentencing. It offers more direct and adequate restitution to the victim; it offers a constructive punishment to the offender which may lead to more acceptable and productive social behavior; it supplements tax revenues or community services rather than depleting them; it prevents nonviolent offenders from mixing with violent criminals in the prison setting; and it alleviates prison overcrowding.

There are also liabilities: Determining an adequate alternative is not always easy; monitoring the offender's alternative sentence is not always done adequately; and some offenders may violate the terms of the alternative sentence. Moreover, stereotypes of offenders and fear of crime in society inhibit the use of alternative sentencing.

Mayors recommend that the federal government play a leadership role in making available information regarding alternative sentencing programs now in operation in the United States and assisting in funding through this proposed grant those methods that have the highest success rates.

PRISON INDUSTRIES

When offenders are sentenced to a prison term, there is frequently nothing constructive for them to do. Idleness in prison breeds a dehumanizing atmosphere and negatively conditions an inmate, who will return to society with no job skills, no attitude change, and no prospect for improvement. The approach of merely warehousing offenders for a period of time does not repay any debt to society; in fact, it virtually ensures that the debt will grow larger as the cycle of crime continues.

One potential source of change in this situation is prison industry. There has been a long-standing practice of prison manufacture but it usually involves a small percentage of the inmates. Moreover, sale of the goods produced in prison is severely restricted by interstate commerce laws (to keep outside firms from being underbid by cheap prison labor), a condition that curtails production of goods at prison industries and consequently depresses the numbers of inmates who can be employed.

Initial efforts to encourage private sector companies to establish prison industries have been encouraging in building prison industries to levels where larger proportions of prison residents may work. This concept, which Chief Justice Warren E. Burger has called "factories with fences," is being promoted by the National Center for Innovation in Corrections (NCIC) at the George Washington University in Washington, D.C. The aim of the NCIC is to stimulate a holistic approach to corrections using prison industries as the focus.

Mayors recommend that the federal government review existing laws and support changes that will encourage prison industry. In addition, there are incentives that can be offered to businesses to make their participation more attractive and profitable to them without exploiting inmates or violating fair labor practices.

The ten elements of an expanded criminal assistance program discussed above are not being developed at a pace or level needed to produce sufficient results when compared to the magnitude of problems in our criminal justice system. With expanded federal support this ten-point plan should make a major contribution to crime control.

FIREARMS CONTROL

In addition to the above grant proposal, a federal partnership for firearms control is needed. In 1972, in response to the growing violence in U.S. cities, the U.S. Conference of Mayors passed a resolution calling for national legislation that would ban the manufacture, sale, importation, and private possession of handguns, except for use by law enforcement personnel, the military, and sport clubs. The policy also called upon the Congress to adopt a national handgun registration law. Finally, the policy called upon the states to adopt legislation that would require the registration and licensing of all firearms. Many jurisdictions have enacted their own gun control laws, but they have had limited success because, without federal legislation, they can offer no real control of the transportation of weapons across jurisdictional lines. As a National Institute of Justice (NIJ) study states: "There are roughly 20,000 'gun laws' already on the books; the wide variability of provisions across jurisdictional lines tends to vitiate the effects of these laws."[16]

There are approximately 120 to 200 million guns in the United States, at least half of U.S. households possessing a firearm.[17] As the above-referenced study indicates:

> Whether for sport or self-defense or illicit criminal purposes, the United States is, without any reasonable doubt, among the most heavily armed private populations in the history of the world. A second American "distinction," rather a dubious one, to be sure, is that the incidence of violent crime, and violence in general, is also higher in the United States than almost any-

> where else in the industrialized West. . . . The idea of putting one's fellow citizens to death, and using firearms to do it, seems rather more widespread and firmly established in the United States than in any other advanced industrial civilization.[18]

As an example of the disparity, the gun homicide rate in the United States is about forty times that of the United Kingdom.[19] In 1983 firearms were used on 58 percent of U.S. murder victims, and in 75 percent of those cases a handgun was the weapon used.[20]

The American public should be educated to the dangers of private possession of handguns. Moreover, mayors have urged mandatory minimum sentences on firearms-related crimes. The Conference's 1972 policy, even today, represents the strongest stand against handgun violence taken by any national organization of elected officials. Over thirteen years later, mayors continue to support these positions strongly. Violent crime remains at unacceptable levels in our cities. The major weapon used in violent crime is the handgun. Handgun control is an effective way to reduce the incidence of violent crime.

CONCLUSION

Mayors believe that the nation should no longer complacently accept excessive levels of crime in our cities and the nation as a whole. Consequently, the U.S. Conference of Mayors takes a comprehensive view of crime in our cities and offers recommendations that address this crisis honestly, realistically, and creatively. Anything less will threaten the safety and future prospects of our nation's cities.

NOTES TO CHAPTER 14

1. Statement of the Honorable Thomas H. Cooke, Jr. before the Subcommittee on Juvenile Justice, Committee on the Judiciary, U.S. Senate, April 14, 1983.
2. U.S. Department of Justice (DOJ), *Third Annual Report of the Justice System Improvement Act Agencies* (Washington, D.C.: DOJ, 1982).
3. U.S. Conference of Mayors (USCM), *The Federal Budget and the Cities* (Washington, D.C.: USCM, February 1985), p. 77.
4. U.S. Department of Justice (DOJ), Bureau of Justice Statistics, *Report to the Nation on Crime and Justice: The Data* (Washington, D.C.: DOJ, October 1983), p. 13.
5. U.S. Department of Justice (DOJ), President's Task Force on Victims of Crime, *Final Report* (Washington, D.C.: DOJ, December 1982).
6. John C. Ball, John W. Shaffer, and David N. Nurco, "The Day-to-Day Criminality of Heroin Addicts in Baltimore—A Study in the Continuity of

Offense Rates," *Drug and Alcohol Dependence*, Vol. 12 (Ireland: Elsevier Scientific Publishers, 1983), pp. 119, 125.

7. U.S. Department of Justice (DOJ), Bureau of Justice Assistance, "Special Report on Family Violence" (Washington, D.C.: DOJ, April 1984), p. 2, citing a study by Straus, et al., *Behind Closed Doors: Violence in the Family*.
8. Ibid., p. 3.
9. U.S. Department of Justice (DOJ), Bureau of Justice Statistics, "Bulletin: The 1983 Jail Census" (Washington, D.C.: DOJ, November 1984), p. 1.
10. Pretrial Services Resource Center, *The Pretrial Reporter* (Washington, D.C.: Pretrial Services Resource Center, August 1983), p. 12.
11. U.S. Department of Justice, "Bulletin: The 1983 Jail Census," p. 1.
12. U.S. Department of Justice, *Report to the Nation on Crime and Justice: The Data*, p. 78.
13. U.S. Department of Justice," Bulletin: The 1983 Jail Census," p. 7.
14. Comments of Stephen R. Schlesinger, Director, Bureau of Justice Statistics, before the National Conference of the National Association of Pretrial Services Agencies, September 1983.
15. U.S. Department of Justice (DOJ), Bureau of Justice Statistics, *Prisoners, 1984* (Washington, D.C.: DOJ, April 1984), p. 5.
16. James D. Wright et al., *Weapons, Crime and Violence in America* (Washington, D.C.: U.S. Government Printing Office, November 1981), p. ii.
17. Ibid., p. 17.
18. Ibid., pp. 2, 3.
19. Ibid., p. 3.
20. Federal Bureau of Investigation, *Uniform Crime Reports, 1983* (Washington, D.C.: U.S. Government Printing Office, September 1984). p. 10.

15 URBAN TRANSPORTATION
A Key to Economic Development, Environmental Quality, and Energy Conservation

Mayors call for a reaffirmation of the intergovernmental and private partnerships that have created in the United States the most effective total transportation network in the world. Mayors urge, particularly, a recommitment of the federal government to sustaining and improving all aspects of our transportation network in the nation's cities.

Transportation is essential to our national social, economic, and environmental well-being. It is the circulatory system which simultaneously achieves a wide variety of goals for city, suburban, and rural residents and businesses. Effective, well-balanced transportation facilities and services provide basic mobility, ensure and support economic development, contribute to a cleaner environment, and provide for more efficient use of land and limited energy resources.

Just as effective, well-balanced transportation is critical in achieving these national goals, it is critical to the very essence of our cities, bringing people and goods to the urban marketplace, increasing access to educational and cultural centers, and strengthening the fabric of our city-suburban environments. The entire nation directly or indirectly relies on our cities to sustain and expand our economy, enrich our cultural heritage, and open opportunities for personal achievement of all types. The responsibility for improving urban transportation, therefore, rests in the hands of the entire public as well as with all levels of government.

All modes of transportation play an important role in achieving the related goals of our cities and the nation as a whole. Public transportation, streets, roads and highways, passenger and freight rail transportation, airlines and airports, and ports and waterways together form the vital transportation system that has both shaped U.S. cities and been shaped by them.

HISTORICAL PERSPECTIVE

Transportation has always been a principal issue on our national agenda. U.S. history can be charted by significant federal attention to the transportation needs of a new and growing society. The U.S. Constitution makes specific references to "post roads," establishing a national responsibility for a transportation system to improve communications and commerce. In the nineteenth century an extensive program of federal land grants was one of the most critical factors in the rapid development of the nation's rail systems. An active federal stance in harnessing water resources contributed extensively to the growth of shipping and waterborne commerce. In the twentieth century the federal government took the lead in the creation of the aviation industry and air travel system as well as our national system of highways. Recent federal legislation has enacted for the first time a federally dedicated source of funds to support transit capital investment. All of these steps were taken with conscious recognition of the important national goals to be served.

In cities this national commitment has been particularly evident and important. Most city transportation systems and basic development patterns are greatly affected by the combination of federal transportation resources, investments, and regulations. Although this national role has not always been consistent nor federal resources sufficient, it has always been a critical factor in the well-being of our nation's cities.

Despite the critical nature of the federal role in the transportation network, the federal government has planned to disband much of the federal partnership. The president's 1986 budget proposed to reduce federal support for public transportation by two-thirds from 1985 levels, including a complete end to operating assistance. Congress did not support these large-scale reductions in its actions on the 1986 federal budget, but it did enact an 11 percent reduction. Nonetheless, these differences in viewpoint between the executive and legislative branches with respect to public transit assistance are certain to surface in 1987 budget discussions and beyond. This chapter discusses the need for all members of the federal-state-local partnership to fulfill their responsibilities.

SEVEN PRINCIPLES OF URBAN TRANSPORTATION POLICY

A number of critical principles must guide urban transportation policy in the coming years if it is to be comprehensive and effective. These principles and policy directions form the foundation of a workable approach to solving our transportation problems.

Balance

Transportation policies and the investments that flow from them have frequently created large imbalances between modes, often with unanticipated, seemingly irreversible consequences. As an example, postwar suburbanization was hastened by, and gave rise to, the massive federal commitment to highways. One related consequence was the demise of private mass transit operators and our near total dependence on private automobiles; another was the coincidental rise of trucking and the decline of our national freight railway system. The implications are clear. Transportation policy and programs, particularly at the federal level, must be based on the broad principle of balanced transportation investment and with the objective of meeting critical needs through a consistent long-term federal commitment.

The Transportation Partnership

Transportation is not the domain of any single level of government or sector of society. Nor can any level of government or sector be totally exempt from the partnership that is required to meet our transportation goals. The federal government in particular has a pivotal, catalytic, and unique role to play. But the federal role must complement rather than contradict or supersede these shared responsibilities.

There has been a tendency in recent years for the federal government to assume a roller coaster approach to urban transportation policy. There have been wide swings in financing policy, regulatory approaches, and assertions of responsibility for particular problems. One of the great needs is for a consistent, long-term reaffirmation of the federal role, supported by adequate resources at the federal level to help sustain capital and operating requirements. In particular, capital decisions are made years in advance of capital construction and purchases at the local level, and considerable local funds are budgeted. Rational decisions cannot be reached if the federal share is uncertain or made just a year in advance. Federal funds must be long term and "bankable" to optimize local effectiveness. An unstated, uneven, or faltering federal commitment greatly weakens the ability of local governments, states, and the private sector to identify and fulfill their responsibilities to meet our transportation needs.

As will be seen in the following pages, mayors and public transit officials believe that local transit systems can raise sufficient funds to meet the vast majority of capital needs, if the federal government will simply uphold its share of the partnership by appropriating funds at the federal funding share already enacted.

Moreover, clearly articulated and consistently applied criteria are needed at the federal level on which to base their investment decisions. Not only would these criteria clarify decisionmaking, but they would also enable local officials to plan and program projects with a better understanding of the likelihood and level of federal support to be expected.

The state role in transportation finance must also be broadened and enhanced. There has been sustained growth in recent years' funding for urban transportation coming from state capitals. This is a trend that should continue, recognizing that while the states must contribute a fair share to urban transportation, responsibility for urban transportation *policy* must be focused at the local level.

There is also a major creative role that can be undertaken by the private sector. Underwriting transportation costs for specific projects, participating in financing plans, and helping to create the community consensus for transportation improvements are all key aspects of transportation policy that the private sector, both business and community groups, can undertake.

Finally, local governments must continue to make the major decisions for all aspects of transportation within their borders. The local role is all-encompassing and must coordinate planning, development, finance, and operations. Local governments can only sustain their role, however, if the broader partnership remains intact—including active federal participation and support.

New Financing Techniques

All levels of government must explore the expansion of transportation financing sources to include nontraditional techniques. The recent inclusion of dedicated funding for public transportation from the 1982 federal gasoline tax increase was an important step in this direction. The federal government should also look at other uses of the federal tax code as a source of funding incentives for transportation projects. Local governments must also seek new dedicated funding sources and encourage less reliance on often unpredictable and uneven commitments from general fund sources. Dedicated revenue streams for urban transportation from various sources have been successful in a number of communities. These forms of taxation should be extended to other communities, along with an exploration of ways to lift artifical or outdated state limitations on local revenue-raising capacity. In particular, regional taxation to support metropolitan area transit systems can provide sufficient funding for capital needs and keeping fares low while not imposing an unfair and uncompetitive tax burden on any one jurisdiction in the region.

Flexibility to Meet Unique Needs

No two communities are alike, particularly in their transportation needs. To the extent that federal resources are committed to solving urban transportation problems, federal policy should provide each community, to the maximum extent possible, with the ability to tailor and target all resources to meet the special needs of that community. Federal policy should also enable the use of federal funds for capital or operating purposes, as the need arises, rather than necessarily locking communities into federally specified forms of expenditures.

Safety as a Priority

Regardless of the mode of transportation in question, safety should remain an important priority and a local responsibility. In the transportation of goods and people, as transportation becomes increasingly deregulated, additional attention must be given to establishing and enforcing safety standards.

Intermodalism as a Key to Efficiency

Productivity and innovation will be keys to ensuring the success of urban transportation in coming years. In order to ensure the greatest possible levels of service per dollar committed, intermodalism should be greatly encouraged where practical and economical, particularly in downtown areas. The coming together of various transportation modes to extend and enhance the transportation system will allow cities to take greatest advantage of their natural densities and the efficiencies of all transportation systems and services. Joint or shared terminal and transfer facilities, integrated schedules and fare structures, and coordinated financing mechanisms are vital if maximum efficiency and use is to be achieved.

Coordinating Transportation with Other Urban Goals

The basic goal of our transportation systems and services is to enhance mobility for all citizens. But improved transportation is not a goal in itself. If properly viewed, transportation can be a natural catalyst for and integral factor in the achievement of other key urban goals. Transportation improvements can help enormously with downtown economic development and neighborhood community development. They can also be used as one of the key tools in achieving the national goals in the areas of air quality, energy efficiency, and economic stability. Jointly harvesting the many benefits of improved transportation requires forethought, cooperation, and active participation by all levels of government.

With these seven principles as a backdrop, if goals are properly defined, partnership roles maintained, and fiscal resources committed, balanced transportation policies and programs will continue to make an enormous contribution to the future quality of life in our urban areas. This contribution has been profound in our nation's past, but not without complications. Below is a specific mode-by-mode discussion of the problems cities now encounter with respect to transportation and the Conference of Mayors' policy outline for solutions to these problems.

PUBLIC TRANSPORTATION[1]

For more than twenty years the federal government has established an important and growing commitment to public transportation. From the Urban Mass Transportation Assistance Act of 1964 through the Surface Transportation Assistance Act of 1982, our national government has recognized how central public transportation is to the life of our cities and, as a consequence, to the achievement of our national goals. Growth of the federal commitment to public transportation has had bipartisan support and has been sponsored by five administrations.

Since 1964 the programs of the Urban Mass Transportation Administration (UMTA) have grown to where they currently support over $4 billion in annual investments in critically needed transit development and improvements. Since 1975 the federal UMTA has been able to provide communities with broad-based assistance for planning, capital investment, and operations. Since 1981, however, federal transit funding has declined 17 percent in current dollars and over 25 percent in real terms—despite broad-based support for public transit in Congress and strong, unified opposition to reductions from local officials. Moreover, an abrupt drop of 67 percent in federal support for public transit was proposed by the executive branch for 1986 from 1985 levels. While these drastic reductions were not sustained in Congress, they signal a serious retrogression in the federal executive branch's commitment to public transit. Meanwhile, highway programs and, especially, aviation programs continue to receive substantial increases.

The role of the federal partner in the provision and support of public transportation must be reinforced and strengthened significantly if the mobility needs and related social, economic, and environmental goals of our cities and nation are to be fully realized. This role includes both capital and operating assistance.

Figure 15-1. Public Transit Capital Needs, 1984-1988.

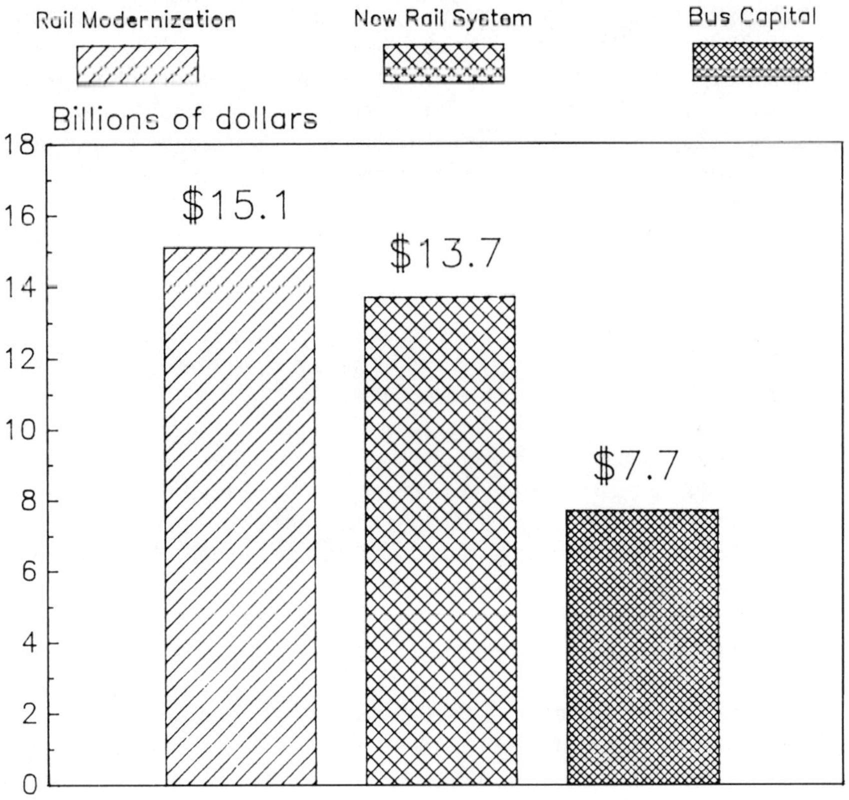

Source: American Public Transit Association, Testimony of April 25, 1984 before the House Committee on Appropriations, Subcommittee on Transportation, p. 1.

Federal Capital Assistance

Estimates indicate that nearly $36 billion in transit capital investment is required by 1988 (see Figure 15-1). Most cities in the country will require major capital investment to rehabilitate, replace, or construct new bus maintenance facilities; nearly 23,000 new bus vehicles must be purchased to replace aging vehicles. The average fleet age is 8.6 years; 30 percent of the bus fleet is over twelve years old. Over 82 percent of the bus capital needs, according to an American Public Transit Association survey, involve maintaining current levels of service.[2]

Cities with existing rail systems, particularly those that have been in operation for some time and on which major cities are highly dependent, require extensive capital investments for modernization. Modernization of existing rail systems represents over 50 percent of all rail needs. In addition, over two-thirds of new rail system and extension projects are designed, in large part, to serve current travel demands which are overwhelming local capacities. Taking bus and rail together, over 80 percent of public transit capital needs would simply sustain existing facilities and services and meet current travel demands.[3] Together, our cities' bus capital needs and rail modernization needs represent an enormous backlog. Substantial increases in capital funding commitments are necessary if progress is to be made in reducing this backlog.

Other cities throughout the country are in various stages of planning and designing major new transit systems. Today, there is more new rapid transit development taking place than at any time since the turn of the century. Over forty major new transit system projects are being pursued in thirty-two cities around the country. The question of new rail starts has emerged as one of the most significant and controversial issues in recent years.

The current administration originally opposed the use of federal funds for new system development. Although this stance was modified in 1984, it is clear that the executive branch continues to be reluctant to commit federal dollars to new subway or light rail projects. Despite this climate of restraint, these projects are of critical importance to urban regions the current and projected growth or economic development objectives of which leave them no option other than to provide new, high-capacity systems and services. New system development projects also have substantial support in Congress and have met the tests of adequacy and political support in their local communities. New transit system projects in cities such as Detroit, Los Angeles, Buffalo, Milwaukee, Pittsburgh, Seattle, Houston, Miami, Baltimore, Atlanta, and the District of Columbia must go forward as an important part of national transit policy. Detailed planning and analysis efforts in dozens of other cities should also be allowed to proceed to logical conclusions based on local goals and needs.

Full funding of capital needs up to authorized levels plus release of all gas tax receipts that are earmarked for public transit would go a long way toward meeting the mayors' transportation goals. These urban goals are well within reach, without the need to enact mammoth new programs.

In fact, a survey of local transit systems indicates that the vast majority of these systems state that they already have the resources or can secure the necessary matching amounts if the federal government would uphold its end of the funding agreements. As transit officials testified in 1984 congressional hearings, "the enactment of appropriations at full authorized levels is the central element in meeting the nation's transit needs."[4]

The 1986 proposed federal budget included a reduction of over 60 percent in capital funding. Should such major reductions in capital assistance be enacted, a survey of transit systems officials indicated that 70 percent of the systems

Figure 15-2. Sources of Support for Mass Transit, 1984.

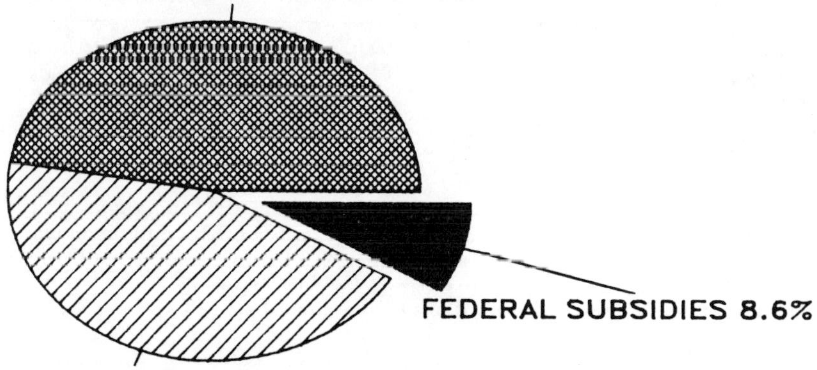

Source: American Public Transit Association, Testimony before House Subcommittee on Housing and Urban Affairs, March 1985, p. 11.

could not buy new buses, despite the advanced age of the average bus fleet; 60 percent forecasted declines in quality and reliability of service; and 58 percent projected service level cutbacks.[5]

Federal Operating Assistance

Similar to federal education assistance, federal assistance to mass transit constitutes a relatively small share of total needs, but it makes the difference between a successful and an unsuccessful system.

As can be seen from Figure 15-2, federal support for public transit is a small, but critical, fraction of total funding. State and local governments provide the vast majority of subsidies, and that share is growing. Considering operating assistance only, the federal share of total revenues is about 10 percent.

Over many years, federal operating assistance has been instrumental in keeping transit fares relatively low. Between 1960 and 1981 fares increased 2.9 times, and overall consumer prices increased 4.5 times.[6] However, federal operating aid has been reduced over 30 percent in real terms from 1981 levels. During this time fare levels have soared and ridership in many cities has declined drastically (see Table 15-1).

The executive branch proposed a total elimination of operating assistance in 1986 and beyond. Such a proposal is in conflict with the president's approval of

Table 15-1. Changes in Fares and Ridership, Selected Cities, 1981-1984.

City	*Fares*	*Ridership*
Chicago	+50%	down 194,000 daily
Cincinnati	+100	down 8.5 million annually
Detroit suburbs	+67	down 14,000 daily
Memphis	+21	down 9.5 million annually
Richmond	+33	down 3.3 million annually
Rochester	+40	down 26,000 daily
San Diego	+30	down 9.8 million annually
Washington, D.C.	+56	down 13.4 million annually

Source: American Public Transit Association (APTA), Testimony before the House Subcommittee on Housing and Urban Affairs (Washington, D.C.: APTA, March 25, 1985), p. 18.

Table 15-2. Personal Consumption Expenditures on Public Transit Systems as a Percentage of Expenditures on Private Cars, Selected Years.

1960	*1970*	*1975*	*1982*
3.3%	2.1%	1.6%	1.4%

Source: U.S. Bureau of the Census, *Statistical Abstract: 1984* (Washington, D.C.: U.S. Government Printing Office, 1983), p. 605.

the Surface Transportation Assistance Act of 1982, which maintains a consistent level of operating assistance at approximately \$875 million per year. To enable public transit to have a reasonable chance to compete with the automobile, Congress must continue to sustain federal operating assistance.

This reasonable operating assistance goal falls far short of what one could construe an ideal level. A national consensus seems to have evolved over the last decade or more to make a commitment to clean air and energy conservation. Nonetheless, as a society, we are placing ever greater levels of support for the private automobile, with diminishing assistance for mass transit. Table 15-2 shows the U.S. public's expenditures on public transit systems as a ratio of our expenditures on the private automobile, including the cost of new and used cars, gasoline, oil, tires, parts, accessories, repair, washing, parking, tolls, and insurance.

Since 1960 expenditures on cars have increased 6.4 times, and public transit spending has only increased 2.7 times. We seem to be sliding backward from the national commitments to energy conservation and clean air through mass transit.

The importance of federal programs to increase public transit use and achieve national environmental and energy policies is clear. During 1970 to 1975, before the federal operating program was instituted, productivity measures declined.

Table 15-3. Productivity Measures, Public Transit Systems in the United States.

Measure	*1970-75*	*1975-80*
Passengers per employee	-7.6%	+14.4%
Passengers per vehicle mile	-2.0	+18.0
Operating expenses (constant $)	+36.6	+ 5.0
Expenses per passenger (constant $)	+36.0	-14.9
Expense per vehicle mile	+33.3	- 0.5

Source: American Public Transit Association (APTA), Testimony before the House Subcommittee on Housing and Urban Affairs (Washington, D.C.: APTA, March 25, 1985), p. 8.

From 1975 to 1980, when the federal program grew considerably, productivity measures showed improvement (see Table 15-3).

Even with the federal operating assistance, public transit systems provided wage increases to bus operators equal to or less than workers under other major labor contracts. The operating assistance was used to increase service and keep fares as low as possible.

When considering whether or not to subsidize public transit, the characteristics of the passengers should be kept in mind. The administration estimates that 71 percent of riders have annual incomes under $20,000 and 40 percent have incomes under $10,000. Nearly 60 percent of the riders are female; 40 percent are minority. The majority of trips, 54 percent, are for travel to work, emphasizing the economic nature of public transit. The remaining trips support the commercial, social, and cultural fabric of the nation.[7]

Without federal operating assistance, 88 percent of 140 transit systems surveyed indicated that they would have to cut service, one in three systems estimating a cut of more than 50 percent. Moreover, 82 percent of the systems would be forced to raise fares. Of these, one-quarter projected increases of 90 percent or more. Nearly one-half projected fare increases of greater than 50 percent.

Further, 87 percent projected major declines in ridership, with 60 percent of the systems projecting a passenger loss of 20 percent or more.[8] Gains and losses in public transit ridership are closely correlated to the level of federal commitment; nonetheless, it should be acknowledged that the nation has yet to launch a comprehensive campaign to make public transit sufficiently attractive and affordable to alter driving habits. Table 15-4 is of metropolitan areas that have more than 800,000 workers. In these areas, many more people *drive alone* to work than use public transit. In fact, in only one area, New York City, do we find that mass transit users outnumber those who drive alone.

Table 15-4. Percentage of Workers Who Drive Alone and Use Public Transit, in All Metropolitan Areas Having More Than 800,000 Workers, 1980.

Metropolitan Area	*Drive Alone to Work*	*Take Public Transit to Work*
Anaheim, California	74.8	2.1
Atlanta, Georgia	68.7	7.6
Baltimore, Maryland	59.8	10.3
Boston, Massachusetts	56.0	15.7
Chicago, Illinois	57.6	18.0
Cleveland, Ohio	67.9	10.6
Dallas, Texas	71.2	3.4
Denver, Colorado	65.4	6.1
Detroit, Michigan	75.1	3.7
Houston, Texas	69.5	3.0
Los Angeles, California	68.7	7.0
Minneapolis, Minnesota	63.1	8.7
Nassau-Suffolk, New York	63.7	12.5
New York, New York	30.7	45.1
Newark, New Jersey	64.0	10.7
Philadelphia, Pennsylvania	59.1	14.0
Pittsburgh, Pennsylvania	60.7	11.5
St. Louis, Missouri	67.3	5.7
San Diego, California	63.8	3.3
San Francisco, California	57.9	16.4
Washington, D.C.	53.7	15.5

Source: U.S. Bureau of the Census, *Statistical Abstract: 1984* (Washington, D.C.: U.S. Government Printing Office, 1983), p. 622.

Certainly the proposals advocated by mayors to support authorized capital expenditure levels and 1985 levels of federal public transit operating assistance would not alter the existing transportation patterns. The policies are primarily intended to prevent further deterioration of support for public transit. Mayors therefore recommend that the executive and legislative branches work closely with state and local governments, citizens, and the private sector to develop long-term transportation strategies, and expenditure levels, that achieve explicitly stated goals for clean air, energy conservation, and relief of traffic congestion. Without such actions, the jurisdictions that can least accommodate an excessive reliance on the automobile—namely, congested cities—will suffer the most.

Transit for the Elderly, Handicapped

In addition to the provision of traditional, broad-based transit services, services to the elderly and handicapped must be provided and enhanced by all levels of government. Local experiences indicate that no single method of providing services for the disabled is effective in meeting the needs of all communities and all users. It is necessary, therefore, that services be tailored to meet special community needs with the local option to provide service through a variety of methods. Today, nearly 25 percent of our cities' transit systems are providing services through the development of lift-equipped regular transit vehicle fleets; another 40 percent are providing such services through the use of special vehicles and "demand responsive" systems using specially equipped vans, taxis, and other small vehicles; remaining cities are providing elderly and handicapped services through a combination of these methods.[9]

Because the cost of such services may range from $10 to $50 per trip, compared to $1 to $2 per trip for traditional services, it is important that government at all levels support local decisions on the appropriate mix and balance of services to all transit users, including the elderly, the disabled, and other transit-dependent groups.

STREETS, ROADS, HIGHWAYS, AND BRIDGES

Cities are greatly concerned with the physical state of streets, roads, highways, and bridges. Indeed, when discussing their infrastructure problem, invariably the highest priority concerns of cities fall into the streets, roads, highways, and bridges category.

A sound surface transportation system is an essential link to an effective economy. The federal government now spends approximately $12 billion annually for a variety of roads systems, including the interstate and related highways. Although this is a sizable sum, it is clear that considerably more attention needs to be paid to urban, local systems in the coming years. For example, the Federal Aid Urban System (FAUS) is the only program to provide direct federal assistance to major city streets. This program has been targeted for elimination by the executive branch but saved by Congress. However, unlike all other major road systems, FAUS has received no funding increases. As another example, the federal Priority Primary System was designed to assist highway construction between communities where substantial growth has occurred after the initial development of the highway program in the 1950s. This program has been eliminated. Most mayors would readily support restoration of the Priority Primary System and an increase in funding for FAUS.

Moreover, there are several national infrastructure programs under consideration that would provide direct federal assistance to urban capital construction and renovation needs and which would include streets, roads, highways, and bridges, as well as public transit, as major components. The National Urban Development Bank, proposed in Chapter 3, is one financing mechanism for these needs, although direct funding to state and local governments would provide the necessary assistance as well.

Finally, safety should be an important urban transportation policy in coming years. Heavy trucks, which cause some concern for safety, should be closely controlled in terms of routes within cities. The 1982 legislation that loosened oversight of heavy trucks on urban roads should be corrected. Many cities simply do not have roads that can sustain these extra long and heavy trucks. They potentially threaten not only transportation infrastructure but human life as well.

RAILROAD TRANSPORTATION

Cities are greatly concerned about railroad transportation, both passenger and freight. Passenger railroad service is vital to many cities across the country for mobility and energy efficiency purposes. AMTRAK also plays an important economic development role for many cities. There are almost annual efforts on the part of the administration to trim AMTRAK substantially, but these have been largely resisted in the past and should be in the future. In the president's 1986 proposed federal budget, the executive branch proposed eliminating funding for AMTRAK altogether. However, Congress voted to retain 90 percent of AMTRAK funding. AMTRAK appropriations should be retained at a level of at least $750 million per year, which roughly approximates its historic financing level over recent years. This is necessary to sustain a reasonable pace in the AMTRAK capital renovation program and prevent massive abandonments on most parts of the AMTRAK system if federal assistance were eliminated.

Railroad stations also are of great importance to cities. In addition to being historic structures in many instances, railroad stations have the potential of being key contributors to movement of people downtown as intermodel facilities. Efforts should be focused on revitalizing these stations so that they can make a maximum contribution to urban life, coordinated when possible through AMTRAK. Cities, working with the private sector, can do much of this redevelopment on their own. But the federal government can be an important catalyst to get these projects underway.

Freight railroads will continue to be critical to the movement of goods in the United States. They have certain efficiencies and transportation qualities, particularly in long-haul movements, which prove their worth to communities. However, left to itself, the marketplace may ignore the rail needs of many cities, particularly the small communities, thereby abandoning longer term national needs for short-term profit. Public policy should therefore focus on the adequacy of such service to all communities.

In addition, unused freight railroad land, such as yards and terminals, could play an important role in urban revitalization. They lie dormant because their location is not considered profitable enough to produce a conversion. Economic development programs such as EDA grants (see Chapter 3) or the federal Urban Initiatives program, which was in effect in past years, would provide the catalytic incentive to turn these now blighted land uses into jobs and revenue opportunities. (The Urban Initiatives program, which ended in fiscal 1982, provided Urban Mass Transit Administration grants to link transit improvement to economic development.) Projects such as these are prime candidates for private-public cooperation.

AIRPORTS AND AIR TRANSPORTATION

The capital needs of the nation's airports will continue to be great in the years ahead. The executive branch and some members of the Senate in years past sought to eliminate large and medium-sized cities from eligibility to receive federal assistance for airport construction and rehabilitation needs. This "defederalization" was swept aside in 1982 legislation when it became clear that it would hurt local airport financial capacity and threaten air travel growth. The ticket tax which rules the Airport and Airway Trust Fund has contained considerably more funds than the executive branch is willing to allocate for aviation construction needs. Mayors advocate expenditure of all funds collected for such purposes. We are fast approaching a crisis of space and facilities in the nation's airports. In the absence of expansion or rehabilitation of airports, greatly increased passenger inconvenience will inevitably ensue, and the likelihood of air disasters will increase dramatically.

Many medium and smaller cities have lost air service or had it sharply reduced since the advent of airline deregulation. The impact of airline deregulation should be closely studied to assess the adequacy of airline service to these communities.

Airline noise continues to plague many communities. Considerable increase in federal efforts to assist cities coping with aircraft noise is necessary.

CONCLUSIONS

In recent years the U.S. Conference of Mayors has adopted transportation policies on an annual basis which are reflected in the preceding pages. Those policies call for a partnership of all parties to bring about a transportation renaissance in our cities, recognizing that mobility and economic growth are the ultimate results of transportation improvements. These improvements are among the keys to the success of our cities in the years ahead.

In 1982 an historic commitment to public transit was made through passage of the Surface Transportation Assistance Act (STAA) of 1982. Legislation for the first time specifically earmarked federal gasoline tax monies for public transit—one cent per gallon, or $1.1 billion per year. The commitment of gas tax funds to transit is the first tangible recognition at the federal level that our cities' mobility needs, economic development objectives, tax policy, energy conservation goals, and so on can and must be linked and supported through a dedicated federal funding source for transit. At the same time, it remains critical that the federal partner appropriate the full level of funds authorized under Section 9 of the STAA. This formula program for both capital and operating assistance is the cornerstone of the federal transit program, on which virtually every city now depends for basic transit improvements.

Retaining the enacted level of federal commitment can also help achieve economic development goals of the nation. As estimated by the American Public Transit Association, for each $100 million in capital funding lost, a loss of 7,600 jobs and $327 million in business revenues would result.[10] The federal government in the 1986 budget proposed a decline in support for public transit of $2.8 billion, which would mean a loss of 203,000 jobs and $8 billion in private business revenues from the national economy. Economic development in urban centers should be enhanced by broadening existing economic development programs such as Economic Development Administration and Urban Development Action Grants, and linking them more closely to transit-related projects, as well as through full funding of the Surface Transportation Assistance Act.

NOTES TO CHAPTER 15

1. Preparation of the material addressing public transit needs and policy was assisted by Robert G. Stanley, Director of Planning and Policy Analysis, American Public Transit Association, Washington, D.C.
2. American Public Transit Association, Testimony before the Subcommittee on Transportation, House Committee on Appropriations, April 25, 1984, pp. 2, 3.
3. Ibid., p. 3.
4. Ibid., pp. 4, 22.
5. American Public Transit Association, Testimony before House Subcommittee on Housing and Urban Affairs, March 25, 1985, pp. 13–14.
6. U.S. Bureau of the Census, *Statistical Abstract: 1984* (Washington, D.C.: U.S. Government Printing Office, 1983), p. 624.
7. American Public Transit Association, Testimony of March 1985, p. 11.
8. Ibid.
9. American Public Transit Association (APTA), "Public Transit: Meeting the Mobility Needs of the Elderly and Handicapped" (Washington, D.C.: APTA, November 1982).
10. American Public Transit Association, Testimony of April 1984, pp. 19–20.

16 FEDERAL PROCUREMENT IN ECONOMICALLY DISTRESSED URBAN CENTERS

The federal government is one of the nation's greatest economic forces, its budget amounting to 23 percent of the gross national product. Obviously the federal government is more than a passive monitor of economic growth and equity; its own actions determine who fares well and who does not.

As has been amply documented, federal policies in recent years have shifted substantial funds away from older central cities and toward areas of the nation that already have had relatively low unemployment levels and good economic growth performance.[1] These shifts have occurred because of (1) domestic spending cuts which adversely affect cities and regions having extensive poverty; (2) federal tax reductions which add disposable income to the economic stream of those areas having high proportions of upper and upper-middle income people; and (3) defense spending increases, all of which favorably impact on those areas already experiencing economic vitality and relatively low unemployment levels.

U.S. mayors emphasize that federal investment in our strongest economic sectors is sound economic policy, since sustained growth of these sectors can lead the way to a new level of U.S. prosperity. Nonetheless, in the process of stimulating these sectors, the central cities, which have thus far built U.S. prosperity, must have the opportunity to regain full employment levels and economic well-being.

Targeted federal procurement is one route to achieve balanced growth, so that areas of currently heavy unemployment can better participate in economic recovery and growth. All signs indicate that areas experiencing heavy structural unemployment will continue to do so, even in times of economic expansion, unless specific actions are taken.

In this chapter ways are explored to target federal procurement to high-unemployment areas in such a manner that minimal costs are added to federal budgets with no sacrifice to the quality of goods and services purchased. The employment increases achieved will be much lower in cost per new job created in high-unemployment areas than any federal employment and training program could produce. The overall cost to government, from reduced public assistance, housing, and human service needs, is likely to be less once these policies are implemented.

These policies apply to defense and other federal procurement practices. The defense procurement primarily applies to goods and services outside of strategic weapon systems, so that no military objectives are compromised.

TARGETING DEFENSE EXPENDITURES: OVERVIEW

National defense is the only substantial part of the budget (other than interest on the federal debt) that is experiencing significant growth. In fact, from fiscal year 1979 to FY 1990 (projected), defense is proposed by the executive branch to grow from 23 percent to 36 percent of federal budget outlays. Over the next five years defense budget authority is proposed to total \$2.3 trillion. Meanwhile, grants to state and local governments are rapidly declining, from an 11.7 percent share of the budget in 1979 to 5.5 percent by 1986 to a projected 4.1 percent share by 1990.[2]

Therefore, mayors of distressed central cities are increasingly concerned about receiving a healthy share of defense expenditures to help revive their cities' economies and combat unemployment, since this is one source of funds that is not drying up. The needed remedy is to direct increased defense procurement toward areas experiencing structural unemployment and sluggish economic growth or decline; however, defense procurement funds have been flowing away from these areas for decades.[3]

Often those who are opponents of "government solutions" to our nation's social and economic problems will assert that the federal government should remain neutral, not directing particular assistance to any group of persons or area, regardless of need. Nonetheless, defense policies explicitly direct the flow of expenditures away from hard-pressed, high-density, older urban areas.

DEFENSE PROGRAMS AIDING LABOR SURPLUS AREAS

Defense Manpower Policy Number Four (DMP-4), nominally in effect since 1952, assigns purchasing preference to areas classified by the Labor Department as "labor surplus areas." However, the Maybank Amendment, added routinely to each defense appropriations bill since 1953, prohibits the Department of Defense (DOD) from paying a higher price for goods and services to help relieve economic distress. This amendment prevents DMP-4 from going into effect for defense procurement.

The President's National Urban Policy Report of 1978 recognized the harmful effects on cities which were not benefiting from federal procurement policies and the potentially powerful effect of revised policies:

> To ensure that federal procurement is used to strengthen the economic base of our nation's cities and communities, I will:
>
> - strengthen the implementation of the existing procurement set-aside program for labor surplus areas, by directing the General Services Administration (GSA) to work with each agency to develop specific procurement targets and to monitor their implementation. GSA will report to me every six months on the progress of each agency.
> - direct the Defense Department to implement an experimental program to target more of its procurement to high unemployment areas.[4]

Relative to the latter policy, the 1981 Defense Appropriations Act, Section 724, established a test program to direct the Pentagon's supply operations—the Defense Logistics Agency (DLA)—to target up to $3.4 billion in nonstrategic services and supplies to businesses in high-unemployment areas. These labor surplus areas have unemployment rates 20 percent higher than the national average over a period of two years (e.g., if the national rate is 7 percent, a rate of 8.4 percent is needed to qualify). To aid in achieving the goal, these firms received a 5 percent price advantage in bidding for the set-aside defense contracts. As of fiscal 1985, the ceiling on the amount to be set aside under this program was $5 billion, and the allowable price differential was reduced from 5 percent to 2.2 percent. Indications are that DLA may not be achieving even this modest $5 billion-a-year goal. Between 1981 and 1984, the total dollar volume of targeted procurement was $6.8 billion, compared to a cumulative 1981-1984 goal of $16.4 billion. Moreover, this defense procurement program for economically distressed areas is apparently being terminated as of fiscal 1986.

Studies have shown that a significant price differential is not necessary. The Defense Department can target its expenditures toward high-unemployment areas, helping to heal our nation's most critical economic problems without sacrificing DOD financial objectives. Between 1981 and 1984, there were 61,203 contracts awarded under this procurement preference program. However, it was only necessary to pay a price differential on 1,194 of those contracts. The total value of the 1,194 contracts was $131 million, and the value of the price differential was just $2.2 million. Therefore, it cost a total of $2.2 million plus an additional $3 million in administrative expenses to achieve $6.8 billion in targeted procurement. No price differential at all was necessary in 98 percent of the contract awards, and even when a price differential was needed, it amounted to only 1.7 percent, on the average, of the contract value.

As a result of paying this price differential on the 1,194 contracts, 3,923 jobs were created. The cost per job created was $561. By adding in the administrative expenses of the DLA procurement preference program, the total cost per job created is $1,326. This figure is substantially lower than the $3,500 cost of many direct jobs creation programs, and the $1,356 cost figure could be lowered further by considering savings in income maintenance programs' costs.[5]

RECOMMENDED DEFENSE PROCUREMENT POLICIES

Reforms should be considered in defense procurement policies that build further the successful DLA efforts, develop procurement strategies beyond the DLA, improve minority business contracting, and increase competition in defense contracting so that firms in high-unemployment areas have a better chance to participate. Moreover, a new and promising federal procurement outreach policy establishes offices in high-unemployment areas, at a modest cost, to show local firms how to bid successfully on defense contracts.

Enlarge the Highly Successful DLA Procurement Program

DLA procurement for FY 1984 amounted to $19.7 billion out of a $274 billion defense budget. Of this amount, $9.8 billion is for fuel, which does not lend itself well to targeting. Much of the remaining amount is suitable for targeting, especially since explicit targeting programs outside DLA have not been developed. U.S. mayors call for targeting $7 billion of DLA procurement to labor surplus areas. The current preferential price differential in bidding of 2.2 percent should be sufficient to accomplish this goal.

Target Procurement in Defense Expenditures Outside of DLA

There has been little effort thus far to target DOD procurement outside of DLA. The strategic weapon systems and other military prime contracts (over $10,000 each) totaled $103.8 billion in FY 1983. Targeting of expenditures in this area requires a lifting or modification of the Maybank Amendment (discussed above). In view of the serious need to boost job opportunities in distressed urban centers, U.S. mayors call for development of a plan, within a year, to target some significant portion of outside-of-DLA procurement to high-unemployment areas.

Mayors recognize that much of this category of defense procurement may not be well suited for targeting in those cases where national security clearly dictates production of the good or service outside of heavily populated areas or by certain defense suppliers not located in high-unemployment areas. However, all of this category of procurement should not be considered out of bounds for targeting, as is presently the case. An impartial panel should be convened to develop a plan to target expenditures to labor surplus areas in the most feasible categories. Perhaps components of strategic weapons are suitable for targeting (e.g., seats for aircraft), and perhaps some contract categories are suitable for split sourcing, a portion of the contract or subcontract going to a firm in a labor surplus area.

Improve Minority Business Contracting

Nearly everyone concerned with equal opportunity among all Americans agrees that our nation will never fully achieve the equal opportunity goals for which we are supposedly striving unless business ownership, as well as jobs, is opened to minorities. Today only 2.7 percent of businesses in the United States are owned by blacks, and the vast majority of these (89%) are operated with no full-time employees other than the owner. Black firms account for less than 1 percent of sales and gross receipts.[6] Among firms that have a number of employees, minority-owned businesses are much more likely to hire, train, and promote minorities than majority-owned firms.

The DLA set-aside program makes no provision for minority firms. The panel recommended above should also review and set targets for federal procurement from minority firms (e.g., 10 percent). To help ensure fairness, minorities should, of course, be fully represented on the panel.

Increase Competition in Defense Contracting

Congress has historically required the federal government to purchase goods and services with the benefit of competition, whenever feasible. However, in FY 1981, 59.3 percent of the dollar value of Defense Department procurement was awarded on a "sole source," noncompetitive basis. Sole sourcing was made in 51.9 percent of all DOD contracts.[7] Several of these awards were made out of necessity, because of the lack of cultivation of a variety of suppliers.

Competition is often restricted by means of vertical integration among prime contractors; that is, they buy subcontractors. This enhances these firms' ability to underprice competition, eventually squeezing them out of the market. In the area of defense-related aerospace manufacturing, for example, the number of suppliers has decreased from 6,000 in 1967 to about 3,000 today.[8] In several critical areas there are just one or two suppliers (e.g., tank hull castings and aircraft navigation systems). When the subsidiary becomes a sole source, substantial price increases inevitably follow.[9] A city that is attempting to retrain its workforce and retool its industries will find it exceptionally difficult to break into defense contracting given the above trend limiting the number of suppliers with which DOD does business.

The following strategies should be considered to enable DOD to increase competition, include more small and minority businesses, and better employ workers in labor surplus areas:

Limit Sole Sourcing. Some buying installations, such as the Navy Aviation Supply Office, have initiated "breakout" programs to encourage greater competition for system components and spare parts. Mayors support these programs. In addition, Congress has introduced legislation in recent years to limit sole sourcing, and mayors support the intent of such legislation.

Track Subcontractors. The Northeastern-Midwest Senate Coalition estimates that about half of the $103.9 billion spent in military prime contracts in a recent year went to subcontractors. However, the coalition reports that DOD does not track or report on the flow of these subcontract dollars.[10] By requiring DOD to do so, the federal government and the American people can gain a better understanding of the impact of federal expenditures and better direct policies to assist high-unemployment sectors.

Hold Procurement Conferences in Labor Surplus Areas. The mayors support DOD's frequently holding procurement outreach conferences in labor surplus areas to: cultivate potential contractors and subcontractors in these areas; make firms more aware of their potential for doing business with DOD; overcome as many concerns as possible about excessive and costly paperwork requirements in doing business with DOD; and resolve problems firms may have in relating to DOD. Confusion, misinformation, and pessimism in overcoming the DOD bureaucracy excessively limit the number of firms seeking to do business with DOD, and active steps must be taken to turn this situation around.

Initiate a Targeted Procurement Outreach Program. Local procurement outreach programs, targeted to areas experiencing high unemployment, are promising developments. These programs help small and medium-sized companies enter or expand their participation in federal prime contract and subcontract markets.

During the last three and a half years, successful procurement outreach programs have been established in large cities, including Baltimore, Buffalo, Cleveland, New York, and Philadelphia as well as in smaller cities, including Altoona, Pennsylvania; Hammond, Indiana; and Lewisburg, Pennsylvania.

These programs, administered and staffed by various local economic development agencies, are based on an evaluation of the local economic environment, careful assessments of the capabilities of individual firms, and an understanding

Table 16-1. Budgets and Dollar Value of Contracts Generated by Selected Procurement Outreach Centers.

Program	*Annual Budget*	*Value of Contracts per Year*
Cleveland	$150,000	$15 Million
Buffalo	$150,000	$25 Million
New York City	$400,000	$25 Million
New York State	$470,715	$138 Million
Down River Community Conference, Michigan	$225,000	$10 Million
Bid Center Beaumont, Texas	$240,000	$21.5 Million in one six months period
Florida Small Business Development Centers	$100,000	$7.3 Million

Source: Academy for State and Local Government, "Planning a Government Procurement Outreach Center" (Washington, D.C.: Academy for State and Local Government, September 1985), p. 4.

of the requirements for effective participation in the federal marketplace. Procurement outreach programs help companies make best use of both existing federal support services and local economic development services. Though each program is customized to local requirements, they share a common goal: to guide and monitor each company's activities to ensure successful, independent, long-term participation in the federal market.[11]

The procurement outreach track record, to date, is impressive. The Buffalo Procurement Outreach Program, for example, has been in operation for over four years. During this period over $44 million in contracts have been brought into the Buffalo economy, directly due to assistance provided by the local procurement outreach program. As a result, over 450 jobs have been created or retained annually, at an average cost of less than $300 per job. The federal government has also benefited from increased competition and a broadened base of suppliers.[12]

Table 16-1 demonstrates that procurement outreach centers can generate contracts for their localities far in excess of the usually small administrative costs involved.

The DOD appropriation act for fiscal 1985 provided $2 million for DOD to share in the cost, up to $150,000, of establishing or retraining twenty-six procurement outreach centers around the nation. Indications are that this effort will be expanded to $5 million during 1986. This new effort is likely to prove highly beneficial in stimulating a broader base of DOD suppliers, greater competition for DOD contracts, and therefore lowered costs of the goods and services that DOD procures. The program should pay for itself through these benefits.

The DOD has established six criteria for awarding funds to states and cities for procurement outreach centers, with the level of unemployment as the fifth priority in ranked importance. Currently, the primary purpose of the federally subsidized procurement outreach centers is to stimulate competition for DOD contracts, not to reduce problems of structural unemployment. Better targeting of these funds to areas that need assistance the most would help achieve broader national objectives for balanced economic growth. After all, more affluent areas already have the funds to establish procurement outreach centers on their own. An improved targeting policy would reduce, albeit to a minor extent, the current imbalance where the overwhelming majority of DOD contracts go to areas having lower than average unemployment.

Improve Competition through Other Measures. A number of other steps may be taken by the federal government to include more contractors and subcontractors in procurement programs. In particular, adoption of the National Urban Development Bank proposal, discussed in Chapter 3, would enable funds to be targeted directly to firms in labor surplus areas, enabling those firms to compete better for federal contracts.

Additionally, DOD and other federal agencies could help small businesses by further streamlining its procedures. Some firms have mastered the complex art of federal contracting, and they obtain a healthier share of contracts; others fear the maze of regulations. The new Federal Acquisition Regulations that went into effect in 1984 help alleviate some of the duplication. This attempt to establish uniform federal procurement procedures will undoubtedly lead to further progress.

A primary outreach tool to businesses that is currently employed is the *Commerce Business Daily*, a publication intended to list all nonclassified defense contracts over $10,000 that are open for bid. However, this tool is underused. Several defense agencies do not publish their procurements, even in nonclassified areas. Others publish too late to meet the typical ten-day time period for bidding.[13] The process of advertising bid opportunities should be reformed and directed in particular toward small and minority businesses in high-unemployment areas, so that excessively restrictive bidding practices can be reduced or eliminated.

Another area of potential reform involves milspecs, or military specifications. Milspecs are necessarily rigid for much military procurement, requiring components to function under the most arduous conditions with little or no maintenance. In some cases, however, milspecs could be reviewed to see if they are essential to the uses for which they are intended. Revisions to milspecs for certain products could increase the number of suppliers and lower costs considerably.[14]

Procurement in Other (Nondefense) Federal Agencies

The President's National Urban Policy of 1978 called for agency-by-agency targets for their procurement to labor surplus areas.[15] Subsequently targets were established for each agency to spend approximately 10 percent of its procurement budget for labor surplus area set-asides. Under the program, a labor surplus area must have a two-year unemployment rate at least 20 percent greater than the national average to qualify for set-aside procurement. This policy was designed to steer a minimum of $10 billion in procurement to areas of high unemployment, out of a total base of $100 billion.[16]

A goal of targeting 10 percent of a $60 billion rather than a $100 billion base may be more realistic since much government procurement is nondiscretionary. However, even this lower $6 billion targeting goal is not being achieved. Some federal agencies such as Interior, Agriculture, Energy, NASA, and GSA are achieving procurement targeting goals, while others are not. A modest $1.3 billion government-wide goal was established for 1985.

The executive order establishing targeted procurement for labor surplus areas is not being enforced, according to several procurement officials. Moreover, federal legislation designed to achieve targeted procurement lacks specificity.[17]

Targeting a minimum of 10 percent of all nondefense federal procurement to high-unemployment areas would help meet urban economic development goals. With top-level leadership in the federal government, this minimal goal can be achieved. Moreover, expansion of the types of federal procurement considered for inclusion in these targeted goals should be considered. The current amount of under $30 billion, which constitutes the universe of federal procurement that is subject to targeting, is considerably less than the over $100 billion universe of 1979 when the program began.[18]

CONCLUSIONS

The targeting of federal procurement is an example of a policy that can reduce severe economic distress in central cities at low cost and in a natural, productive manner. The proposal is in contrast to an artificial government program that provides temporary income maintenance and keeps citizens in a dependent condition. Rather, with well-targeted procurement the productive capabilities of the free enterprise system are strengthened, providing permanent jobs to those who need them the most.

The tools to implement this policy are already in place. All that is needed is a new executive order and strong enforcement.

Defense procurement is a huge amount—2.7 percent of our 1985 gross national product.[19] Often military expenditures are considered a diversion from domestic resources needed to achieve critical national economic and social goals.

They need not be. If a portion of those expenditures is properly targeted, it would be of considerable value to urban citizens.

NOTES TO CHAPTER 16

1. Thomas L. Muller, "Regional Impacts," in John L. Palmer and Isabel V. Sawhill, eds., *The Reagan Experiment* (Washington, D.C.: The Urban Institute Press, 1982), pp. 448–57. The heavily urbanized Northeast and Midwest are experiencing per capita domestic spending reductions of $145 to $151, compared to the national average of $138. Muller notes further that federal tax reductions favor areas of personal income growth and new construction. For example, those in the west-south central region receive a $194 per capita tax reduction, $185 in the mountain region and $205 in the Pacific region, compared to the $172 national average. Moreover, the Pacific region is receiving a 36.5 percent increase in defense expenditures, more than double the increases of any other region.
2. U.S. Conference of Mayors (USCM), "The Federal Budget and the Cities" (Washington, D.C.: USCM, February 1985), p. viii.
3. Northeast-Midwest Institute (N–MI), "The Pentagon Tilt, Regional Biases in Defense Spending and Strategy" (Washington, D.C.: N–MI, January 1983), pp. 1–3 and Tables I, II; Northeast-Midwest Institute, "Pentagon Tilt, A Statistic Update" (Washington, D.C.: N–MI, May 2, 1983), p. 3; and Northeast-Midwest Congressional Coalition, "Defense Spending 'Tilts' to South, West," *Report* 2, no. 2 (May 1985), pp. 1, 6–8. The FY 1983 Defense budget for all items aside from weapons procurement sent more than twice as many dollars to the South and West as to the heavily urbanized Midwest and Northeast. Sixty-seven percent of defense installations and 80 percent of defense personnel are located in the South and West. Moreover, the South and West received 85 percent of the $2.7 billion in military construction expenditures, which support the future direction of military activities and expenditures.

   Procurement of major weapon systems is still directed to a considerable extent toward the Midwest and East, although those regions' share of military prime contracts decreased from 72 percent in 1951 to 37 percent in 1983.

   In 1983 the nation spent $122 billion in defense expenditures outside of procurement of major weapon systems—for research and development, testing and evaluation, operations and maintenance, and military construction—or $539 per capita. Of these expenditures, the South and West received $754 per capita compared to the Northeast and Midwest's $279. From 1981 to 1983, the South and West gained $293 per capita, compared to $114 for the Northeast and Midwest. Taking into account all defense expenditures, the Northeast and Midwest, with 45 percent of the nation's population, received only 31 percent of expenditures in 1983, or $565 per capita. The South and West received $987 per capita.

   California has 10 percent of the nation's population, compared to the Northeast and Midwest's 45 percent share of the nation's population. Yet

California received $81 million more in FY 1983 military construction funds than the entire region of the Midwest and Northeast combined.

To cite another example, Michigan has among the nation's highest unemployment rates. However, Michigan received $922.1 million fewer in prime contract dollars in 1982 than it did in 1951, a decline of 37 percent. With over 4 percent of the nation's population and considerable manufacturing capability, Michigan received 2 percent of prime contracts in 1982. In all defense expenditures outside of prime contract procurement of major weapon systems, Michigan received $119 per capita defense expenditures, well below the national average of $539.

4. U.S. Department of Housing and Urban Development (HUD), *The President's National Urban Policy Report* (Washington, D.C.: HUD, August 1978), p. 137.
5. Phone conversation with Defense Logistics Agency, Policy Office, November 1985.
6. U.S. Bureau of the Census, *1982 Survey of Minority-Owned Business Enterprises* (Washington, D.C.: U.S. Government Printing Office, 1985), Table 1. For further discussion, see Chapter 6 of this book.
7. Northeast-Midwest Senate Coalition, *Report to the Chairman* (Washington, D.C.: Northeast-Midwest Senate Coalition, February 24, 1983), p. 1.
8. Peter J. Ognibene, "In Military Procurement, More Bucks Don't Always Produce a Bigger Bang," *National Journal* (December 12, 1981): 2197.
9. Jacques S. Gansler, *The Defense Industry* (Cambridge, Mass.: The MIT Press, 1980), pp. 69-70, 130.
10. Northeast-Midwest Senate Coalition, p. 4.
11. For a more detailed description of procurement outreach, see Warren H. Suss, "Tapping the Federal Market, the Procurement Outreach Approach," *NCUED Economic Development Commentary* 6, no. 4 (Winter 1982): 19-23.
12. U.S. House of Representatives, House Subcommittee on General Oversight of the Committee on Small Business and the Federal Procurement System, 97th Congress, 1st session (Washington, D.C.: U.S. Government Printing Office, 1981), pp. 11-15.
13. Ibid., pp. 23-25.
14. Gansler, p. 280.
15. U.S. Department of Housing and Urban Development, p. 137.
16. George E. Peterson, The Urban Institute, "The Impact of Federal Fiscal Policies on Urban Economic Development," *Urban Consortium Information Bulletin* (Washington, D.C.: U.S. Department of Commerce, September 1980), pp. 29, 30.
17. Phone interview with U.S. Government Services Administration officials, November 1985.
18. Peterson, p. 30.
19. John L. Palmer and Isabel V. Sawhill, eds, *The Reagan Record: An Assessment of America's Changing Domestic Priorities* (Cambridge, Mass.: Ballinger Publishing Company, 1984), p. 120.

INDEX

ABOUT THE CONFERENCE OF MAYORS

The United States Conference of Mayors is an organization of city governments. It is the national forum through which this country's cities with populations of 30,000 or more share ideas, express ideals, and actively meet the challenges facing today's urban leadership. The principal role of the United States Conference of Mayors is to provide a policy development and legislative action force in federal-city relationships to ensure that federal policy meets urban needs. Each member city is represented by its chief local elected official, the mayor.

The President of the Conference of Mayors, through June 1986, is Mayor Ernest M. Morial of New Orleans. The organization's Vice President is Mayor Joseph P. Riley, Jr., of Charleston, South Carolina. The Conference has an extensive, bipartisan Board of Trustees and Advisory Board comprised of mayors of cities in all sections of the nation.

Municipal cooperation among the major cities of the country, as achieved by the United States Conference of Mayors, began in 1932 during the Depression. First steps to organize the municipalities on a national level were taken in June of that year in Detroit. The Conference was formally established in Washington in February 1933. The constantly increasing problems growing out of the Depression literally forced the cities to organize into the United States Conference of Mayors. Local governments had no effective means for working together to meet their common needs.

For more than fifty years the United States Conference of Mayors has taken the lead in directing attention to the nation's urban challenges and in shaping landmark legislation of significant benefit to cities and their people. While mayors must provide direction and leadership for their city governments within the framework of the law and tradition provided by their own states, they must also deal with many issues which can only be approached through nationwide study and action. As an everyday working alliance, the Conference is the instrument established and maintained by mayors to provide for this common purpose.